As I read these brilliant  and interesting they would be for all serious readers, and for writers — perhaps especially young writers, many of whom want to know more about why they are indebted to the work of the four literary geniuses Peter Stine so generously illuminates here. Babel, surely the least read of the four writers today, is revealed as a highly contemporary sensibility aware that identity in and outside of literature is often a deliberate blending of fiction and memoir. Stine shows how his work implicitly asks a question of the Russian Revolution that all of these writers ask: What do we do with violence? How do we express the worst of humanity as artists determined to stay awake? And how does all the work examined here shed light on the perversion of masculinity that war and revolution have created? Hemingway's famous faults are reconsidered in the light of Stine's deep compassion for the writer's lifelong effort to assimilate into a fragile psyche the bloodshed he witnessed and suffered as an ambulance driver in World War I. Kafka seems especially a man of our time, in his absurd and rudderless sense of himself in a personal isolation that deepens while he intuits the collapse of Judeo-Christian culture that gives rise to Nazism. Conrad, filled with contradiction, investigator of the heart from which spring the crimes of imperialism, writes about the world in a letter, "If you take it to heart it becomes an unendurable tragedy." But these are men who took their world to heart, and managed to endure, at least for a while, even as they were ravaged by such endurance.

This is literary criticism at its translucent best, a meditative investigation into the work and lives of writers who were branded by some of the worst crimes civilization has witnessed, artists who did not have the luxury to hold themselves apart from the violence that shaped and shattered their consciousness. The essays in *The Art of Survival* are written in utterly luminous, quotable prose, by a writer who is asking all the right questions.

— JANE MCCAFFERTY, *author of* Thank You for the Music *and* Director of the World, *winner of the Drue Heinz Literature Prize.*

THE ART OF SURVIVAL

Essays on
Isaac Babel, Ernest Hemingway,
Franz Kafka and Joseph Conrad

PETER STINE

Rocky Shore Books
Marquette MI

ISBN 978-0-9823319-3-4

Copyright © 2011 Peter Stine
All rights reserved.

Designed by Doug Hagley

Printed in the United States by
McNaughton & Gunn, Saline, MI

PUBLISHED BY

Rocky
Shore
Books
Marquette MI

For Zan and Nick

Contents

ix
PREFACE

1
ISAAC BABEL
Violence and the Russian Revolution

59
Ernest Hemingway
The Great War

113
Franz Kafka
Metamorphosis and the Holocaust

167
Joseph Conrad
Survivor Guilt and the Politics of Duplicity

PREFACE

THIS COLLECTION OF ESSAYS on Isaac Babel, Ernest Hemingway, Franz Kafka, and Joseph Conrad highlights the impact upon their fiction of violent cataclysms each survived, with special attention to the undercurrent of survivor guilt that informs their respective visions. For Babel that cataclysm was the violence of the Russian Revolution, for Hemingway the trenches of World War I and its ten million dead, for Kafka the collapse of the Hapsburg Empire amidst rising anti-Semitism and the war in which he wished to become a soldier. Roughly contemporaries, these three writers were perfectly placed to register the birth of the most murderous century in human history. Conrad, whose novels were preferred reading in the trenches, warrants inclusion in this study because his political fiction, so influenced by the Polish Insurrection of 1863, anticipates the nihilistic urgencies of the next literary generation.

The watershed was the Great War itself, a catastrophe that, in Paul Fussell's words, was "perhaps the last to be conceived as taking place within a seamless, purposeful 'history' involving a coherent stream of time." Babel, Hemingway, and Kafka came of age in the aftermath of this loss; all of them explore in their narrative art its consequences to the human spirit. As Virginia Woolf wrote, "Personality changed after the war." In his masterwork, *The Great War and Modern Memory*, Fussell reveals how the conditions of trench warfare are reflected in the characteristic modes of modern literature — ironic understatement, gross dichotomizing, exploded versions of pastoral, paranoid melodrama, and absurdity. In truth the Great War is a precondition of that literature, and one need not be a survivor to be influenced by it. At the age of twelve I was hiding from friends in an attic in Ohio and found my cheek resting on a dusty hardcover edition of Erich Maria Remarque's *All Quiet on the Western Front*. Reading the novel that summer changed my view of reality forever, and perhaps one consequence is the writing of this book.

These essays do not adhere to any particular critical method, but I do assume continuity between the psychic life of a writer, his creative work, and the historical moment that claimed him. One will find no ideology in tow here, no interpretative doctrine, no trace of poststructuralism. These four Modernists, each of a different nationality and each a stylistic original, present a wide range of literary responses to a central Western malaise—survival in a time of panoramic chaos and violence. Unfortunately, this is still the air we breathe. In drawing a bond of responsibility between survivor and fallen brother, these writers establish a grounding for morality once modern war and revolution undermined the authority of a once-proud culture. More specifically, I seek to illuminate the impact of history on literary genius, the link between literary experimentalism and cultural trauma, and both the possibilities and hazards of fictionalized autobiography.

There are comprehensive Notes at the conclusion of each essay that serve as a selective bibliography. The writings that make up this book—here significantly revised and expanded—originally appeared as articles in *Modern Fiction Studies, Contemporary Literature, Fitzgerald/Hemingway Annual, The South Atlantic Quarterly, The Cambridge Quarterly, Conradiana*, and Harold Bloom's *Modern Critical Views*. I am grateful to many people who influenced and supported me in this project. In particular I would like to thank two literary mentors, the late Mark Schorer and Roger Sale, and my friend and designer, Doug Hagley.

ISAAC BABEL

Violence and the Russian Revolution

B Y TEMPERAMENT ISAAC BABEL was a spy in the service of eternity. When asked why he was drawn to figures like NKVD executioner Nikolai Yezhov and their merchandise of death, he replied, "I don't want to touch it with my fingers — I just like to have a sniff and see what it smells like."[1] It became his mission as a man and writer to breathe this polluted air, feigning impassivity for close access in order to bear witness to the violence of the Revolution. But never to touch it. Babel sprang from a mercantile Jewish family in Odessa into the romantic *élan* of the October insurrection of 1917 and embraced the early course of events. They seemed at one stroke to free the Russian population, including its Jews, from the czarist prison into an arena of limitless social possibility. They also promised to emancipate Babel from the prison of an exclusively Jewish destiny held in place by anti-Semitic practices. But as a reign of terror set in, sealed with the emergence of Stalin in 1924, his origins became manifest in a complex pacifism, and a more subversive role became clear. "I can't make anything up," he admitted to Konstantin Paustovsky. "I have to know everything down to the last wrinkle, or I can't even begin to write. *Authenticity*, that's the motto, and I'm stuck with it... What I do is get hold of some trifle, some little anecdote, a piece of market gossip, and turn it into something I cannot tear myself away from. It's alive, it plays. It's round like a pebble on the seashore. It's held together by the fusion of separate parts, and this fusion is so strong that even lightning can't split it."[2] Such truth-telling through the metamorphosis of found trifles and anecdotes into literary gems was something the Revolution could not long afford to tolerate.[3] Getting "to know everything," an impulse driven in his case by gargantuan curiosity, Babel refined his loot of perceptions into an art of epiphany that would explode all Soviet ideology in a restorative act of literary violence.[4] Drawing a bond of brotherhood between himself and the Revolution's victims, this *agent provocateur* forged the ironic secret of his art and so revived the ancient biblical proscription — Thou Shalt Not Kill — that had been banished by the theory of "historical necessity" to the dustbin of history.[5] That such a reverence for life led to his execution by firing squad in the Lubyanka in 1940 during Stalin's purges seems now a tragic, yet inevitable destiny.

Babel's stories of his childhood, which began to appear in 1925 after the publication of *Tales of Odessa* and *Red Cavalry*, are worth looking at now, for while a mixture of fact and fiction, they offer a glimpse into his spiritual origins. Babel was always mischievous about the facts of his own life. For instance, he never worked for the Cheka nor is there evidence that he fought on the Rumanian front in World War I, as he claimed. Nor was his family personally touched by the 1905 pogrom in Nikolaev described in "The Story of My Dovecot." His daughter Nathalie wrote that her father was a man "of bewildering contradictions who enjoyed mystifying others and sometimes deluded himself. Whether as a conscious strategy or not, Babel wrapped himself in enigmatic ambiguities, which has led to confusion, errors, and gross discrepancies even in the records and studies that attempt to be factual."[6] This phenomenon — his lies about his life, posturing, and masquerading identities — can be explained as a blend of factors ranging from a conflicted identity to an artist's penetration of reality to self-protection from Stalin's totalitarian regime. His second wife, Antonina Pirozhkova, relates how her husband was always improving upon incidents from his childhood: "On another occasion in Odessa I broke my rule of never discussing Babel's literary work with him and asked: 'Are your stories autobiographical?' 'No,' Babel said. From his account, it turned out that even such stories as 'In The Basement' and 'Awakening,' which seemed to reflect his childhood, were not actually autobiographical. Perhaps a few details were, but not the whole story plot."[7] Andrei Sinyavsky offers the most insightful perspective on this matter:

> In a general way, the problem of truth and fiction has always obsessed Babel, especially in that new, transitory period of his career as a writer, when his style was changing and when the realistic vision of the world was taking the upper hand. But for Babel, fiction was not the opposite of reality. The truth of fiction helped to penetrate the truth of life and to recreate it much more compellingly than a vulgar copy could. "To invent" is not "to deceive," but neither is it to copy facts just as they were or "are ordinarily." Art is the quest

for the unexpected, the unaccustomed, the unique, themselves the source of veracity, for real experience always contains new elements and assumes discovery, creation, and not the repetition of what is already known.[8]

In any case, from his childhood stories we may conclude that Babel knew death as illumination from an early age. It came with an outbreak of anti-Semitism in 1905. "I didn't choose to be born a Jew," he told Paustovsky. "I think I can understand everything. Only not the reason for that black vileness they call anti-Semitism. I came safely through a Jewish pogrom as a child, only they tore my pigeon's head off. Why?"[9] Indeed his indelible images of violence seem to suggest a state of lucid, mesmerized incredulity. In "The Story of My Dovecot" the short, weakly, ten-year-old prodigy passes his exams into the secondary school of Nikolayev, whose *numerous clausus* allows just 5% of its enrollment to be Jewish, only to be victimized by a czarist-sponsored pogrom the day he goes to claim his reward. The reward is pigeons for his dovecot, a gift from his jubilant father. All his elders, including his granduncle Shoyl, a "simple-minded liar" but great storyteller, herald his feat as comparable to David's defeat of Goliath, a victory over "the foes who had encircled us and were thirsting for our blood."[10] But this Jewish faith in learning is exploded when the boy is assaulted with his beloved pigeons by Makarenko, a normally kind, legless cigarette vendor transmogrified in the murderous streets. As Makarenko's wife hisses, "Their seed ought to be destroyed. I cannot abide their seed and their stinking men," he strikes the boy:

> I lay on the ground, and the guts of the crushed bird trickled down from my temple. They flowed down my cheek, winding this way and that, splashing, blinding me. The tender pigeon-guts slid down over my forehead, and I closed my solitary unstopped eye so as not to see the world that spread out before me. This world was tiny, and it was awful. A stone lay just before my eyes, a little stone so chipped as to resemble the face of an old woman with a large jaw. A piece of string lay not far away, and a bunch of feathers that still breathed. My world was tiny, and it was awful. I closed my eyes so as not to see it, and pressed myself tight into the ground that

> lay beneath me in soothing dumbness. This trampled earth in no way resembled real life, waiting for exams in real life. Somewhere far away Woe rode across it on a great steed, but the noise of the hoofbeats grew weaker and died away, and silence, the bitter silence that sometimes overwhelms children in their sorrow, suddenly deleted the boundary between body and the earth that was moving nowhither. The earth smelled of raw depths, of the tomb, of flowers. I smelled its smell and started crying, unafraid. I was walking along an unknown street set on either side with white boxes, walking in a getup of bloodstained feathers, alone between the pavements swept clean as on Sunday, weeping bitterly, fully and happily as I never wept again in all my life. (262-63)

Here violence tears a veil from reality, compelling wonder, as the boy dies from innocence, even selfhood, into a zone of knowledge and perceptual joy beyond fear or shame. Such is the mental state of one upon returning, as it were, from the dead — and this would be the ground of the *joie de vivre* and sunlit aesthetics of this deeply eschatological writer. Yet if the world for the survivor is renewed in a cosmic embrace, he also has special obligations. Returning home through a gauntlet of looted shops, a parade of banners celebrating Czar Nicholas II on a day allotted to the selection of a Constitution, the boy comes upon his granduncle murdered, fish stuck in his mouth and trousers, one "still alive, and struggling." The yardman Kuzma prepares the corpse and tells the boy proudly that Shoyl "cursed them right and left" before he died. This symbol of degradation and defiance would take voice in the undercurrents of Babel's art: a subterranean link with the victims of violence affixed forever.

Yet the clairvoyant spy must be attracted to a degree by the deeds he is exposing. "First Love" traces the purely psychological impact of this trauma on Babel's nascent sense of manhood. First love is Galina, an erotic Russian woman whom the boy has spied upon sexually dominating her husband (an army officer) and who harbors the Babels for the duration of the pogrom. From her window, the boy witnesses his father pursued by Vlasov, a drunken workman railing against the "God of the Old Believers who took pity only on the Jews" (268). When an officer of a Cossack patrol appears riding on horseback "as though through a mountain pass," his father falls to his knees and pleads for protection, but the officer, "raising his hand in its lemon-colored chamois glove to the peak of his cap" (269), divinely ignores the looting of their store. Such a dispersion of parental authority sends the boy into hysterical hiccups. To blot out the day's nightmarish revelations he now imagines himself as *someone else*, "a member of the Jewish Defense Corps" shooting at the murderers with a "useless" rifle, an antiquated one that "shoots badly" as the murderers with "beards and white teeth" approach stealthily.[11] This fantasy of resistance then fades into a feeling of "immanent death" and a vision of Galina being seduced "high in the world's blueness" by her "half-dressed" officer. "O foolish fancies," the boy exclaims, "that helped me forget the death of the pigeons, and Shoyl's death!" (271) The fantasy, after passing from vengeance to his own voyeuristic nonexistence in a world of morbid sexuality and military force, is interrupted by the impotent grief of his father, and the boy's verging mental breakdown soon dictates a family retreat to Odessa. In such memories, Babel concludes, "I find . . . the beginning of the ills that torment me, the cause of my early fading" (274).

Babel's emergence as a passionate ironist, then, was in part a reflection of a deeply divided psyche. On one hand, he was baptized into moral and aesthetic consciousness by violence, which provides the radiant backdrop ("a bitter silence that sometimes overwhelms children in their sorrow") to his retrospective fiction. Yet as a persona inside his own narratives, he was also seduced by the spectacle and held a captive to its model of manhood. This he suffered, quite consciously, as the "incomprehensible ailment" of a vulnerable Russian Jew who desired to escape his fate as a traditional victim. Babel's awestruck admiration for aspects of the Cossack ethos, most notably in *Red Cavalry*, can best be grasped as a dream of rescue — born of imagining his father's humiliation before that Cossack officer's life-dispensing power. Fortunately, this "ailment" opened the portals of discovery, enabling Babel as an artist to keep his sense of identity fluid and open, receptive to the historical moment. Indeed his *repulsion/attraction* to violence ran parallel to the moral self-debate of a revolutionary generation in its often parricidal struggle with its own past.[12] But there the parallel ends. The Revolution was to resolve this struggle with the homicidal paranoia of Stalin's reign, his campaign of genocide against his own people.[13] For Babel there was no severing of his roots without merging with the agency of his earlier oppression. Whatever we make of the complex ground of his pacifism, his rifle remained forever "useless," his flight from his origins an eager and outgoing interest in the world anchored in love for his spiritual kin.

Babel's stories of his Odessa childhood trace the trajectory of this flight, but only to anticipate the return of a "repressed" reservoir of Jewish humanity that made his vision of reality whole. In "In the Basement" the boy, solitary, bookish, and hyper-imaginative, has "let slide everything that really mattered, such as playing truant in the harbor, learning the art of billiards in the coffeehouses on Greek Street, going swimming in Langeron" (294). He courts with mendacities the friendship of Mark Borgman, a wealthy schoolmate, whose father is a cosmopolitan bank manager. Their mansion he gets invited to fills the boy with the vision of a lush exotic world: "Card addicts and sweet-tooths, untidy female fops with secret vices, scented lingerie and enormous thighs, the women snapped their black fans and staked gold coins . . ." (296) But when the visit is reciprocated, the boy must stash away at neighbors' homes his own loony relatives, especially crazy grandfather Leivi-Itzkhok and loudmouthed Uncle Simon, since he has portrayed them to Borgman as worldly adventurers and "nothing I had told him about really existed. What did exist was different, and much more surprising than anything I had invented, but at the age of twelve I had no idea how things stood with me and reality" (297). At first all goes smoothly as he shows Borgman his grandfather's ingenious alarm clock, his barrel of boot polish, and the two read a few pages of his manuscript:

> It was written in Hebrew on square yellow sheets of paper as large as maps. The manuscript was entitled "The Headless Man," and in it were described all the neighbors he had had in his seventy years, first at Skvira and Belaya Tserkov and later on at Odessa. Gravediggers,

> cantors, Jewish drunkards, cooks at circumcisions, and the quacks who performed the ritual operation — such were Leivi-Itzkhok's heroes. They were all as mad as hatters, tongue-tied, with lumpy noses, pimples on their bald pates, and backsides askew. (299)

This human carnival from "The Headless Man" will populate Babel's *Tales of Odessa*, but for now, Uncle Simon invades the basement drunk, raving, and carrying a coat hanger made of antlers — leaving the boy "dead" and hysterically shouting Mark Anthony's funeral oration as his guest takes flight. The boy is too young to realize his family legacy will prove more precious than Borgman's. Later his inept, mock-heroic attempt at suicide by drowning himself in the water barrel only generates epiphany ("I opened my eyes and saw on the bottom of the barrel the swollen sail of my shirt and two feet pressed against one another. Again my forces failed me, again I surfaced. By the barrel stood grandfather, wearing a woman's jacket. His sole tooth shone greenly") and provokes his grandfather to remark scornfully on his gesture of defeat: "Grandson, I am going to take a dose of castor oil, so as to have something to lay on your grave" (304).

Such a tribal injunction to endure with an abiding joy in sheer existence would not be lost on the mature artist. Yet early on, Babel's need to escape the stunted aspects of his Jewish upbringing steered him toward the voyaging invisibility of exile. This is exposed in "Awakening" as the young boy, burdened by his father's own displaced ambitions, awaits liberation from Zagursky's violin school, "a factory of infant prodigies, a factory of Jewish dwarfs in lace collars and patent-leather pumps" (305). With no musical talent, but a taste for literature, he reads books by Turgenev and Dumas on his music stand, now out of step with the "big-headed, freckled children with necks as thin as flower stalks and an epileptic flush on their cheeks" (307). Soon he skips violin school for the more manly pursuits of the Odessa harbor. Here he learns to admire the hand-crafted pipes of an old English sailor, for "in each one of them thought was invested, a drop of eternity." Here he battles the heavy sea waves that "swept me further and further away from our house, impregnated with the smell of leeks and Jewish destiny" (309).

Here his literary talent is recognized by Yefim Nikitich Smolich, a proofreader at the *Odessa News,* who replaces his father's passion for fame and "protested bills of exchange" with a feeling for nature, a love of the physical universe: "I came to love that man, with the love that only a lad suffering from hysteria and headaches can feel for a real man" (310). Yet the boy can't conquer the hydrophobia of his ancestors, and once his truancy from Zagursky's is discovered, he is pressed to take refuge from his raging father in a locked privy.

"I was thinking of running away . . ." So Babel concludes this story, and when he did, it was into bohemian poverty as an illegal resident in war-depressed Petrograd in 1916. Now his patron saint became Maxim Gorky who, recognizing both his precocity as a writer and his lack of experience, would soon advise that he abandon literature and go among the people to harvest raw experience that might inform and deepen his art. This was Gorky on the eve of the Revolution, before his conversion to Party rectitude — a voice already warning against Bolshevik abuse of power and recognizing Vladimir Lenin as "not an omnipotent magician, but a cold-blooded trickster who spares neither the honor nor the lives of the proletariat."[14] He was able to stand up to Lenin: "There is something frightening about the sight of this great man, who pulls the levers of history on our planet as he wishes."[15] Yet when Gorky petitioned him about a young sailor who was going to be shot, Lenin replied, "Alexey Maximovich, for God's sake — don't come to me with all these trifles. Don't you understand — this is *one* boy. There's a revolution going on."[16] Babel's own whereabouts during these early years is uncertain, though he claimed to have served in the Civil War with the northern army against Yudenich in 1918. He was certainly in Petrograd to savor the dominant mood of elation in the Revolution's wake. And yet Babel's early journalistic pieces from this period, appearing in Gorky's *New Life,* soon to be shut down by Lenin, focus upon subjects that forecast his later work of moral espionage: the wretched Bolshevik homes for juveniles and orphans, the neglect and abuse of blinded war veterans, the cruel dislocations and death visited upon the peasantry by enforced economic "evacuations," the emaciation of wet-nurses caused by corruption in the State nurseries. Too often these investigations led Babel to police stations and morgues. Out of his indignation grew a standard by which he would measure the achievements of the new era: "We must see to it that children are born properly. This is real revolution — of this I am quite sure" (72).

Babel's earliest stories from this time appeared in the short-lived *Lava*, and marked the beginning of his observations on war. With subject matter borrowed from books written by French officers who saw action in World War I, they reveal his bent for impersonation and his voyeuristic loss of self into others.[17] "On the Field of Honor" tells of a shell-shocked village idiot in uniform who, caught masturbating in a crater, refuses a punitive order to go over the top. His captain urinates in his face, driving him in despair into no man's land where he is killed by fire both from the Germans and the officer. "The Deserter" focuses upon a young French soldier, tired of the carnage and ready to surrender, who is executed by his commanding officer when he refuses the "honorable" option of suicide. In "Old Marescot's Family" a French *pere* wanders into a graveyard under bombardment with the bodies of his family in a sack, searching for his burial vault until he finds himself standing in it.[18] "The Quaker" traces the exhausting duties of a driver at the front, a Quaker named Stone who keeps his "inviolable promise to God" to avoid "the mortal sin of murder." Leaving his beloved, ailing horse in the hands of a sadistic stable boy, he is summoned away to a fresh battle:

> After a change in the position at the front, the division to which Stone belonged was transferred to a more dangerous place. His religious beliefs did not allow him to kill, but they permitted him to get killed himself. The Germans were advancing toward the Isere. Stone was transporting the wounded. Round about him people of various nationalities were dying fast. Old generals, their faces clean and knobby, stood on hilltops and spied out the land through field glasses. The big guns roared incessantly. The earth gave off a stench and the sun poked around in the mangled corpses. (93)

In this Quaker we can see a forerunner of Lyutov in *Red Cavalry*. Stone returns from the engagement to find his horse starving, and when he drives up a dangerous road to find oats for the creature he take a sniper's bullet in the forehead. In each of these vignettes, Babel strips away the vainglorious and jingoistic flourishes of the original, all the while restraining his genius for metaphor, so that his dry matter-of-fact narrative generates compassion for the common soldier — who emerges as a camouflaged alter ego. "A soldier has no time for mysticism," he observes. "A field of skulls has been churned up into trenches. That's war" (87). As exercises in compression, these stories bespeak the grainy, tight-lipped silence of the fallen dead. Already they forecast the moral issue of Red Cavalry, which, as Lionel Trilling has observed, is not whether the author-protagonist can confront violence and death with honor, but whether he can endure killing his fellow-men.[19]

Two other stories from this period deserve mention as a measure of Babel's own development — the maturation of his curiosity from voyeurism to moral discovery. In "Through the Fanlight" a boy pays the madam of a brothel five roubles to spy through a fanlight upon Marusya, a young prostitute. All goes well until one day when, while she services a routinely disengaged client, who "undid his collar, took a look in the glass, found a pimple under his mustache, gave it a thorough examination and squeezed it out with his hanky" (364), the boy slips and is discovered hanging from the ledge. Marusya arrives to scold him while comforting her client with kisses, and suddenly the boy wonders: "Why was she kissing him?" (365) He had been watching, but not seeing the real event. The next day he rescales the ladder for ten roubles and witnesses Marusya with the same client, now giving herself "with the passion of one in love," while her protector "the lanky bloke wallowed in business-like bliss." Out of a shallow interest in the prurient, the boy discovers a tragic incalculable of life: love is the big surprise from which there is no protection.

Nor is there protection from lust in "The Sin of Jesus," Babel's wonderful contribution to proletarian literature. The earthy Arina, a hotel servant, is three months pregnant again by Seroyga, who must go into the army for four years. "It's like walking around with your skirt up, working at the hotel," she tells the janitor's helper. "Whoever stops here, he's your master, let him be a Jew, let him be anybody at all" (245). For this reason she can't wait for her boyfriend. When he proceeds to beat her, Arina takes a seamless narrative leap into heaven and tells her story to Jesus. This neurotic deity, who would keep Seroyga out of the army were He not afraid of dealing with the police, counsels Arina to live in purity for a while. "For four years?" she cries. "To hear you talk, all people should deny their animal nature . . . And where will the increase come from? No, you'd better give me some sensible advice" (246). So Jesus gives her Alfred as a husband for four years, a hale young angel chaffing under rules of celestial chastity, with "two wings fluttering behind his pale-blue shoulders, rippling with rosy light like two doves playing in heaven" (247). Jesus blesses the union, then instructs Arina how to take off the angel's wings each night, which "were attached to hinges, like a door," so they would not snap when Alfred tossed in bed. After she has prepared him a supper and plied him with vodka, the angel "keeled over in a deep sleep," whereupon Arina removes his wings and carries him to bed in her arms:

> There it lies, the snowy wonder on the eiderdown pillows of her tattered, sinful bed, sending forth a heavenly radiance: moon-silver shafts of light pass and repass, alternate with red ones, float across the floor, sway over his shining feet. Arina weeps and rejoices, sings and prays. Arina, thou hast been granted a happiness unheard of on this battered earth. Blessed art thou among women! (248)

The omniscient narrator, operating midway between human and celestial realms, changes his tune when Arina accidentally suffocates Alfred: "Not enough for her to sleep with an angel, not enough that nobody beside her spat at the wall, snored and snorted—that wasn't enough for the clumsy, ravening slut. No, she had to warm her belly too, her burning belly big with Seroyga's lust" (249). Presenting the corpse to Jesus, she pleads her innocence: "Was it I who made my body heavy, was it I that brewed vodka on earth, was it I that created a woman's soul, stupid and lovely?" (249) But His condemnation is even more wrathful than the narrator's: "I don't wish to be bothered with you . . . You've smothered my angel, you filthy scum" (249).

13

Arina is "thrown back to earth on a putrid wind," but just before she is laid up she addresses the Lord in the back yard of the hotel: "See, Lord, what a belly! They hammer at it like peas falling into a colander. And what sense there's in it I just can't see. But I've had enough" (250). In an astonishing reversal of roles, Jesus falls on his knees before her and begs, "Forgive me, little Arina. Forgive your sinful God for all He has done to you . . . ," but she replies: "There's no forgiveness for you, Jesus Christ. No forgiveness and never will be" (250). What is unforgivable is the abuse of ordinary people by powerful authority, whether the police or a deity, for the crime of being themselves. Lenin might have no problem in killing one boy for the Revolution, but through a single hotel servant Babel gives voice to an uncompromised and timeless sense of individual justice.

The *Lava* stories were the last Babel published before he joined Semyon Budyonny's First Cavalry for the Polish campaign of 1920. They exhibit a variety of styles ranging from the documentary realism of "The Quaker" to the descriptive symbolism of "Through the Fanlight" to the ribald humanity and lyrical metaphors of "The Sin of Jesus." Babel's love of language is apparent at every turn, his virtuosity astonishing, and what he learned in writing his diary of the Polish campaign must have only completed his literary self-development. "It was only in 1923," he said, "that I learned to express my ideas clearly and at not too great length. Then I set about writing again."[20] This maturation happened to coincide with Lenin's New Economic Policy, the "breather" that allowed a degree of capitalistic enterprise, personal freedom, and artistic experimentation as the country rebounded from the turbulence of the Civil War. But its promise was an illusion. "It is a very great mistake to think that NEP means the end of terror," Lenin reassured one of his commissars. "We shall resort to terror again."[21] Yet a remarkable generation of young Russian writers would step forward before Lenin's dark prediction for the future would materialize to silence them.[22]

Perhaps in some unconscious adaptation to that future, the "ideas" that Babel had learned to express with clarity and precision would be presented as concrete images that speak for themselves. "A simile," he said, "must be as precise as a slide rule and as natural as the smell of dill."²³ To allow this to happen, he had to cleanse the doors of perception through relentless revision, creating vignettes that are in effect prose poems. He would explain his writing method to Paustovsky this way:

> If you use enough elbow grease even the coarsest wood gets to look like ivory. That's what we have to do with words and with our Russian language. Warm it and polish it with your hand till it glows like a jewel . . . The first version of a story is terrible . . . It's clumsy, helpless, toothless. That's when the real work begins. I go over each sentence time and time again. I start by cutting out all the words I can do without. Words are very sly. The rubbishy ones go into hiding . . . ²⁴

While Babel admitted to Paustovsky that his complaint about asthma in his puny body as a child was a falsehood, his working on the shortest story was like trying "to dig up Mount Everest all by myself with a pick and shovel . . . I have heart spasms when I can't manage a sentence."²⁵ Indeed his aesthetics of compression might be viewed as a kind of asthma before what W.B. Yeats called in "Easter 1916" the "terrible beauty" of the new century. While the Revolution during the 1920s went about its leisurely and grotesque "revaluation of all values," Babel would excruciatingly revise his art by paring away all ideological skin, all moral didacticism, leaving only flash-like seizures of a passionate moment.²⁶ His irony, based on the naked juxtaposition of opposite modes of being, cancels out nothing. True to the law of contrasts, that irony transcends the historical moment from which it arises. Babel's own captivation by the will to violence floats like a mere psychological mote in the rays of a higher vision. By such techniques, he preserved what Nadezhda Mandelstam felt his artistic contemporaries were gradually losing to the Revolution, for "what causes anguish in an artist is not longing for eternity, but a temporary loss of his feeling that every second of time is, in its fullness and density, the equal of eternity itself."²⁷ Quite rightly his literary credo, embedded in a later story, "Guy de Maupassant," is couched in military terms, for, minus any intervening intellect, his art is calculated to penetrate consciousness like a bullet: "I began to speak of style, of the army of words, of the army in which all kinds of weapons may come into play. No iron can stab the heart with such force as a period put just at the right place" (331-332). Honoring a limitless respect for the reader, Babel draws no conclusions, makes no value judgments. The right or wrong of what is witnessed is either self-evident or lost. There is an awesome aspect to this kind of art, for its use of epiphany moves beyond morality only to recover its intuitive presence in a primitive and joyous embrace of the sensuous universe.

FOR BABEL, THEN, the only legitimate form of violence was pure perception. "There is no greater joy for me," he said, "than to follow impassively the play of passions on human faces."[28] Nowhere is this joy more manifest than in the wholly imagined world of *Tales of Odessa*. These stories were composed concurrently with *Red Cavalry*, mischievously linked with that work, but clearly anterior in inspiration. In an early piece, "Odessa," Babel had expressed his love for the city, its "sweet and oppressive spring evenings, the spicy aroma of acacias, and a moon filled with an unwavering, irresistible light shining over a dark sea."[29] Odessa offered the promise of "new blood," a world of "lightness and sunshine," a cosmopolitan assimilation of ethnic groups in its harbor, a tradition of artistic excellence, even a "Literary Messiah" who will come "from the sunny steppes washed by the sea" to replenish the national literature. Perhaps Babel himself? But there remains one political obstacle: "In Odessa there is an impoverished, over-crowded, suffering Jewish ghetto, an extremely self-satisfied bourgeoisie, and a very Black Hundred city council" (72).[30]

Tales of Odessa can be understood as an escape from the bloody Polish campaign that matches fable and pure literary pyrotechnics against the existence of violence. Here Babel elaborates a jaunty, erotic dream of how violence might be contained without killing in the Jewish ghetto, the Moldavanka, now transformed in imagination, yet still laboring under czarist Russia of the 1890s. His single hero,

Benya Krik, is a richly brocaded anti-self, a mask of physical potency and anti-traditional authority, an image placed *inside* the ghetto but not originating there, a gangster in orange pants who prevails because he "was passionate, and passion rules the universe" (207).* Placed in a frame of age addressing youth, most stories of the cycle insinuate the form of a Jewish wisdom book — but the law is revised to meet the exigencies and lawlessness of the Great Pale. While Babel was steeped in the Talmud and the Bible, as well as European literature, there is no evidence in any of his writings that he had any religious faith. Appropriately then, Benya Krik is an heir to messianic echoes now turned ironic in an age of unbelief. At every stage, Babel's virtuoso narrative techniques both proclaim his "unreality" and

---

*Lev Nikulin, a childhood friend and fellow writer, has observed that Babel took a famous Odessa gangster from the Civil War days, nicknamed Mishka the Jap, and projected him into the creation of Benya Krik, now placed in the period of his own childhood. It is doubtful that Babel knew the details of Stalin's youth in Georgia, but as a man who aspired to "know everything," perhaps he did, and it is worth contemplating, if only to draw a contrast, that the man who murdered the creator of Benya Krik was a Mafioso figure himself in 1905, working in Tiflis and Batumi for the Bolsheviks. In his biography *Young Stalin*, Simon Montefiore writes: "Stalin became the effective godfather of a small but useful fundraising operation that really resembled a moderately successful Mafia family, conducting shakedowns, currency counterfeiting, extortion, bank robberies, piracy and protection-rackets – as well as political agitation and journalism." Stalin was no Benya Krik, however, no king in a redemptive fable, but rather a cunning, paranoid, vendetta-ridden street thug. He recruited a gang of criminal toughs and psychopathic killers he had first known as a teenager at Tiflis Seminary – the same types he would later bring to the Kremlin's Central Committee and the NKVD upon seizing power after Lenin's death in 1924. Losing his beloved wife Kato in 1907, Montefiore cites Stalin as saying at the funeral that she "had softened my heart of stone. She died and with her died my last warm feelings for humanity." By 1908 the police had tracked Stalin down and exiled him to northern Russia, but Montifiore reckons there were eight escapes from arrest, forty different aliases, years on the run, a life of amorality and sexual promiscuity, then four years of exile in Siberia, whereupon the Georgian reemerged in 1917 as an important and shadowy figure in Party politics in revolutionary Petrograd.

elevate him to personal myth. Again the irony cancels out nothing. Benya is meant to be his creator's own dream of liberation from the prison of Jewish tradition, the czarist police, and the pogromniks that terrified his youth, and also, as John Berryman has observed, "the King that history had denied the exiled, dispossessed, persecuted, and suffering Jews."[31]

Babel uses his own lavish metaphoric excess to sustain a new and magical world in "The King." Here Benya, an apostate who reigns by turning a rabid Jewish business ethic into straightforward extortion in the service of the community, presides over his sister's wedding in the uterine folds of the Moldavanka. The omniscient narrator's lens is a kaleidoscope of color and sensuality:

> The living quarters had been turned into kitchens. A sultry flame beat through the soot-swathed doorways, a flame drunken and puffy-lipped. The faces of the old crones broiled in its smoky rays — old women's tremulous chins and beslobbered bosoms. Sweat with the pinkness of fresh blood, sweat as pink as the slaver of a mad dog, streamed this way and that over those mounds of exorbitant and sweetly pungent flesh. (203)

But Benya's spies learn of a police raid timed to interrupt this most venerable of Jewish ceremonies. In clipped gangster lingo that mimics Homeric dialogue, he accepts the news with stylish sang-froid in a pose of clairvoyance.[32] Suddenly a flashback to how Benya tamed the avaricious Zender Eichbaum establishes the basis for this confidence. His extortion letters getting no response, Benya raided the old man's farm, where "on the blood-flooded ground the torches bloomed like roses of fire" as his men put a dairy herd to the knife, then fire shots in the air — for as the narrator interjects: "If you don't fire in the air you may kill someone" (206). Yet one glimpse of Eichbaum's beautiful daughter Tsilya "wearing naught save her V-necked shift" in the yard and Benya is "defeated": he returns two days later to return Eichbaum's extortion money and ask him for his daughter's hand. Violence in this world only begets sons-in-law, not corpses, at least not on stage.

Now we are swept back to the mock-epic wedding, where "wines not from these parts warmed stomachs, made legs faint sweetly, bemused brains, evoked belches that rang out sonorous as trumpets summoning to battle" (208). Benya's chivalric *mafiosi* are in attendance, "aristocrats of the Moldavanka...tightly encased in raspberry waistcoats," while his sister, "a virgin of forty summers who suffered from goiter," hungrily awaits her miserable, purchased bridegroom. But the threat of the police raid remains. Parallel to their cow-blood-flooded but victimless raid on Eichbaum, and again reversing Jewish history, Benya's men strike first. Soon pogrom-like flames have the police station "blazing like a house on fire" with the officers "rushing up smoky staircases and hurling boxes out of windows, while prisoners, unguarded, were making the most of their chance" (210). As Jerome Charyn has observed, "It's a parody of a pogrom — a pogrom that will never happen," as indeed was the raid on Eichbaum, and one might add a burlesque of revolution as well.[33] Finally Benya ambles up to the police captain to remark upon what has been ordained by his own invisible hand: "What do you say to this stroke of bad luck? A regular act of God!" (211)

The secret of Benya's rise to power is narrated by the elder Arye-Leib in "How It Was Done in Odessa." In a self-referential aside, Babel has the elder exhort his young listener to "forget for a while that you have spectacles on your nose and autumn in your heart," to "quit playing rowdy at your desk" and to imagine a "rowdy in public places" who started his climb by overthrowing the legacy of a brutish father: "What would you have done in Benya Krik's place? You would have done nothing. But he did something. That's why he's the King, while you thumb your nose in the privy" (212).[34] What Benya does is seek to join the gangsters, who order him to shake down the corrupt Tartakovsky, old "Jew-and-a-Half" who has "the soul of a murderer" but "is our blood" — an acknowledgement of reasons other than prejudice for the sufferings of the Moldavanka. We learn that earlier, during a pogrom, the gangsters had *staged* the burial of Tartakovsky, then at the cemetery "produced a machine gun from the coffin and started plastering the Sloboda thugs" (214). The contrast between passive accommodation and militant resistance to the Black Hundreds could not be more starkly drawn.

This time Jew-and-a-Half's letter responding to Benya's demand for protection money is lost in delivery, but the haphazard only produces a feeling of inevitability. The tone now turns dubious with an insistence on the theatrical as "the curtain rose on a three-act opera." First, in the ensuing raid on Tartakovsky's place, his clerk Muginstein is accidentally shot and killed by Butsis, a gang member who lacks "sang-frwa." Benya's ascendancy begins now in putting things right with justice, as Tartakovsky is forced to pay compensation and a pension to the clerk's Aunt Pesya. Second, Benya, now "wearing a chocolate jacket, cream pants, and raspberry boots," pays a visit to the grieving aunt in an automobile that "cast thunderbolts with its wheels, spat fumes, shone brassily, stank of gasoline, and performed arias on its horn" (218). He rationalizes the death of Muginstein with an oration that compares his own mistake with those of Jehovah:

> Aunt Pesya, if you need my life you may have it, but all make mistakes, God included. A terrible mistake has been made, Aunt Pesya. But wasn't it a mistake on the part of God to settle Jews in Russia, for them to be tormented worse than in Hell? How would it hurt if the Jews lived in Switzerland, where they would be surrounded by first-class lakes, mountain air, and nothing but Frenchies? All make mistakes, God not excepted. (219)

And finally, at the lavish funeral Benya ushers in a new reign of protection ("on that day the cops wore cotton gloves") and the community is united in earthly glory ("honorary dairymaids . . . wafted the odors of the sea and of milk") as Arye-Leib orates the proceedings like "the Lord God spoke on Mount Sinai from the Burning Bush" (220). This parody and appropriation of the Law also extends to revolutionary ideology when Benya eulogizes Muginstein as a hero who "perished for the whole working class" and will be buried next to the unmarked grave of his slayer. This eclipse of religion and every *ism* by the sheer force of personality earns Benya the title of "king" from the lips of Little Lisping Mose, an attending gravedigger. Yet when Arye-Leib is done, his young listener remains silent, still with spectacles on his nose and autumn in his heart.[35]

We must be wary, then, when Raymond Rosenthal calls Benya

Krik a "Jewish Cossack."[36] Structural ironies explode such a claim. Benya is a mock-epic figure who eschews killing, and gradually fades from view as the cycle moves on. Indeed Babel will reserve that ethnic nickname for Lyubka Shneiveis whose inn is a rowdy hangout for Odessa's exotic smugglers, foreign traffic, and gangsters. In "The Father" the superannuated gangster Ephraim Rook is spurned by Capon when he tries to negotiate a marriage between the grocer's son and his gigantic daughter Basya. Looking for revenge, Ephraim turns to Lyubka, who suggests Benya, by the way also a bachelor. "Splice him with Basya," she advises, "give him some dough, make something of him" (232). Lyubka tells what she knows to Benya, but while he's "thinking it over," Ephraim waits all night outside her inn while the King makes indefatigable love with the Russian prostitute Kate:

> The landlady gave Ephraim a chair, and he plunged into measureless expectancy. He waited patiently, like a peasant in a government office. Beyond the wall Kate moaned, beyond the wall Kate choked with laughter. The old man snoozed for two hours at her locked door, two hours and maybe more. Evening had long since turned to night, the sky had grown black, and its milky ways were filled with gold, glitter and coolness . . . Then music came from the sea: French horns and trumpets from the English ships. Music came from the sea and then fell silent, but Kate, the whole-hogging Kate, was still heating up for Benya Krik her many colored, Russian and rubicund paradise. She moaned beyond the wall and shouted with laughter. (233)

This broadly comic scene belies a future reality when Benya will be purchased to marry Basya and begin "the story of the fall of the House of Capon, the tale of its slow ruination, of arson, and of shots fired in the night" (234). Once the deal is made, as Benya and his future father-in-law stroll by the Russian cemetery, "Lads were then dragging lasses behind the fences, and kisses re-echoed above the tombstones" (234).

It's revealing that Benya makes no appearance in "Lyubka the Cossack" where the tough landlady is won over by the humanity of a wise old Jew. Again the issue is the proper raising of a child. In her various professions as innkeeper, wine dealer, madam of a brothel, and dealer in smuggled goods, Lyubka is a resume of her creator's own youthful dreams of liberation. In real terms, however, this amounts to neglecting her son. In her absence, Tsudechkis has been detained due to unpaid bills of a rich client he brought to the inn. He likens his captivity to being "in the hands of Pharaoh," but trusts "in God, who will lead me out of here as he has led all Jews out — first from Egypt, and then from the wilderness" (236). Once more Babel updates Jewish destiny, now with the Cossack ethos (embodied in Lyubka) assuming the role of traditional oppressor — and so projects the resolution of his own split psyche upon the fate of Little Dave. Upon her return, Tsudechkis scolds the woman for having "ridden off for three years on business" and leaving him "at the mercy of a famished babe in arms..." (236) But despite her barbs, he strikes up their friendship by weaning Little Dave from her breast with a fine-toothed comb.[37] This feat earns Tsudechkis a role as Lyubka's manager for fifteen years and, indeed, is a wry forecast of Babel's own "management" of the Cossack ethos by an ineradicable Jewish heritage that is one underlying dynamic of *Red Cavalry*.

Written after Babel had witnessed the early work of the Revolution, *Tales of Odessa*, despite its humor and verbal exuberance, has a distinctly elegiac tone. Though its magically sustained world has florid color and bizarre people, historical reality has been suspended: the cycle of stories projects a nostalgic, pre-revolutionary graveyard. Irresolvable conflicts and incipient violence lie in the shadows cast by its bright plumage. The Homer of the cycle is still Arye-Leib, an old man balanced on a cemetery wall, whose youthful listener, "you who snip coupons on other people's shares," remains wrapped in silence and alienation. Benya may be an improvement on Jewish traditions: "Not according to their years did the wedding guests take their seats. Foolish old age is no less pitiable than timorous youth. Nor according to their wealth. Heavy purses are lined with tears" (205). Yet the King is also debunked by his presentation in defiant, yet defunct literary tropes. There are weddings, feasts, and funerals, the ceremonies of a rich Jewish tradition, but now secularized by the reign of masculine virility. There is the sanctification of real values, such as parenthood and community, many of them the ancient possessions of Jewish life, but now they are dependent for their protection on the raids of a dream-figure like Benya Krik — and that is no protection at all.

BABEL'S MASTERPIECE, *Red Cavalry*, based on his five months of service as a transport officer and war correspondent with Budyonny's First Cavalry in 1920, tells the saga of another kind of raid — a furious, endless campaign, spreading social justice through looting, rape, and slaughter, trampling on horseback across a prostrate Poland. On this expanding edge of the Revolution, the unfolding of "historical necessity" is reduced to a relentless pursuit of war and death. In this campaign, during the third year of the Civil War, the Red Army was repelling an invasion of western Ukraine by nationalistic Polish forces, led by Josef Pilsudski, attempting to reclaim territory seized by Russia in 1772. Lenin also saw an opportunity to spread the Revolution into the doomed cities and shtetls of eastern Poland, perhaps into Germany itself. Most land-owning Cossacks sided with the Whites in the Civil War; however, Budyonny was a committed Bolshevik and friend of Stalin who had campaigned in southern Ukraine. In a move that his family felt was suicidal, Babel, recently married, sought the help of a Party Committee member in Odessa to serve with the Cossacks. He concealed his mission of espionage and his Jewishness with a Russian surname, Lyutov (meaning "ferocity"), the name he gave to the narrator of *Red Cavalry*.

This narrator, cultural *naïf* and urban intellectual, a stranger to the world he describes, cannot be accurately equated with the real "I" of the author, which, as Sinyavsky remarks, "is hidden, camouflaged under the twists and turns of the action."[38] Any authorial presence is not primarily psychological, but effortlessly manifold, like the emotions and actions of the campaign. As a fragment of autobiography, Lyutov is viewed ironically, as a masquerader, often subject to humiliation, one among an astonishing range of characters and actions in *Red Cavalry*. Polished vignettes of battlefield violence are etched in a remarkable calm. What is least expected is rendered with a lucid sense of inevitability, what is familiar, for instance the Cossack banners, sabers, and horses, with a romantic glow. This "violence" between form and content generates a sense of wonder, tableaux frozen in a tension of being. "The special effect," says Patricia Carden, "is of being placed outside time, of being caught in a single, recurring event, of going from innocence to knowledge in a flash."[39] Silence acquires a maximum expressiveness. Babel uses the traditional Russian *skaz* (written or spoken monologues of others) to broaden and deepen his range of witness. But either mode of narration is sounding the moral resonances of his own double allegiance to the ideals of the Revolution and to the eternal suffering of its victims.

This tension is struck immediately in "Crossing into Poland." As the Red cavalry wades across the Zbruch River, carrying with them "the smell of yesterday's blood, of slaughtered horses," only the neutral physical universe is expressive of the violation of a territory: "The orange sun rolled down the sky like a lopped-off head, and mild light glowed in the cloud gorges" (41). In Novograd, Lyutov billets in the ransacked home of three Jews, who, when ordered to clean up the filth, "skipped about noiselessly, monkey-fashion, like Japs in a circus act . . ." But playing the invader is a kind of sacrilege, a cruel masquerade, and as Lyutov beds down on a disemboweled mattress, "the moon, clasping in her blue hands her round, bright, carefree face, wandered like a vagrant outside the window" (42). That night in a dream Lyutov sees VI Division Commander Savitsky shoot a retreating Brigade Commander between the eyes. When the pregnant Jew awakens him from the nightmare with fingers groping his own eyes, we recognize the link between the Brigade Commander and his inner situation. Indeed Lyutov's bedfellow, upon inspection, is the woman's father, slain by the retreating Poles after begging them to kill him out of sight of his daughter: "His throat had been torn out and his face cleft in two; in his beard blue blood was clotted like a lump of lead" (43). Now she has the last word, a cry of "terrible violence," a lament of irremediable loss that rises unanswered above the bloody work of revolution: "And now I should wish to know where in the whole world you could find another father like my father?"

This cry, in endless variations, provides the chorus of *Red Cavalry* and invades Lyutov's consciousness via troubled dreams that universalize his sympathies. The Polish peasants, with an unquenchable hatred for the Polish aristocracy, are natural recruits for the Soviets; yet despite the courage they display as infantry, these "partyless masses" are scorned by the Red military staff, abused in general by their "liberators," their property looted, horses stolen, women despoiled. "Tired, shattered," Babel wrote in his diary. "The system. Army stores and foraging parties give us nothing. Red troops arrive in a village, ransack the place, cook, stoves crackling all night, the householders' daughters have a hard time."[40] Many of the shtetl Jews in the towns of Galicia and Volhynia, long victims of pogroms conducted by the Poles, seem inclined to see the Bolsheviks as a lesser evil, perhaps liberators — yet they too suffer a similar fate at the hands of the Cossacks. "Same old story," Babel wrote in his diary, "the Jews have been plundered, their bewilderment, they expected the Soviet regime to liberate them, and suddenly there were shrieks, whips, cracking, shouts of 'dirty Yid'" (12). After the slaughter at Brody, Lyutov finds that the "chronicle of our workaday offenses oppressed me without respite, like an ailing heart" (81). And for moral ballast, despite himself, he starts to drift toward the peacemakers.[41]

Already in Novograd, Lyutov has met a wandering Polish artist, a heretic and mystic whose "wise and beautiful life" intoxicates him and whose religious frescos reflect Babel's own literary credo by elevating the commonplace faces around him to sainthood. Apolek's story of the marriage of Jesus and Deborah depicts a savior of sorrow and compassion — juxtaposed beside the *skaz* of Sidorov, a murderous Red anarchist billeted with Lyutov, whose letter to his wife dreams of Italian sunshine only as an opportunity to assassinate King Victor Emmanuel and spread the Revolution. "I then made a vow to follow Pan Apolek's example," Lyutov says. "And the sweetness of meditated rancor, the bitter scorn I felt for the curs and swine of mankind, the fires of silent and intoxicating revenge

— all this I sacrificed to my new vow" (55). This vow of mystical acceptance opens up a multiplicity of worlds for the spy. At first repelled by the Hasidic communities and shtetl Jews of Galicia, by their excremental settlements and warped physicality, Lyutov soon discovers "their capacity for suffering is full of a somber greatness, and their unvoiced contempt for the Polish gentry unbounded" (86). His revulsion is a means to distance himself from the terror and maintain sanity, as when after the Jew-killing at Berestechko "a violent smell of rotten herrings emanates from all its inhabitants. The little town reeks on, awaiting a new era, and instead of human beings there go about mere faded schemata of frontier misfortunes" (120). In Zhitomir, from their ranks, he meets old Gedali, the owner of a curiosity shop, who resumes for him on Sabbaths the lessons of "the rotten Talmuds of my childhood." Gedali welcomes the defeat of the Poles ("that is splendid, that is Revolution") but not the voice of the new regime: "You don't know what you are fond of, Gedali. I'll shoot you and then you'll know. I cannot do without shooting, because I am the Revolution" (71). As a participant in the invasion, all that Lyutov can do in response is repeat these words in a faint-hearted appeal to the laws of expediency.[42] Then the elder replies:

> But the Poles, kind sir, shot because they were the Counter-Revolution. You shoot because you are the Revolution. But surely the Revolution means joy. And joy does not like orphans in the house. Good men do good deeds. The Revolution is the good deed of good men. But good men do not kill. So it is bad people that are making the Revolution. But the Poles are bad people too. Then how is Gedali to tell which is Revolution and which is Counter-Revolution? (71)

Gedali's dream of an "International of good people" is dismissed by Lyutov as a sentimental impossibility — yet he is forced to admit with deepening disaffection that the real world is "eaten with gunpowder . . . and spiced with the best-quality blood" (72).

This issue of violence is what undercuts Lyutov's desire, born of fancied inadequacies, to identify with the Cossacks and their alluring valor, boldness, and grace. Upon joining the brigade in "My First

Goose," he stands in voyeuristic awe of Savitsky, whose "long legs were like girls sheathed to the neck in shining riding boots." But he is snubbed and hazed by the men as a "brainy type," told to "go out and mess up a lady . . . and you'll have the boys patting you on the back" (74). What Lyutov does to earn their acceptance and homoerotic company is seize the goose of a peasant woman and kill it in brutal fashion with his sword. "What with all this going on," the woman laments, "I want to go and hang myself . . ." That night Lyutov reads the *Red Cavalryman* aloud around the campfire and "rejoiced, spying out exultingly the secret curve of Lenin's straight line." But later: "I dreamed: and in my dreams saw women. But my heart, stained with bloodshed, grated and brimmed over" (77). Such rites of initiation into the Cossack brotherhood involve a violation of the soul. Babel's imagined childhood trauma of having his pigeon smashed against his face during the 1905 pogrom in Nikolayev is both normative and ineradicable.

Hence when the issue is killing humans, Lyutov turns stillborn. In "After the Battle," he is accused by the ribless, epileptic Akinfiev of taking an unloaded revolver into battle, of secretly being a Molokan pacifist who "worships God" and "ought to be wiped out." Lyutov drives his antagonist away, but that evening "I felt my strength all ebbing away . . . I continued on my way, imploring fate to grant me the simplest of proficiencies — the ability to kill my fellow-men" (187). This incapacity operates beyond psychology, is an ontological grounding, and under some circumstances is recognized as a moral weakness. In "The Death of Dolgushov," during the retreat from Brody where "bullets struck the earth and fumbled in it, quivering with impatience," Lyutov comes upon a wounded telephonist by the roadside: "His belly had been torn out. The entrails hung over his knees, and the heartbeats were visible" (89). Dolgushov asks to be mercifully dispatched to escape Polish torture, but Lyutov leaves the chore for Alfonka, to whom he explains ("with a wry smile"): "I couldn't, you see" (90). This admits an element of squeamishness in Lyutov's abstention, as well as something else. "Get out of my sight," his friend mutters with justifiable rage, "or I'll kill you. You guys in specs have

27

about as much pity for chaps like us as a cat has for a mouse" (90).

This charge may be rebutted by the expansive pity shown for the plight of the Cossacks, but only to a degree. An element of exploitation, of cold fact-gathering neutrality remains. Good and evil interpenetrate in *Red Cavalry*, and Lyutov is no exception. Ultimately he must accept the charge leveled against him by the bloodied, walleyed Galin that the Red cavalry is "busy shelling and getting at the kernel for you" (129). *Red Cavalry* is utterly free of self-righteousness or hypocrisy on this matter. Any witness of stature knows he is as responsible for what he sees as for what he does. "What is our Cossack?" Babel wrote in his diary. "Layers of trashiness, daring, professionalism, revolutionary spirit, bestial cruelty. We are the vanguard, but of what? The population await their saviors, the Jews look for liberation — and in ride the Kuban Cossacks" (28). And Lyutov rides with them, a propagandist for the cause, with or without a loaded revolver.[43] His only defense lies in espionage. In "Berestechko," as posters are being put up to announce a lecture on the Comintern, Lyutov records the immediate present:

> Right under my window some Cossacks were trying to shoot an old silvery-bearded Jew for spying. The old man was uttering piercing screams and struggling to get away. Then Kudrya of the machine gun section took hold of his head and tucked it under his arm. The Jew stopped screaming and straddled his legs. Kudrya drew out his dagger with his right hand and carefully, without splashing himself, cut the old man's throat. Then he knocked at the closed window.
> "Anyone who cares may come and fetch him," he said. "You're free to do so." (119)

Such realities are now what this spy knows, for our sake. By delivering in silence his stunning images of the Cossacks at war, Babel runs the risk of becoming a scapegoat for their misdeeds. Richard Hallett speaks of the "basic heartlessness" of *Red Cavalry*.[44] Frank O'Connor, himself a master of the short story, is skeptical of Babel's eager "romanticization" of violence and wonders if he should be regarded "as a real writer or a dangerous lunatic."[45] We are in the habit of equating silence with complicity, but this silence is the opposite, inviting us as readers to exercise what the Revolution had interdicted: *individual moral judgment*. There is the trashiness of the Cossacks drunkenly looting St. Valentine's Church at Berestechko, cursed by its bell ringer, then confronted at the altar by a barefooted figure of Jesus in an orange Polish overcoat, "pursued by hatred and overtaken by the chase," his uplifted hand "a purple stream," his mouth "torn like a horse's lip" (142). There is the daring of Kolesnikov leading the "great noiselessness of a cavalry charge" at Brody, and an hour after wiping out the Poles, "riding on a dun stallion at the head of his brigade, alone and dreaming" (92). There is the professionalism of Budyonny, who smiles and smokes behind the lines, ready to shoot anyone who turns back. Revolutionary spirit burns in the Kurdyukov brothers, "dull, broad-faced, goggle-eyed" giants who enter the stream of history by beating to death their father, who before the Revolution was a village policeman, only then to become a renegade White who killed their brother Theodore. There is bestial cruelty in Balmashev's letter to the *Red Cavalryman* relating how he threw a peasant woman off a moving troop train for smuggling salt, then "took my faithful rifle off the wall and washed away that stain from the face of the workers' land and republic" (126). Or the demented savagery of Afonka Bida, who, losing his beloved horse in battle, searches for a new one in an endless, homicidal raid against the Polish peasantry. Or the vengeance of Prishchepa, a "carefree syphilitic, and happy-go-lucky fraud" who ran away from the Whites, then returned to his village where his parents had been held hostage and put to death:

> He went out into the street in a black felt cloak, a curved dagger at his belt. The cart plodded along behind. Prishchepa went from neighbor to neighbor, leaving behind him the trail of his blood-stained footprints. In the huts where he found gear that had belonged to his mother, a pipe that had been his father's, he left old women stabbed through and through, dogs hung above the wells, icons defiled with excrement. The inhabitants of the settlement watched his progress sullenly, smoking their pipes. (108-09)

Finally, in another *skaz* narrative, Matthew Pavlichenko, a former serf, now bellicose Red division commander, still smelling of the milk of dairy herds, tells how he sought out his former master and exacted that class-bred vengeance that will continue to fuel the Revolution: [46]

> There in the parlor was Nadezhda Vasilyevna, clean off her head, with a drawn saber in her hand, walking about and looking at herself in the glass. And when I dragged Nikitinsky into the parlor she ran and sat down in the armchair. She had a velvet crown on trimmed with feathers. She sat in the armchair very brisk and alert and saluted me with the saber. Then I stamped on my master Nikitinsky, trampled on him for an hour or maybe more. And in that time I got to know life through and through. With shooting — I'll put it this way — with shooting you only get rid of a chap. Shooting's letting him off, and too damn easy for yourself. With shooting you'll never get at the soul, to where it is in a fellow and how it shows itself. But I don't spare myself, and I've more than once trampled an enemy for over an hour. You see, I want to get to know what life really is, what life's like down our way. (106)

As Lyutov, by proxy, also gets to know life through and through, the tenor of *Red Cavalry* grows more grim and elegiac. "This isn't a Marxist revolution," Babel wrote in his diary, "it's a Cossack rebellion, out to win all and lose nothing" (64). And again from the diary: "The hatred is the same, the Cossacks just the same, the cruelty the same, it's nonsense to think one army is different from another. The life of these little towns. There's no salvation. Everyone destroys them — the Poles gave them no refuge. The girls and women, all of them, can scarcely walk. In the evening — a talkative Jew with a little beard, used to keep a shop, daughter threw herself out of a second-story window to escape a Cossack, broke her arms, one of many" (84-85). These recognitions leave Babel and his proxy consumed in loneliness: "Why can't I get over my sadness? Because I'm far from home, because we are destroyers, because we move like a whirlwind, like a stream of lava, hated by everyone, life shatters, I am at a huge never-ending service for the dead" (56). Outside Brody is the harvest of this invasion, a "dreadful field . . . sown with mangled men, inhuman cruelty, unbelievable wounds, fractured skulls, naked young bodies gleaming white in the sun, jettisoned notebooks, leaflets, soldiers' books, Bibles, bodies amid the wheat" (50).

Parallel to Lyutov's rising revulsion at the work of Revolution, we witness the gradual expulsion of 16,000 Cossacks, the last cavalry campaign in European history. All this is telescoped with special horror in "Squad Commander Trunov." The story opens with Trunov, a "long corpse with its mouth stuffed full of broken teeth," being eulogized as a "world hero" by Pugachov. As a worshipper of heroes, Lyutov also pays his respects: "I would be the last of all to judge him" (46). But earlier that day the two of them had clashed over the treatment of prisoners.[47] Half-crazed by a head wound, Trunov had executed an old man, nearly shot a Cossack comrade over the corpse's trousers, then turned his rifle on another prisoner and "sent the Polish lad's skull flying, and bits of his brains dripped over my hands" (149).[48] Afterward, when told by Trunov to cover up the atrocity by rubbing the two prisoners' names from his official list, Lyutov shouts back what has been his creator's daring policy throughout: "I'm not going to rub out anything" (150). After this Trunov is strangely resigned to his own death, and to provide cover for his brigade, he wanders off to a suicidal encounter with strafing American warplanes — now just a heroic anachronism, both in the war and in Lyutov's expanding consciousness. Replacing him as an emerging authority is the white-clad Galician, a mysterious figure who wanders through the story radiating a Christ-like charity and humility, "his gibbet-like frame cleaving the burning brilliance of the skies" (145).

Lyutov may have dismissed Gedali's "International of good people," but he is drawn as the campaign grinds on to an informal one of his own composed of those, Cossack, Pole, and Jew, who become secret selves, dark doubles. There is Brigade Commander Khlebnikov, whose beloved white stallion is taken from him by the virile Savitsky. When the Division Commander is replaced, the Army Staff orders the horse to be returned — but Khlebnikov is spurned once more by Savitsky, who stands brandishing a revolver beside his Cossack woman, her bosom stirring "like an animal in a bag" (111). Khlebnikov withdraws without his horse, tries unsuccessfully to quit the Communist Party, and at last, due to head wounds, is declared unfit for service.[49] "And that was how we lost Khlebnikov," Lyutov says.

"I was very upset about it, for he was a quiet fellow whose character was rather like mine . . . We were both shaken by the same passions. Both of us looked on the world as a meadow in May — a meadow traversed by women and horses" (114). There is Sandy the Christ, so named by the Cossacks because of his simplicity and good nature, who, infected with syphilis through the misguidance of his brutish stepfather, leaves home to become a herdsman before mobilization: "Foolish old peasants would come to the pasture to wag their tongues with him, women would run to Sandy to recover from the everyday brutality of the peasants, and because of his love and because of his illness they were never angry at him" (98-99). Pronounced unfit for combat due to wounds, Sandy serves on the transport wagons where Lyutov gets to know him, and "whenever the capricious chance of war has brought us together, we have sat down of an evening on the bench outside a hut, or made tea in the woods in a sooty kettle, or slept side by side in the new-mown fields, the hungry horses tied to his feet or mine" (99). There are the voiceless dead. Lost on a night battlefield at Khotin with his own horse killed, Lyutov by accident spatters a Polish corpse with urine: "I wiped the skull of my unknown brother, and went on, bent beneath the weight of the saddle."[50]

And finally there is Elijah, the precocious son of the Rabbi of Zhitomir, who bravely led Volhynian peasants against the Poles at Leszniow, only to have Commander Maslak's brigade charge the peasants and whip them "for fun." When the front collapses at Kovel, his naked and wasted body is dragged by Lyutov aboard a retreating Cossack troop train. Elijah's scattered belongings objectify as well as anything the warring coordinates of the narrator's own psyche:

> His things were strewn about pell-mell — mandates of the propagandist and notebooks of the Jewish poet, the portraits of Lenin and Maimonides lay side by side, the knotted iron of Lenin's skull beside the dull silk of the portraits of Maimonides. A lock of woman's hair lay in a book, the Resolutions of the Party's Sixth Congress, and the margins of Communist leaflets were crowded with crooked lines of ancient Hebrew verse. They fell upon me in a mean and depressing rain — pages of the Song of Songs and revolver cartridges . . . (192-93)

Elijah whispers to Lyutov that his initial inability to leave his mother kept him from joining the Party's military forces, but now "when there's a revolution on, a mother's an episode." But the elevation of Party discipline over family roots cannot save him. "We buried him at some forgotten station," Lyutov says. "And I, who can scarce contain the tempests of my imagination within this age-old body of mine, I was there beside my brother when he breathed his last" (193). Elijah's death is the symbolic loss of his hopes for the Revolution. Replacing the Party's belief in "historical necessity" is a personal religion of universal brotherhood, washed in the compassion expressed by old Gedali in Zhitomir four months earlier: "All is mortal. Only the Mother is destined to immortality. And when the mother is no longer among the living, she leaves a memory which none yet has dared to sully. The memory of the mother nourishes in us a compassion that is like the ocean, and the measureless ocean feeds the rivers that dissect the universe" (77).

By the end of *Red Cavalry*, this compassion has been all but blotted out by the oozing red chloroform skies of the campaign. A brigade prostitute cries out after the slaughter at Chesniki, "Everything that's gone on today makes me want to go and hide my face" (187). As an historical experiment, the grafting of straight Party doctrine onto the Cossacks has proven a failure. All that is "liberated" is an ideological paranoia ("Nowadays everybody judges everybody else") and a license to conscience-free killing.[51] Outside of Zamoste, Lyutov falls asleep in a rainy field and dreams of his own death, only to awaken to the "smoke of secret murder" in the town. "The Poles are killing the Jews," a peasant tells him. "The Jews are to blame for everything, on our side and yours. There'll be mighty few of them left after the war" (170).* Even the Cossacks have lost

---

*Babel seemed to have sensed that genocide was to descend upon Eastern European Jewry in two decades. He wrote in his diary on July 23: "Dubno synagogues. Everything destroyed. Two little vestibules left, centuries, two tiny rooms, everything full of memories, four synagogues, close together, then pasture, plowed fields, the setting sun . . . I go into the Hasidic synagogue. It's Friday. Such misshapen little figures, such worn faces, it all came alive for me, what it was like three hundred years ago, the old men running

heart. Undersupplied, riddled with defections, demoralized by the futility of hurling cavalry against trenches, machine guns, artillery, and warplanes, ridden with syphilis, they retreat into what forecasts the next stage of the Revolution: a suspicion of "winking" treason everywhere.[52] In "Treason," a syphilitic and wounded Balmashev, whose "savage bayonet" was turned by Lenin and Leon Trotsky to "predestined guts and viscera," informs the Party about the slackness of recovering patients in a military hospital that led him to shoot out some windows in protest. Now the "enemy" has become his own wounded comrades. Balmashev will eagerly embrace his next role as executioner of Russian "traitors." He does not know that the Cossacks, embracing a defiant ethnic identity, will themselves be liquidated by Stalin over the next decade.

We get a glimpse of the new breed of executioners, those of the revolutionary tribunals and the NKVD, with the sinister appearance of Baulin in "Argamak," the concluding story that Babel appended six years after the first publication of *Red Cavalry*. Young, tough, stubborn, Baulin "had never known worry," a quality that "formed an important element in the victory of the Revolution" (194). When Tikhomolov kills some captured Polish officers, the Squadron Commander punishes him by giving his horse to Lyutov, who has now joined the active forces. But his "hatred reached me across forests and rivers," nor can Lyutov train Argamak to accept him as a new rider. When he returns the horse after Tikhomolov is amnestied for bravery in the attack at Rovno, the Cossack will not accept his offer of friendship. Now Lyutov turns and asks the Squadron Commander why he created this animosity. "I see the whole of you," Baulin replies. "You're trying to live without enemies. That's all you think about, not having enemies" (200). We accept the justice of this charge but

---

corner to corner, their worship could not be less formal . . . There are no adornments in the building, everything is white and plain to the point of asceticism, everything is fleshless, bloodless, to a grotesque degree, you have to have the soul of a Jew to sense what it means. But what does the soul consist of? Can it be that ours is the century in which they perish?" *1920 Diary*, 33.

also now recognize it as a precious, vanishing virtue.⁵³ There is dark menace and prophecy in Baulin's claim that "boredom comes of it." In the fading moments of *Red Cavalry*, Lyutov does fulfill his dream of riding a horse before the approving eyes of the Cossacks, but ironically this feat has paled into insignificance before the advancing Revolution's new god of violence.

"I'M PULLING BACK NOW, but what does it matter," Babel wrote in his diary in the last month of the campaign. "Others will make the Revolution . . . and once again I am thinking my own thoughts."⁵⁴ No doubt these thoughts, with Babel now liberated from his official straightjacket as Party propagandist during the war, were pressing for artistic expression. Over the next four years in Kiev, he wrote most of the stories that appear in *Tales of Odessa* and *Red Cavalry*, works which won him immediate fame across Russia. Babel seems to have embraced his new celebrity, social mobility, and privilege with the same curiosity and merriment that he brought to everything he did. Yet there must have been other thoughts, more private and disaffiliated, that were attuned to a changing political climate. Judging from Budyonny's renewed attack on *Red Cavalry*, and more generally from the suspension of Lenin's NEP, the eclipse of Trotsky, and the expansion of state terror under Stalin, Babel had to recognize the risk in his continuing literary witness.⁵⁵ A head-hunting mentality was taking root, a brand of "official" spying and "informing" that travestied the modus operandi of his own art. Moreover, Stalin had imposed upon Russian writers the aesthetic of socialist realism, which erased any distinction between propaganda and art, and aimed to engineer a new proletarian man through the copulation of clichés. Still, Babel had gained an immense popularity and was under the protective sponsorship of Gorky. While the grand old man of Russian letters had a puzzling fondness for Stalin, he defended his protégé from Budyonny by declaring *Red Cavalry* "has no parallel in Russian literature" and justified Babel's literary eccentricities as "revolutionary romanticism."⁵⁶ Most likely Soviet censors, blind to the very spirit they were trying to eradicate, were

35

deaf to the subversive silences of his fiction. One imagines a real if shrinking margin of freedom here.

Then why did Babel's productivity drop off sharply after 1925? We can dismiss the simple answer of fear. He could have left Russia several times, having been granted permission to travel to Paris in 1927 and again in 1934 to visit his first wife and daughter living in exile, but chose instead to be wrenched from his family in order to pursue his "hellish trade" inside the Soviet regime. He "was convinced that a writer mutilates himself and his work by leaving his native country," his daughter Nathalie writes. "He always refused to emigrate; on top of which, his sense of honor and love of the limelight demanded that he stay among his own people . . . What in so many people would have produced only fear and terror awakened in him a sense of duty and a kind of heroic fatalism."[57]

Nadezhda Mandelstam, in noting the silence of her husband, Boris Pasternak, and Anna Akhmatova in the late 1920s, speaks of "a hypnotic trance," the "onset of a kind of numbness, the first symptoms of lethargy," born of a pressure "to submit to historical inevitability . . . another name for the dreams of all those who had ever fought for human happiness."[58] But what if historical inevitability arrived as a bullet in the back of the neck?[59] Mandelstam speculates that writers, in order to find their voices again, "had first to determine their places in the new world being created before their eyes—and this they could only do by learning from experience how it affected everybody else."[60] And exactly how Stalin's brand of totalitarianism affected everyone else would become Babel's new area of espionage, although by now he likely knew where he stood with the New Era: outside it. His declining productivity, then, his "early fading" had probably more to do with forging a new narrative art to speak to new realities. And with one other issue as well. Judging from his often-expressed dissatisfaction with *Red Cavalry*, it can be surmised he was chagrined by the prominence he had given to his own captivation by violence. What had become a monolithic tool of the Revolution was for him now an exploded romanticism.

At any rate, the stories Babel wrote in the last decade of his life reflect a new directness, a faith in psychological realism to explore the shaping influences of his childhood and the depredations of the Revolution. The link between these two spheres is drawn in "With Old Man Makhno."[61] Here the narrator spies with a disinterested curiosity ("I would see how the woman looked after her sixfold ravishing") upon a Jewish servant maid the morning after her rape by six young Cossacks. "And it seemed to me that of yesterday's virginity there remained only the cheeks, more than usually inflamed, and the eyes, thrust downward" (279). A retarded Cossack urchin, Kikin, who held the Jewess' head during the assault, is protesting to her with an aggrieved sense of injustice that he was not allowed his turn until after the syphilitic Matvey Vasilyich, an opportunity he declined lest he "regret it all my life." The maid listens impassively as he goes on with his short-circuited moral algebra: "People go around saying all sorts of fine things about the Makhno crowd, about what stout lads they are, but knock around with them for a while and you'll soon find that each has a heart of stone" (280). Kikin's inability to convert this truth into personal guilt, indeed recognize anyone but himself as the "victim" of the rape, feel any compassionate solidarity with the servant maid, signals the moral myopia of his creator's early voyeuristic ties with the Revolution. All of this is rendered symbolically when suddenly Kikin, in an astonishing portrait of the artist, "pressed his palms to the floor, threw his legs in the air and, his protruding heels rigid, started walking quickly about on his hands" (280).

By the early 1930s the Party commissar enforcing collectivization had replaced the Cossack on the cutting edge of the Revolution, and Russian writers were all expected to spread the official doctrine or perish. Four years earlier Babel had written a screenplay, *Benya Krik* — the date is 1919 and the Odessa gangster has joined the Revolution and learned to kill. But things go badly in the chaos of Ukraine, and ultimately Benya and his "revolutionary" regiment are executed by a Party commissar and his hatchet men. The screenplay, as Charyn says, "is a form of suicide, not because Benya dies, trapped within a Revolution that is worlds away from his cosmology, but because

Babel ravaged his own fairy tale, sacrificed the King, surrendered him to the Revolution's song of the common man."⁶² Antonina Pirozhkova writes movingly of their lonely wanderings through the same region at this time. The couple often went to Kabardino-Balkari in Ukraine to stay with Betal Kalmykov, a Regional Secretary of the Party who fascinated Babel, a pure revolutionary he called "a new man, a great man of the sort we haven't heard before" who "by sheer determination and vision" is "turning a small, semi-savage alpine land into a real gem."⁶³ In 1937, Kalmykov was summoned to Moscow and disappeared.

Babel worked on a novel about Stalin's enforced collectivization, but all that survives is a first chapter, "Gapa Guzhva," the name of a bawdy vodka-drinking widow who has slept with all the husbands in her impoverished Ukrainian village. During the wild celebration of six simultaneous weddings, Gapa invites Ivashko, the frustrated head of the Regional Commission for Collectivization, to join in. "It would be inappropriate for me to break bread with you," he says. "You people aren't human — you bark like dogs!"⁶⁴ An old woman pilgrim, Rakhivna, spends the night at Gapa's, telling of a judge named Osmolovsky who "collectivized the whole of Voronkov in a single day," of the nine squires he arrested and sentenced to a chain gang but who then escaped the next morning: "Nine squires dangling from the rafter on their belts!" (411) When Party authorities appear to arrest Rakhivna for her "propaganda campaign about the world coming to an end" and penalize the village, Gapa explains the problem with twinkling eyes to the corrupt Osmolovsky: "The good people of the village say that in the collective farm everyone is to sleep under the same blanket! . . . We like sleeping in twos, and we like our home-brewed vodka, goddamn it!" (414) Later, when she returns at midnight to ask the judge what is going to happen to the whores, Gapa learns that her fate will be not unlike the nine squires: "They will no longer exist."

More and more, then, Babel's witness returned a tragic sense of life. For instance, in the retrospective "The S.S. *Cow-Wheat*," set against the rich ethnic diversity and pastoral fecundity of the

Volga region during the Civil War, he measures the price of the Revolution's cold-blooded efficiency. The skipper of the *Cow-Wheat*, Korostelyov, a vodka-swilling mystic of pre-Revolutionary days, delivers guns to the Red Army at Baronsk, and during the layover is "tortured" by political tutorials using copies of *Pravda* as he lies drunk and wallowing in "green trails of vomit." When the *Cow-Wheat* slips out on a secret night journey to procure liquor, Korostelyov has occasion to echo a complaint against the Revolution made by Babel earlier in his career: "'Jew,' said the helmsman to me, 'what will come of the children? . . . The children are getting no schooling,' said the helmsman, spinning his wheel. 'The children will all turn out thieves'" (324). Once back in Baronsk he is summarily executed by the Red Army. As Party head Malyshev explains: "It's all very well to be a fine fellow three times over, to have spent time in hermitages, to have sailed the White Sea, to be a desperate fellow generally; but please don't waste fuel . . ." (328)

The romantic gangster world of the Moldavanka in *Tales of Odessa* is starkly changed in "The End of the Old Folks' Home," where Babel's former gallery of Jewish wise men (Arye-Lieb and others) are reduced to gravediggers pinched in poverty. They resist an order making inoculation for smallpox mandatory because, as Meyer Engless complains, "there's nothing to prick." "Life is a dung heap," he mumbles, "the world a brothel, and people a lot of crooks" (355). Initially the old folk survive by washing and burying the dead in the nearby cemetery, using a recycled coffin — quaint ironic symbol of an intact community — but at the funeral of a Soviet military man they are ordered to bury the coffin too. With timber for another coffin not available and harassed by Soviet authorities, they are evicted from the poorhouse:

> The sun stood high in the sky, and its rays scorched the rags trailing along the road. Their path lay along a cheerless, parched and stony highway, past huts of rammed clay, past stone-cluttered fields, past houses torn open by shells, past the Plague Mound. An unspeakably sorrowful road once led from the cemetery to Odessa. (363)

All of these developments lie latent in "The Road," where the young Babelesque narrator leaves the "crumbling front" during the Civil War, reaches Kiev, and then boards the train to Petrograd only to witness and endure Soviet atrocities. A telegrapher climbs on board, checks the travel permit of a young Jewish teacher, just married, and shoots him in the face. A hunchbacked muzhik nearby "unbuttoned the dead man's trousers, sliced off his sexual organs with a pocketknife, and stuffed them into the wife's mouth," cackling that she can now eat something kosher.[65] Next, Jews are thrown out of the cars and onto the rails. The muzhik takes the narrator's boots and coat, and the boy runs barefoot through the snow: "I felt him mark a target on my back, the nip of his aim cutting through my ribs" (424). By late next morning he reaches a shtetl: "There was no doctor at the hospital to amputate my frostbitten feet" (425). The Soviets move the Jewish patients out on a cart in the darkness, and the narrator now trudges the freezing destitute road. Boarding another train and sleeping under the muzzle of a howitzer, he reaches Petrograd. "The Nevsky Prospekt flowed into the distance like the Milky Way. Dead horses lay along it like milestones. Their legs, pointing upward, supported the descending sky" (426). The boy finds Cheka headquarters, in search of Kalugin, his former sergeant and now an investigator for the Party police. He is directed to Anichkov Palace, former residence of Czar Alexander III and Nicholas II, where the two soldiers reunite. After Kalugin carries the narrator into a hot bath, the two pass the night smoking cigars and reading the diaries of former royalty. The next day Kalugin takes his friend to the Cheka, where he is issued a military uniform and given a position in the Foreign Division "translating depositions of diplomats, *agent provocateurs*, and spies." The narrator concludes: "Within a single day I had everything: clothes, food, work, and comrades true in friendship and death, comrades the likes of which you will not find anywhere in the world, except in our country. That is how, thirteen years ago, a wonderful life filled with thought and joy began for me" (430). Such elation is another example of Babel's complex use of irony, and his taste for unreliable narration. Charyn believes that "the tag he places at the end reads like a kiss to Comrade Stalin and the Central Committee, as if Babel were preparing his own progress report as a Bolshevik pilgrim."[66] But only apparently. Everything that has happened to the narrator between Kiev and Petrograd, every Soviet atrocity undercuts his hymn to revolutionary comradeship. The irony cancels out neither his desperate, almost hysterical need to believe so nor the darker truth that prompts it.*

A last story from this period, "Guy de Maupassant," offers a brilliant summary of Babel's spiritual odyssey. Once again the place is Petrograd, 1916, with himself as a young bohemian writer, spending his mornings "hanging around the morgues and police stations," his days abiding by the wisdom of his ancestors that "we are born to enjoy our work, our fights, and our love; we are born for that and for nothing else . . ." (329) He takes no pause in dismissing Tolstoy's conversion to religion as "yellow . . . all fear . . . He was frightened by the cold, by old age, by death; and he made himself a warm coat out of his faith"(332). Marked early on by this callow buoyancy, the narrator finds work in assisting with a translation of Maupassant by Raisa, a handsome Jewess whose wizened husband has grown rich selling war materials to the army. He discovers that "in

---

*Again it is Nadezhda Mandelstam who provides the brilliant insight here. "The one thing that seemed to me an after-effect of his illness," she writes of her husband in *Hope Against Hope*, "was an occasional desire he now had to come to terms with reality and make excuses for it. This happened in sudden fits and was always accompanied by a nervous state, as thought he was under hypnosis. At such moments he would say that he wanted to be with everybody else, and that he feared the Revolution might pass him by if, in his short-sightedness, he failed to notice all the great things happening before our eyes. It must be said that the same feeling was experienced by many of our contemporaries, including the most worthy of them, such as Pasternak. My brother Evgeni Yakovlevich used to say that *the decisive part in the subjugation of the intelligentsia was played not by terror and bribery (though, God knows, there was enough of both), but by the word 'Revolution,' which none of them could bear to give up* (emphasis mine). It is a word to which whole nations have succumbed, and its force was such that one wonders why our rulers still needed prisons and capital punishment." Mandelstam, 126.

her translation not even a trace was left of Maupassant's free-flowing sentences with their fragrance of passion" (331). Soon Raisa ravishes his dreams, and he woos her with his own translation of the French master: "A phrase is born into the world both good and bad at the same time. The secret lies in a slight, almost invisible twist. The lever should rest in your hand, getting warm, and you only turn it once, not twice" (331). Then one night, with both of them drunk, he reads aloud "L'Aveu," and their identities merge into their fictional counterparts: the lascivious Polyte and modestly submissive Celeste. After the apparent seduction ("Of all the gods ever put on the crucifix, this was the most ravishing"), he feels intoxicated with life; yet returning to his room he finds a biography of Maupassant and reads through the night:

> That night I learned from Edouard Maynial that Maupassant . . . was twenty-five when he was first attacked by congenital syphilis. His productivity and *joie de vivre* withstood the onsets of the disease. At first he suffered from headaches and fits of hypochondria. Then the specter of blindness arose before him. His sight weakened. He became suspicious of everyone, unsociable and pettily quarrelsome. He struggled furiously, dashed about the Mediterranean in a yacht, fled to Tunis, Morocco, Central Africa . . . and wrote ceaselessly. He attained fame, and at forty years of age cut his throat; lost a great deal of blood, yet lived through it. He was then put away in a madhouse. There he crawled about on his hands and knees, devouring his own excrement. The last line in his hospital report read: *Monsieur de Maupassant va s'animaliser*. He died at the age of forty-two, his mother surviving him. (337-38)

Now the narrator senses that while honoring Maupassant's techniques of irony, he had missed his mentor's tragic sense, as he had Tolstoy's and Raisa's earlier. "The fog came close to the window, the world was hidden from me. My heart contracted as the foreboding of some essential truth touched me with light fingers" (338). Fifteen years of experience had lifted the fog for the composer of these lines and confirmed their sense of personal foreboding. Like Maupassant, he would die of an "incurable ailment" in his early forties, his mother surviving him.[67]

From this point onward, with a few exceptions, Babel was to

become master of what he called the genre of silence. In 1934, at the first Soviet Writers' Congress, he delivered a speech that was an exquisitely layered theatrical performance: partly a confession of his lack of productivity, partly a mandatory tribute to Stalin and the increasingly paranoid regime, partly an oblique criticism of the state of Russian letters. The aesthetic of socialist realism now held sway, and he rather boldly attacked "the triteness" of "that individual with his government-issued eyes who becomes even more frightening when he feels he has to tell people about his love . . . I am joking, but the serious aspect of it is that, in our profession, it is our duty to help the triumph of the new Bolshevik taste in this country."[68] Balanced between Soviet pieties and slightly incriminating, yet self-protective humor, Babel continued:

> Now, speaking of silence, I cannot avoid talking about myself, the past master of that art. I must admit that if I lived in a capitalist country, I would have long since croaked from starvation and no one would have cared whether, as Ehrenburg puts it, I was a rabbit or a she-elephant . . . But in our country people take into consideration whether you are a rabbit or a she-elephant . . . I am not happy about my silence. Indeed, it saddens me. But perhaps this is one more proof of the attitude toward the writer in this country . . . I think that, as Gorky said yesterday, Sobelev's words, "We have everything" should be written on our flag. The Party and the government have given us everything, depriving us only of one privilege — that of writing badly.[69]

This might be dismissed as subservience to the Party, until one recognizes that to be deprived of the privilege of "writing badly" is to be deprived of literary freedom, period. But we might wonder whether, in addition to the obvious reason that it might keep him alive, Babel's silence wasn't also recognition that his own writing, with its truth-telling radar, could never inhabit the formulas of socialist realism, indeed could now only propagate despair.

These issues are displaced and given a subtle and haunting expression in "Dante Street." Here another Babelesque narrator is shown the restaurants and hotel-brothels of Paris by Bienal, then "spies" on his host by listening through the wall of his hotel room to the used-car salesman making love to a girlfriend. Returning to Paris after a month in Marseilles, he resumes his voyeuristic post only to confront a murder scene — Bienal's throat cut by the girlfriend, gendarmes shaking down the hotel: "Doors were open; men in unlaced shoes had been lined up in the corridor. In the room occupied by the wrinkled Italian racing-cyclist, a barefooted little girl was weeping into a pillow" (351). These sordid realities are subsumed by the narrator into a tragic sense of French history reaching back to another patriot struck down by the Terror of a revolution he had embraced:

> Here dwelt Danton a century and a half ago. From his window he had seen the Conciergerie, the bridges cast light across the Seine, the array of blind-eyed hovels pressed close to the river; the same breath had risen to him. Jostled by the wind, the rusty trusses and the inn signs creaked. (352)

BABEL'S FATE WAS SEALED in 1936 with the death of Gorky, who most likely was poisoned by Stalin. "Now they are not going to let me live," he told Antonina.[70] It would be the loss of more than just a writer. "A tremendous variety of people were drawn to Babel," she writes, "not only because he was a man of high culture and a wonderful storyteller, but also because of his character; his was a delightful nature and his charm worked on absolutely everyone. Babel loved life, believed that people were born for merriment and the pleasures of life. He delighted in funny stories and situations, which he loved to invent."[71] Antonina relished his gift for impersonation, even if she seems unaware of its use in his writings: "Babel loved to try acting out a whole range of roles: a cripple, a miser, a sick man, a jealous lover. If he and I went for a walk around the city, he might suddenly begin limping, and limp in a whole variety of ways, either as if he had one leg shorter than the other, or as if one leg was twisted and had to be dragged. Passersby would look on in surprise, and while he kept the most serious expression on his face, I would be dying of laughter."[72] That same year the couple had a daughter, Lydia, and her birth occasioned another instance of what Antonina called her husband's "kindness that bordered on the catastrophic":

> I remember when Babel came to the maternity hospital to take us home. I was already dressed in my street clothes when I suddenly saw the front vestibule door open and Babel come in carrying so many boxes of chocolates that he had to steady the top of the stack with his chin. He immediately began giving them away right and left, to all the doctors and nurses he met on his way — both to those we wanted to thank and those who had nothing to do with us. That was Babel through and through![73]

Although he loved children and was the father of two daughters and a son, history was not to allow Babel to raise them. His separation from his beloved first-born Nathalie, growing up in France, was for him an irremediable loss. Yet joining them in exile was never an option. "I am a Russian writer," he said. "If I didn't live with the Russian people, I would cease being a writer. I would be like a fish out of water."[74]

Babel continued to labor at his writing, but published little, turning for busy work to drama and film. "Daily I read idiotic screenplay manuscripts and revise them. I do anything — just in order not to write, let alone publish."[75] There were rumors of a novel in progress, probably *Velikaya Krinitsa*, never to be recovered. Babel's play, *Mariya*, was roundly denounced and his new work could not find publishers. The "heroic fatalism" that Nathalie Babel found in her father can be understood as a blend of several passions: a love of the Russian people, a loyalty to the Revolution's fallen victims, a fidelity to his mission of literary espionage, and perhaps even an inability to totally relinquish his early hopes for the Revolution. Babel and Antonina continued their travels to economic projects and villages undergoing collectivization, in search of "proletarian man" whose individual representatives fed his curiosity, but whose literary stereotypes he could never embrace. According to one of Stalin's biographers, Edvard Radzinsky, the head of the NKVD at the time, Genrikh Yagoda, invited members of the Writers Union into the depths of the Lubyanka to "listen in" while interrogators used "special methods," the usual euphemism for torture, upon some wretched member of the *intelligentsia* until he confessed or betrayed a friend. As he had done since the Polish campaign, Babel was among those writers who accepted the invitation.

But once Yagoda was replaced as head of the NKVD by Yezhov, Stalin's "devil dwarf," one of the great killers of a fratricidal century, the Terror moved into full gear. That year five percent of the population was arrested. "Every family was always going over its circle of acquaintances," Mandelstam writes, "trying to pick out the provocateurs, the informers and the traitors. After 1937 people stopped meeting each other altogether, and the secret police were thus well on the way to achieving their ultimate objective."[76] The novelist Boris Pilnyak spoke despondently of the prevailing mood: "There isn't a single thinking adult in this country who hasn't thought that he might get shot."[77] Pilnyak was arrested in 1937, shot in 1938, although not before accusing Babel of espionage. As more writers began to be arrested, Babel showed concern for their wives, now outlawed, and had one of them move in with him and Antonina, telling his wife: "I'll breathe more easily if she lives with us."[78] The Terror would not cease until fifteen hundred writers had been killed, and thousands more imprisoned, their lives either mutilated or destroyed. Babel wrote a screenplay in these dark days that contained a boldly derogatory portrait of Stalin.[79] Finally he was arrested in 1939 when Yezhov, who had married one of Babel's former lovers and nursed a simmering jealousy, went to Stalin and accused him of espionage.

It turned out that the master of the genre of silence had not been idle. Fifteen folders of manuscripts, 18 notebooks, 517 letters, and 245 other loose sheets of paper were confiscated by the NKVD, then destroyed in 1941 as German troops reached the outskirts of Moscow. In the late 1930s, neither Babel nor Antonina could comprehend the confessions made again and again by people they admired. But under unimaginable torture in the Lubyanka he too "confessed" to conspiracies against the Soviet Union, to the slanderous failure of his writings, and implicated fellow artists and innocent friends such as Sergei Eisenstein, Solomon Mikhoels, and Yuri Olesha. In November of 1939, Babel sent two desperate letters to Laventrii Beria, who had replaced Yezhov when the mad executioner was himself arrested by Stalin, declaring that all his statements implicating his friends were "incorrect and invented." His trial was held in Beria's office on January 26, 1940 and lasted twenty minutes. He was convicted of "active participation in an anti-Soviet Trotskyite organization" and of "being a member of a terrorist conspiracy, as well as spying for the French and Austrian governments."[80] Babel's last words were: "I am innocent. I have never been a spy. I never allowed any action against the Soviet Union. I accused myself falsely. I was forced to make false accusations against myself and others . . . I am asking for only one thing — let me finish my work . . ."[81] He was shot early the next morning, his body cremated and the ashes thrown into a common grave, which incidentally only a week later would receive the remains of Yezhov.

"They didn't let me finish," Babel had whispered to Antonina that night the NKVD came for him.[82] Yet there was sufficient time to leave behind works of true literary genius that were incandescent with the nightmare energies of the early twentieth century, yet curiously triumphant over them. In an era of mass cultural suicide, Babel's nascent sense of guilt as a survivor forged a bond of responsibility to his fallen brothers and sisters, providing a basis for morality once the Revolution had embarked on extirpating its memory through sheer terror and violence.[83] This was continuous with his aesthetics. The lucidity and concreteness of his prose links Babel with the poetic school of Acmeism, which Osip Mandelstam defined as "a nostalgia for world culture."[84] Indeed this memory is like a deep sea in the silences of his fiction. In these respects his stories are, as he said of Maupassant's, "the magnificent grave of a human heart." Yet his art also records a timeless present, piercing the heart with the expansiveness and depth of its vision. All of Babel's artistic "violence" is only meant to shock us awake and return us to the precious earth.[85]

In his last story, "Di Grasso," a fourteen-year-old boy, working for an unscrupulous ticket scalper at the Odessa Theater, witnesses a performance by the Sicilian tragedian, who, playing a jealous shepherd in a simple folk tale, springs across the stage and tears the throat out of a rival, galvanizing the audience.[86] During his stay Di

Grasso "played *King Lear, Othello, Civil Death*, Turgenev's *The Parasite*, confirming with every word and every gesture that there is more justice in outbursts of noble passion than in all the joyless rules that run the world" (379). This passion leaps from stage to audience as the wife of the ticket scalper, upon leaving the theater, recognizes that from her husband she can expect only "beastliness today and beastliness tomorrow" (381), but forces him to return the boy's pawned watch. Stunned (like ourselves as readers of Babel), the boy "saw the columns of the Municipal Building soaring up into the heights, the gas-lit foliage of the boulevard, Pushkin's bronze head touched by the dim gleam of the moon; saw for the first time the things surrounding me as they really were: frozen in silence and ineffably beautiful."

NOTES

1 The question was posed to Babel by Osip Mandelstam in 1937, and his reply recorded by Nadezhda Mandelstam in her brilliant memoir of this period, *Hope Against Hope*, translated by Max Hayward (New York: Atheneum, 1970), 321.

2 Konstantin Paustovsky, *Years of Hope*, translated by Manya Harari and Andrew Thomson (New York: Pantheon Books, 1968), 139.

3 According to Cynthia Ozick, Babel "was devoured because he would not, could not, accommodate to falsehood; because he saw and he saw, with an eye as merciless as a klieg light; and because, like Kafka, he surrendered his stories to voices and passions tremulous with the unforeseen." See Ozick's introduction to *The Collected Stories of Isaac Babel*, translated by Peter Constantine (New York: Norton, 2002), 15.

4 Nadezhda Mandelstam makes the same point about this predominant trait of Babel's: "Everything about Babel gave an impression of all-consuming curiosity — the way he held his head, his mouth and chin, and particularly his eyes. It is not often that one sees such undisguised curiosity in the eyes of a grown-up. I had the feeling that Babel's main driving force was the unbridled curiosity with which he scrutinized life and people." *Hope Against Hope*, 321.

5 "We were all the same," writes Mandelstam, "either sheep who went willingly to the slaughter, or respectful assistants to the executioners. Whichever role we played, we were uncannily submissive, stifling all our human instincts. Why did we never try to jump out of windows or give way to unreasoning fear and just run for it — to the forests, the provinces, or simply into a hail of bullets? . . . The end was the same anyway, so that was nothing to be afraid of. It was not, indeed, a question of fear. It was something quite different: a paralyzing sense of one's own helplessness to which we were all prey, not only those who were killed, but the killers as well. Crushed by the system each one of us had in some way or other helped to build, we were not even capable of passive resistance. Our submissiveness only spurred on those who actively served the system. How can we escape the vicious circle?" *Hope Against Hope*, 369.

6 See Nathalie Babel's introduction to *Isaac Babel, The Lonely Years 1925-1939: Unpublished Stories and Private Correspondence* (Verba Mundi/David Godine, 1995), 11.

7 Antonina Pirozhkova, *At His Side*, translated by Anne Frydman and Robert Busch (South Royalton, Vermont: Steerforth Press, 1996), 87.

8 See Sinyavsky's essay in *Isaac Babel: Modern Critical Views*, edited by Harold Bloom (New York: Chelsea House, 1987), 94-95.

9 Quoted by Paustovsky, 141.

10 Isaac Babel, *The Collected Stories* translated and edited by Walter Morison (New York: New American Library, 1955), 257. Further page references in the text, unless otherwise noted, will be to this edition of Babel's stories.

11 "But it's in Odessa where the idea of a Jewish Defense Corps began," writes Jerome Charyn in his brilliant biography of Babel, *Savage Shorthand* (New York; Random House, 2005). "Fifty-five of these corpsmen were killed. As the American consul stationed there said after the pogrom of 1905: 'Odessa presents an appearance more dead than alive.'" 101.

12 Mandelstam's view of this generational and cultural war during the Revolution is insightful: "Who foresaw the disastrous consequences of abandoning humanism in the name of some overriding aim? Who knew

what calamities we were calling down on our heads by adopting the principle that 'everything is permitted'? Only a handful of intellectuals — but nobody listened to them. Now they are accused of 'abstract humanism,' but in the twenties everybody mercilessly heaped scorn on them. The standard epithets for them were 'puny' and 'spineless,' and the word 'intellectual' itself was always given a pejorative ending (*intelligentishka*). They were constantly caricatured in the press, and the thirty-year-old partisans of the 'new era' would have nothing to do with them." *Hope Against Hope*, 325.

13 In his brilliant *The Time of Stalin*, translated by George Sanders (New York: Harper & Row, 1981), Anton Antonov-Ovseyenko estimates the deaths caused by Stalin, from Civil War days to post-World War II executions to deaths in the Gulag, at 100 million.

14 See Gorky's editorial, published in *New Life* on November 7, 1917 and reprinted in Isaac Babel's *You Must Know Everything*, translated by Max Hayward (New York: Farrar, Straus and Giroux, 1966), 50. Page references to Babel's journalism that appeared in *New Life* and to his stories in *Lava* are to this volume.

15 Quoted by Charyn, 190.

16 *Ibid.*, 190.

17 On this matter, Andrei Sinyavsky's remarks on Babel, written from behind the barbed wire of the Gulag, are illuminating: "Babel exhibited a trait common, perhaps, to all writers: he was not merely an observer, he was also a snooper. All his life he spied 'through the keyhole' in the hope of seeing something interesting. As an author, he was always himself off stage, looking from the outside at the bizarre scenes he picked out from some squalid area of life — hence his reticence about his own views and the elusive quality of his biography." *A Voice from the Chorus*, translated by Kyril Fitzlyon and Max Hayward (New York: Farrar, Straus and Giroux, 1976), 140.

18 This story, along with his other observations on war, appears in *You Must Know Everything* and is an example of Babel's genius for finding "objective correlatives" in the lives of others for his own inner situation. Old Marescot and his bag of family remains, for instance, might well serve as an image of Babel's allegiance to his "exploded" family legacy.

19 See Lionel Trilling's excellent introduction to Walter Morison's edition of *The Collected Stories*, especially 25.

20 Quoted by Charyn, 43.

21 *Ibid.*, 12.

22 Along with Babel, the generation of exceptional writers that came of age at the dawn of the Revolution included Anna Akhmatova, Nikolai Gumilev, Osip Mandelstam, Andrei Bely, and Dmitri Mirsky. The majority of these writers were either killed or imprisoned by Stalin, or had their personal and creative lives devastated by the Soviet regime.

23 Quoted by David Remnick, "Laughter in the Dark," *New York Review of Books*, April 10, 1997, 26.

24 Paustovsky, 142.

25 Quoted by Remnick, 26.

26 Hemingway discovered Babel during the Spanish Civil War and was delighted to "find that Babel's style is even more concise than mine," although the American's minimalism lacked the Russian's metaphoric exuberance. "But none of this might have happened," Charyn writes, "if 'Hem' and Babel hadn't gone to war — war would mark them with an ambiguity worse than any wound. Hem liked to brag that he'd served in the Arditi, the Italian shock troops of World War I who were as notorious as the Red Cavalry would become in the Russian Civil War. But Hem was only a boy in the Red Cross, an ambulance driver . . . blown up weeks before his nineteenth birthday, while distributing chocolate and cigarettes in the trenches; he would have pieces of shrapnel embedded in his buttocks for the rest of his life, remain with a little forest of scars on his legs. And Babel would return from Poland with a severe case of asthma and lice all over his body; a few of his friends had even given him up for dead. Hem would adopt the swagger of an air marshal, and Babel would often behave like a man who was still rocking along on a horse, but whatever the pretense and personal fables, they'd absorbed the no-man's-land of military conflict . . . and what that conflict could do on a page of prose." *Savage Shorthand*, 80-81.

27 Mandelstam, 143.

28 Quoted by James Falen, *Isaac Babel: Russian Master of the Short Story* (Knoxville: University of Tennessee Press, 1974), 55.

29 Isaac Babel, *The Collected Stories of Isaac Babel*, translated by Peter Constantine (New York: W.W. Norton, 2002), 72. Page references to "Odessa" are to this edition.

30 The Jewish sector of Babel's Odessa was under severe persecution during this period by the Union of the Russian People and the Black Hundreds, extreme right-wing anti-Semitic organizations responsible for pogroms in the region.

31 John Berryman, *The Freedom of the Poet* (New York: Farrar, Straus and Giroux, 1976), 122.

32 Babel employs the mock-epic technique of having his characters gravely repeat the statements of their interlocutors in oracular confirmation of their truth. Thus Benya appropriates the knowledge of others as his own, as when he ends a conversation with a messenger from an "Aunt Hannah" who has uncovered the plans for the police raid. Messenger: "What shall I tell Aunt Hannah?" Benya: "Tell her: Benya knows all about the raid."

33 Charyn, 101.

34 This line harkens back to "Awakening," which ends with the young and delinquent Babel locked in a privy to escape his raging father. It also reminds us that Babel never hesitates to mock his own persona in the stories, nor underscore his almost ineradicable alienation from the festival of life he evokes there.

35 For all his curiosity about life and love for humanity, Babel remained essentially the isolated artist. "I am an outsider," he writes early in his diary of the Polish campaign, and this declaration was true throughout his life, wherever he went.

36 See Raymond Rosenthal's insightful article, "The Fate of Isaac Babel," *Commentary*, February 1947, 126-31.

37 Is the ironic message perhaps that Babel recognized his own boyhood fantasies of Cossack glamour as vicarious breast-feeding? Tsudechkis' term as Lyubka's manager spans the same length of time as Babel's own hero-worship of the Cossacks — beginning with his father's imagined

humiliation in 1905 and extending through the Russo-Polish campaign of 1920.

38 Sinyavsky, *Isaac Babel: Modern Critical Views*, 88.

39 Patricia Carden, *The Art of Isaac Babel* (Ithaca: Cornell University Press, 1972), 203.

40 Isaac Babel, *1920 Diary*, translated by H.T. Willetts, edited by Carol Avins (New Haven: Yale University Press, 2002), 78. Page references to the diary in the text are to this volume.

41 Revealingly, when Pan Apolek contemplates painting Lyutov's portrait, he promises to cast him as St. Francis.

42 We have seen Babel's use of repetition for ironic "validation" in *Tales of Odessa*. Here Lyutov's repetition of the Revolution's canon of violence works to undercut it. In failing to recognize this mechanism, Renato Poggioli goes seriously astray in his analysis of this passage: "A man with a faith like Babel's will fight out of a sense of ideological duty, and thus will treat any kind of military struggle as a civil war. Strangely enough . . . he feels his own unworthiness before all those martial murderers for whom killing is a natural habit, or a simple routine. Thus he defends the slaughter and the slaughterers from those who fear and condemn them: 'She cannot do without shooting . . . ,' he tells Gedali, 'because she is the Revolution . . .' Without being born a killer, he not only joins the killers, but wishes and tries to become one of them . . ." *The Phoenix and the Spider* (Cambridge: Harvard University Press, 1957), 233.

43 Babel was quite capable of hyperbolic and bloodthirsty journalism in *Red Cavalryman*, for instance the following entry entitled "The Killers Must Be Finished Off," on September 18, 1920 after pogroms had been conducted by Polish forces in Komarow: "The pogrom was, of course, carried out strictly in accordance with regulations. The officers began by demanding that the Jewish population purchase their safety for 50 thousand rubles. The money, and vodka, were immediately forthcoming, in spite of which the officers were in the first ranks when the pogroms began, zealously searching for bombs and machine guns in the houses of the mortally terrified old Jews. This is our reply to howls from the Polish Red Cross about Russian atrocities. This is one fact among a thousand more terrible facts. The dogs whom we have still to put down have let out their hoarse yelp. The murderers who await the final blow have crawled out of their coffins. Soldiers of the Red Army, finish them

off! Beat down harder on the opening covers of their stinking graves!" In Appendix to *1920 Diary*, 106-07.

44 Richard Hallett, *Isaac Babel* (New York: Frederick Unger, 1973), 101.

45 Frank O'Connor, "The Romanticism of Violence," *Isaac Babel: Modern Critical Views*, 61.

46 Lionel Trilling was offended by this brutality, remarking that "we are inclined, I think, to forget Pavlichenko and to be a little revolted by Babel." Yet this would be an error: the brutality was simply there.

47 On August 20, 1920 Babel records what appears to have been routine during the campaign: "An attack in the evening near a farm. A bloody battle. The military commissar and I ride along the line begging the men not to massacre prisoners. Apanasenko washes his hands of it. Sheko's tongue ran away with him — the massacres have played a terrible role. I couldn't look at their faces, they bayoneted some, shot others, bodies covered by corpses, they strip one man while they're shooting another, groans, screams, death rattles, the attack was carried out by our squadron. Apanasenko remained aloof, the squadron dressed itself up as expected, Matusevich's horse was killed under him, he runs around with a terrible, dirty face looking for a horse. It's hell. Our way of bringing freedom — horrible. They search the farm, drag people out, Apanasenko — don't waste cartridges, stick them. That's what Apanasenko always says — stick the nurse, stick the Poles." *1920 Diary*, 73-74.

48 This episode recalls "The Story of My Dovecot" when the crushed guts of his pigeon stream down the temple of the young boy attacked during the pogrom. It is an example of the way Babel uses a recurring image as a thread to knit together his entire canon of stories into a single work of ethical evolution.

49 Another example of one of Babel's secret selves appears in "Two Ivans." Here Ivan Akinfiev holds captive Ivan Ageyev, who had twice deserted the front and feigns deafness as an excuse. On a level of double-entendre, Lyutov is apparently allied with Akinfiev but is actually the spiritual double of Ageyev, who ultimately is deafened by pistol shots fired next to his ear. Interestingly, Babel has a terrible ear infection in the last month of the campaign.

50 Compare with Babel's earlier piece, "On the Field of Honor." Here again, by juxtaposition, Babel links himself in brotherhood with the

retarded French soldier first shamed and ultimately executed by his own officer.

51 It is unlikely that the Revolution could have "liberated" such wholesale killing had it not been preceded by the demoralization of World War I with its unspeakable carnage, its ten million dead, and the moral vacuum of its aftermath — leaving alive only a persisting compulsion to do harm.

52 Babel wrote on July 28: "A terrible truth — all the soldiers have syphilis. Matyazh is getting better (with hardly any treatment). He had syphilis once, got cured in two weeks, he and a friend of his were supposed to pay ten silver kopecks in Stavropol, the friend died, Misha has had it several times, Senechka and Gerasya both have syphilis, they all go to the village women, although they have fiancées at home. The scourge of the soldiery, Russia's scourge. It's terrifying. They eat crushed crystal, drink either carbolic acid or a solution of ground glass. All our fighting men — velvet caps, rape, forelocks, battles, revolution and syphilis. All Galicia is infected." *1920 Diary*, 41.

53 Nadezhda Mandelstam's remarks are relevant here: "Kindness is not, after all, an inborn quality — it has to be cultivated, and this only happens when it is in demand. For our generation, kindness was an old-fashioned, vanished quality, and its exponents were as extinct as the mammoth. Everything we have seen in our times — the dispossession of the kulaks, class warfare, the constant 'unmasking' of people, the search for an ulterior motive behind every action — all this has taught us to be anything you like except kind." *Hope Against Hope*, 134.

54 Quoted by Falen, 154.

55 Trotsky, himself a talented literary writer, had a scathing contempt for the formulaic pieties of "proletarian" literature. By 1932, however, with the school of socialist realism officially inaugurated, writers like Babel were on the defensive.

56 Isaac Babel, *The Lonely Years*, 385.

57 See Nathalie Babel's introduction to *Isaac Babel, The Lonely Years*, 18.

58 Mandelstam, 44.

59 A frightful measure of Stalin's bloodletting appears in Alexander

Solshenitsyn's *The First Circle* as a major character, Innokenty, arrested and slated for execution, contemplates a physical detail of the Lubyanka: "It was there, on the steps of the last flight of stairs, that Innokenty noticed how deeply the steps were worn. He had never seen anything like it in his life before. From the edges to the center they were worn down in oval concavities to half their thickness. He shuddered. How many feet must have scraped over them to wear out the stone to such a depth!" *The First Circle*, translated by Michael Guybon (London: Collins, 1968), 659.

60 Mandelstam, 163.

61 Known for his daring and cruelty, Nestor Ivanovich Makhno was a Ukrainian anarchist guerilla who fought against the Red army during the Polish campaign and is credited with devising the decisive armament of the conflict, the tachanka, an innocent-looking wagon filled with hay that concealed a battery of machine guns. As Babel wrote in *Red Cavalry*, "An army of tachankas possesses undreamed-of possibilities of maneuver." Babel would mischievously nickname his beloved daughter Nathalie "Makhno" because of her spirited nature. Visiting her in Paris in 1932, he wrote to his sister Maria, "I still haven't recovered from the shock I received at the sight of my daughter—I never suspected anything of this sort. It is really quite beyond me where she could have got so much cunning, liveliness and cupidity (from her father, of course). And it is all full of style and charm . . . I haven't been able to find one ounce of meekness or shyness in this tiny tiger cub." Quoted by Charyn, 127.

62 Charyn, 108.

63 Pirozhkova, 31.

64 Constantine, 410. Page references in the text to "Gapa Guzhva" are to this edition.

65 *Ibid.*, 424. Page references in the text to "The Road" are to this edition.

66 Charyn, 90.

67 Babel's "incurable ailment," of course, was not syphilis, but its moral equivalent, the allure of violence, which, he acknowledged, found its psychosomatic expression in his headaches, asthma, and generally poor health. Again Nadezhda Mandelstam has the telling observation: "We

all emerged shaken and sick from the first years of the Revolution ... The men seemed stronger and withstood the first shocks, but then their hearts gave out and very few lived to be seventy. Those spared by war and prison were carried away by heart attacks or the sort of fantastic diseases from which Lozinski and Tynianov suffered. Nobody here will ever believe that cancer is not connected with the shocks to which we are constantly exposed. We have seen too many cases in which someone has been publicly hounded and threatened, only to hear shortly afterward that he has cancer." *Hope Against Hope*, 307.

68 Quoted by Remnick, 27.

69 *Ibid.*, 27.

70 Pirozhkova, 103.

71 *Ibid.*, 97.

72 *Ibid.*, 98.

73 *Ibid.*, 92-93.

74 Quoted by Nathalie Babel in her preface to Constantine's *The Collected Stories of Isaac Babel*, 23.

75 Quoted by Falen, 226.

76 Mandelstam, 34.

77 Quoted by Charyn, 161.

78 *Ibid.*, 140.

79 For a description of the content of Babel's original screenplay, which was unearthed and published in a Soviet film journal in 1963, see Falen, 231-38.

80 Quoted by Remnick, 27.

81 *Ibid.*, 27.

82 Pirozhkova, 113.

83 "It was rather the onset of a kind of numbness, the first symptoms of lethargy," Mandelstam writes. "What was there to talk about when everything had already been said, explained, signed and sealed? Only children continued to babble their completely human nonsense, and the grown-ups — everybody from bookkeepers to writers — preferred their company to that of their peers. But mothers prepared their children for life by teaching them the sacred language of their seniors. 'My children love Stalin most of all, and me only second,' Pasternak's wife, Zinaida Nikolayevna, used to say. Others did not go so far, but nobody confided their doubts to their children: why condemn them to death? And then suppose the child talked in school and brought disaster to the whole family? And why tell it things it didn't need to know? Better it should live like everybody else . . . So the children grew, swelling the ranks of the hypnotized." *Hope Against Hope*, 44-45.

84 Mandelstam, 246. Along with their adherence to the aesthetics of Acmeism, the careers of Osip Mandelstam and Babel had much in common. Both shared the same moral sensibility; both were committed to the ideals but unable to adjust to the reality of the "New Era"; both fell silent in the late 1920s; both ran afoul of the NKVD in the 1930s, Mandelstam for his 1933 poem on Stalin, which included the lines "His cockroach whiskers leer / And his boot tops gleam," and whose first version, which fell into the hands of the secret police, includes the lines "All we hear is the Kremlin mountaineer / The murderer and peasant slayer"; both for a period were under State orders to "isolate but preserve," but finally perished in the purges.

85 An early line of Osip Mandelstam's might serve as Babel's epitaph: "But I love this poor earth, because I have not seen another . . . "

86 Charyn offers a bold and imaginative interpretation of "Di Grasso," seeing Babel poking fun at socialist realism. "Di Grasso's troupe could be likened to Stalin's own troupe of Soviet writers," he surmises, and goes on to compare Di Grasso's murderous leap at his rival to Stalin's policies. Yet this seems doubtful. For instance, one would have to believe that all the Sicilian actors are frauds, which doesn't square with the reaction of the Odessa theater-goers.

ERNEST HEMINGWAY

The Great War

"WE SHOULD NOT ATTRIBUTE a very high degree of reality to the Great War," W. B. Yeats warned, as if sensing the reasonable grounds for insanity there.[1] Ernest Hemingway proved him right by shunning the warning. At the peak of the fighting, Western Europe was scarred by 475 miles of trenches, stretching from the North Sea to Switzerland, and over a four-year period ten million men died there, in holes and ditches smelling of rum and blood and rotting flesh, a stench that carried for miles. The trench system, says Cecil Lewis, was "a prodigious and complex effort, cunningly contrived, and carried out with a deadly seriousness, in order to achieve just nothing at all. It was . . . a fantastic caricature of common sense."[2] Hemingway's engagement in the theater of action was brief, a mere six weeks before he was severely wounded, but like so many survivors, remembering the war became for him a life work. It was perilous work, and if Hemingway himself became a caricature of common sense in the effort, it is likewise true that his claim to be the moral conscience of his generation lies here. His loyalty always remained with the fallen dead; he spoke for them, deviously *as* one of them. It is no exaggeration to say that it is the indelible stench and bloated corpses of the Great War that fill up the deeper reticences of his famous "iceberg" style. That he had no choice in the matter, that it ultimately vitiated his art — none of this detracts from the courage of his meditations or their appeal to a world readership.

It seems right to emphasize this now, nearly five decades after Hemingway's death and as his reputation as a writer continues to go into decline. Dwight Macdonald took his measure long ago, granting him importance as a stylistic innovator and short-story writer, but seeing him as a failed novelist who, after 1930, "just didn't have it anymore . . . "[3] And this seems right too, even though it does not account for that failure nor explain Hemingway's appeal long beyond then. More recently, psychological critics have had a field day scoring on his works, exposing transparent neuroses, gender confusion, or worse everywhere, and they too have their point.[4] But it is a great intellectual irony that these critics, using Sigmund Freud's insights that were refined by study of damaged survivors of the Great War, should have so little sympathy or historical understanding for their subject. In 1987, in a brilliant groundbreaking biography to which I will return, Kenneth Lynn established the specific links between Hemingway's familial past and his fragile, depressive personality.[5] Yet Hemingway's significance is much larger than his literary merits or his complexes. The Great War ushered in a new modern age of violence — sudden, insensate, mechanized, devoid of responsibility — and it was this man, in his very vulnerability, who taught us of its feel and consequences to the human spirit. That his art was contaminated, and himself destroyed, in an effort to forge a dignified response to it is no cause for self-congratulation. We owe a debt to Hemingway, he is part of our buried lives, but it seems more and more apparent that we want to dismiss him, like a perversion we once indulged in but are now over.[6] In the remarks that follow, I would like to resist this self-deception in an effort to imagine the man suffering behind the work. Obviously our maturity is false, and the perversion still alive and virulent in the form of our own history.

Hemingway took with him to the Great War a Midwestern past that makes him seem almost sacrificial. Carlos Baker tells us that among his first spoken words at the age of three were — "Afraid of nothing."[7] His father was a doctor, severely puritanical, who could be alternately charming and suddenly punitive, a lover of the outdoors who was both expert fisherman and merciless hunter, and probably manic-depressive. No doubt Ed Hemingway's authority was compromised in his son's eyes by his submitting to the domination of his wife. Grace, while discreetly taking on a lesbian lover in Oak Park, Illinois, emphasized genteel culture and the enjoyment of life consistent with Christian ideals. As Lynn has shown, Grace's operatic morality, controlling parenting, and preening artistic ambitions, coupled with her dressing and raising her son and his older sister Marcelline as "twins," were to both profoundly influence the future writer's development and earn his mother his eternal enmity. As Hemingway wrote bitterly near the end of his life in *A Moveable Feast*, "With bad painters all you need to do is not look at them. But even when you have learned not to look at families nor listen to them and have learned not to answer letters, families have many ways of being dangerous."⁸

Whatever the deeper impact of these contradictions, Hemingway's early interest in shooting guns, football, and boxing suggest a reactive violence against these stifling pieties, a rebellious urge to break out into the real world. After a brief stint as a reporter in wild and brawling Kansas City, his opportunity came before he was nineteen. Drawn to the Great War, in January of 1918 he volunteered for overseas duty with the American Field Service. But like millions of young men who had preceded him, he had no idea he had chosen in the war a rite of mass cultural suicide as his new authority. "I was an awful dope when I went into the last war," he wrote in 1942. "I can remember just thinking that we were the home team and the Austrians were the visiting team."⁹ This classical analogy between war and sport had lured a generation of young men from both sides into the trenches in 1914, and such innocence was drowned in carnage. We might ponder the famous feat of a British captain, W.P. Nevill, who led his men at the Somme attack by dribbling a soccer ball up to the German front lines. Nevill was killed instantly, as was the spirit he embodied, by an engagement that cost the British 60,000 killed or wounded on that single day alone, for an advance of a hundred yards. By the time Hemingway arrived in 1918, after Verdun, the Somme and Passchendaele, this analogy had turned obscene among the survivors by conditions of an interminable war that resembled a charnel house. With the lineaments of his manhood sensitive, yet unshaped, and armored by nothing but that blank American receptivity to initiatory shock, Hemingway was fated to experience the war in a way that was both normative and ineradicable.

The shock arrived with a kind of preordained swiftness. After a layover in Paris, drinking with his pals and gaping at craters ripped open by the shells of Big Bertha, Hemingway moved on to Italy and his first ambulance assignment: gathering up corpses and human fragments at an exploded munitions factory outside Milan. Years later in *Death in the Afternoon* he was to recall the grim scene:

> I remember that after we had searched quite thoroughly for the complete dead we collected fragments. Many of these were detached from a heavy, barbed-wire fence which had surrounded the position of the factory and from the still existent portions of which we picked many of these detached bits . . . The picking up of the fragments (was) an extraordinary business; it being amazing that the human body should be blown into pieces which exploded along no anatomical lines, but rather divided as capriciously as the fragmentation in the burst of a high explosive shell. (135-37)

Finally, after three weeks treating the wounded at Schio and now restive for the combat zone, the young ambulance driver reached a position a mile behind the front lines at Fossalta: a village along the banks of the Piave River north of Venice. Here for a week he led a charmed life, delivering cigarettes and chocolate to the troops by bicycle, until on July 8, shortly after midnight, a crude Austrian mortar shell landed in a trench. Two soldiers were killed instantly, another critically wounded, and Hemingway's lower torso was riddled with hundreds of metal fragments. An uncanny sense of living his own death to be reborn again is memorably recorded in *A Farewell to Arms*:

> Through the other noise I heard a cough, then came the chuh-chuh-chuh-chuh — then there was a flash, as when a blast-furnace door is swung open, and a roar that started white and went red and on and on in a rushing wind. I tried to breathe but my breath would not come and I felt myself rush bodily out of myself and out and out and out and all the time bodily in the wind. I went out swiftly, all of myself, and I knew I was dead and that it had all been a mistake to think you just died. Then I floated, and instead of going on I felt myself slide back. I breathed and I was back. The ground was torn up and in front of my head there was a splintered beam of wood. In the jolt of my head I heard somebody crying. I thought somebody was screaming. I tried to move but I could not move. I heard the machine-guns and rifles firing across the river and all along the river. (54-55)

Thanks to Lynn's research, we know what happened next, which puts the lie to the myth of Fossalta that was spawned by the young second lieutenant and then embraced by Malcolm Cowley and a generation of literary critics.[10] Gravely wounded by shrapnel, but not critically, Hemingway responded with courage, offering assistance to more seriously wounded Italian soldiers until he was carried to a dressing station. However, his own embellished account reflects the kind of theatrical, if suicidal heroism that would mark his later life. "Our own death is indeed, unimaginable," Freud said in 1915, "and whenever we make the attempt to imagine it we can perceive that we really survive as spectators."[11] Countless Great War soldiers recall this division of the psyche into "actor" and "spectator" under the stress of outrageous hazard, enabling them to perform their duty without seemingly endangering the "real" self. But in Hemingway's case, this happened only as *fiction*, as he would promulgate the legend that he was able to carry another wounded Italian soldier on his shoulders 150 yards to safety before his knees were ripped by machine-gun fire. Yet the "real" self surfaced later, Siegfried Sassoon observed, the one "mainly disposed toward a self-pitying estrangement from everyone except the troops at the front line."[12] Hemingway awoke to his real self in a roofless shed, surrounded by so many dead and dying that he was to say much later that to join them seemed more natural than to go on living. Apparently, for a time he thought of shooting himself with his officer's pistol, as if to grant that night an ultimate integrity.[13]

Instead Hemingway survived, but only to be tyrannized by this compulsion his entire life, returning to it obsessively in his fiction in a kind of hopeless exorcism. On the surface it hardly seemed that way during his convalescence in a military hospital in Milan. It was here that Hemingway found himself, with what must have been dazed delight, a war hero, recommended for the silver Medal of Honor, admired by his comrades for his valor under fire, and displayed by the nurses as a paragon of injured masculinity. But the truth about the medals is revealed in "In Another Country," when Nick Adams is asked in the therapy room by a group of Italian soldiers how he earned them: "I showed them the papers, which were written in very beautiful language and full of *fratellanza* and *abnegazione*, but which really said . . . that I had been given the medals because I was an American" (208). And as for his valor: "I had been wounded, it was true; but we all knew that being wounded, after all, was really an accident" (208). It was in Milan also that the hero fell in love with a lovely American nurse treating his wounds, Agnes von Kurowsky. The association of his wounds with these precious rewards would be lifelong. "It does give you an awfully satisfactory feeling being wounded," he wrote back home at the time. "It's the next best thing to getting killed and reading your own obituary."[14]

This parting spark of gallows humor, however, is revealing of a darker recess of Hemingway's mind, a zone that sensed that his triumph was specious and misrepresented, that in the theater of modern war the brave died there. As his letter continues, "There are no heroes in this war . . . All the heroes are dead . . . Dying is a very simple thing. I've looked at death and really I know."[15] This, then, was the war's terrible paradigm of manhood, and we can guess that despite all the vainglory Hemingway must have experienced his own ongoing existence with a sickening measure of survivor guilt, his wound not as a badge of courage but of shame to be cleansed by death alone.[16] This dimension has been suspiciously overlooked in our efforts to understand the man, and for the same reason, perhaps, that compelled the world to strain to repress the Great War from modern memory. For ultimately it was some nascent sense of survivor guilt that remained an etiological wellspring for morality after the war had undermined the authority of a once proud culture, and by drawing an accusing connection between survivor and fallen brother, it implicated all in the crime. Hemingway was to slip that feeling right past our guard because he felt it so profoundly, if with only partial self-awareness. There was a battle-seasoned captain, Eric Dorman-Smith, who mesmerized him upon his medical release from Milan and would become a life-long friend, and the hobbling American never forgot the Anglo-Irishman's favorite quotation from Shakespeare's *Henry IV, Part II*: "By my troth, I care not; a man can die but once; we owe God a death . . . and let it go which way it will, he that dies this year is quit for the next."[17]

From such a logic there was no armistice. Hemingway was

welcomed back home a war hero, singled out by the *New York Sun* as having received more punishment than any other soldier who had "defied the shrapnel of the Central Powers," but underneath he must have been embarrassed, knowing that he was accepting such adulation in bad faith. More like Harold Krebs in "Soldier's Home," he had secretly been "sickeningly frightened all the time," exposed to a violence that alienated him from a respectable world now grown nauseating in its power to extort "quite unimportant lies" from him that consisted in "stating as fact certain apocryphal incidents familiar to all soldiers" (112). This was a common experience of veterans returning from the front. Sassoon confessed that "the man who really endured the War at its worst was ever-lastingly differentiated from everyone except his fellow soldiers."[18] For Robert Graves, the Armistice "sent me out walking alone . . . , cursing and sobbing and thinking of the dead," and he admitted one legacy of the war was also "a difficulty in telling the truth."[19] For Krebs, "a distaste for everything that had happened to him in the war set in because of the lies he had told . . . In this way he lost everything" (111). Religion is just lifeless cliché, love for his parents has vanished, dating girls is too "complicated," and there remains only his sister who looks like a "twin" to provide Krebs with company.

Similarly, while Hemingway might exaggerate his deeds to listeners back in Oak Park — claiming, for instance that he had been hit 32 times by 45-caliber bullets, or that he joined the Italian shock troops called Arditi after his wounding — one astute friend during this time, sensing a latent disgust and exile, remarked on his resemblance to someone "put in a box with the cover nailed down."[20] For this was the inner truth of his war experience, manhood was earned by death alone, and already we can see that in propagating a legend about himself Hemingway was only pursuing through mendacities what would later be the dominant theme of his fiction: men groping in the aftermath of cataclysmic violence for their lost sense of manhood and air of immortality. In his otherwise reliable biography, Jeffery Meyers would seem to have it exactly wrong in saying that his subject's escape from death at Fossalta "made him feel invincible . . . made him want to challenge fate."²¹ Hemingway's own proclivity in ensuing years for telling apocryphal tales about himself must also be viewed in a darker light. There is an episode from this time that reveals all by way of a visual double entendre. Hemingway was asked to address his old high school assembly, and after holding them spellbound by tales of the war's ferocity, he climaxed the show by holding up as evidence the bloodied, shrapnel-riddled pants he wore that night at Fossalta. The audience could hardly resist taking this as miraculous proof of his own bravery and immortality; yet it might more accurately be seen as evidence of his own death, or at least castration, as if the war hero had suffered his wound as a sexual maiming. On this score matters could hardly have been mollified with the news reaching him shortly afterward that Agnes von Kurowsky had fallen in love with an Italian soldier back in Europe.

In brief this was the march of events issuing from the Great War that shaped Hemingway's vision and would provide his fiction with its entelechy. Of course these events were undeniably stamped upon very ready psychic soil. It hardly seems likely, for instance, that his wound could have affected him as a castration if it had not revived earlier childhood fears of the same kind. The short stories are saturated with evidence, and in particular "Now I Lay Me," titled after the prayer Hemingway admitted he had repeated over and again while awaiting medical aid that night at Fossalta. Here a wounded Nick Adams, trying to cope with night trauma in a makeshift Italian hospital, free-associates back to an episode in his childhood when a fire in the attic set by his mother destroys jars of snakes kept in alcohol as well as Indian arrowheads and other relics of masculinity prized by his father.²² Likewise, the strength of Hemingway's death wish, simultaneously an impulse of loyalty to the war and punishment for surviving it, was no doubt abetted later by the terrible instruction of his father's suicide.²³ But there is a danger in this kind of psychologizing. For instance, Lynn sees Hemingway's death wish as primarily a compulsion engendered by his complex and depressive bondage to his parents. He even goes so far as to suggest that the son might have wanted to die of his wounds at Fossalta for his mother's sake.* But this perspective seems reductive, tends to minimize or ignore the weight of the historical moment on Hemingway's behavior and art. To an uncanny degree, the example of his father's suicide and the lessons of the Great War were woven together in Hemingway's psyche. To collapse his artistic symbols into private symptoms is to evade what he has to tell us. As John Thompson has observed, "The events in these Nick Adams stories are not the results of individual psychology or of complex motives or social situations. The actions, like those in all of Hemingway's best work, are the movement of fate."[24] And that fate was delineated by a war so horrible that even in the quietest of times 7,000 men were killed or wounded daily on the British side alone — "Wastage," as they were called by the staff. The only destiny was death. Anything else was cheating.

IN THE EARLY 1920s Hemingway went back to Paris, where it all started, to learn a style that might recover the feel of this malaise.

---

*Lynn underplays, indeed almost discounts the influence of Hemingway's wound at Fossalta. Because the young American was not as seriously injured as he pretended, because he was photographed in an elated state at the hospital in Milan, because he lied about what happened that night, and because he used those lies to glorify himself, Lynn concludes that the experience was hardly traumatic at all, indeed almost welcome. Of course, the lies may have served many purposes beyond inflating his ego as I will attempt to show, and certainly don't rule out trauma. Lynn is skeptical of the veracity of Hemingway's claim to Lowry in 1948 that "in the first war, I now see, I was hurt very badly; in the body, mind and spirit; and also morally . . . 'Big Two-Hearted River' is a story about a man who is home from the war . . . I was still hurt very badly in that story." Although people with PTSD are prone to misremember traumatic events as worse than they originally experienced them, Hemingway returned to Fossalta in his fiction for over thirty years, and we might heed the testimony of another Great War soldier, Robert Graves: "The memoirs of a man who went through some of the worst experiences of trench warfare are not truthful if they do not contain a high proportion of falsities. High-explosive barrages will make a temporary liar or visionary of anyone; the old trench-mind is at work in all over-estimation of casualties, 'unnecessary' dwelling on horrors, mixing of dates and confusion between trench rumors and scenes actually witnessed." Quoted by Fussell, 207.

Although his time in the combat zone was brief, he read widely and intensely about the war, claiming that knowledge as his own through the medium of his wound. Gregory Clark, an ex-infantryman and features editor at the *Toronto Star*, where Hemingway was filing dispatches on Paris and the Greco-Turkish war, remarked at the time: "A more weird combination of quivering sensitiveness and preoccupation with violence never walked this earth."[25] He had already learned from Pete Wellington, assistant editor at the *Kansas City Star*, to write short, plain, declarative sentences stripped of adverbs, dead metaphors, stale imagery, and all but devoid of adjectives. "Those were the best rules I ever learned for the business of writing," Hemingway told an interviewer in 1940. "I've never forgotten them."[26] From Ezra Pound he learned to perfect the accuracy of the natural image, and from Gertrude Stein the use of repeated words, prepositional phrases, present participles, and a colloquial American style. From both of them he learned to strip away all moral and rhetorical prophylactics from his language, leaving only an emotional positivism with a vengeance, a mode that was consistent with the returning veterans' sense of the incommunicability of their ordeal. The economy of this minimalist style and naked gesture, as Lynn points out, "make a virtue of necessity by packing troubled feelings below the surface . . . like dynamite beneath a bridge."[27] Fussell detects in Hemingway the utter sang-froid or style of British Phlegm of much Great War writings, and suggests he also learned much by imitating the cabelese of the foreign journalist.[28]

Regardless, the result of this discipline and meditation was *In Our Time*. Whether riding the rails with Nick Adams in "The Battler," or reclaiming dead babies in "On the Quai at Smyrna," we attend a sensibility adrift in a no-man's-land ready to deliver violence — murder, suicide, execution, loss of love — with the impersonal suddenness of a mortar shell crashing into a trench. In the former story, Nick, his eye bruised by a brakeman who knocks him off a train, finds the campfire of a punch-drunk ex-prizefighter Al Francis and Bugs, a sadistic Negro who controls his companion with a blackjack. Al's wife, who posed as his sister, has left him, and his face "was queerly formed and mutilated. It was like putty in color. Dead looking in the firelight" (99). Here is Nick's own life fast-forwarded. When Al remarks of him that "he says he's never been crazy," Bugs replies: "He's got a lot coming to him" (100). The narrator of these stories, in Wyndham Lewis's phrase, is "the man that things are done to," and a tightlipped irony of understatement, derived from a trench world where men huddled in a common grave against the chance of a direct hit from an unseen enemy, is the only appropriate interpretive means.[29] Hemingway had simply to make clear what happened; fate was implied in the haunting serenity of the style; the clean act of attention to detail became a modern equivalent of prayer. Hemingway could imagine no other way to record the moral history of his time, and to think him abnormal or diseased is to be blind to our own era. The spectacle of men maiming and killing other men with the numbed insouciance of actors in hell has remained the same, and it all started back in Mons:

> We were in a garden at Mons. Young Buckley came in with his patrol from across the river. The first German I saw climbed up over the garden wall. We waited till he got one leg over and then potted him. He had so much equipment on and looked awfully surprised and fell down into the garden. Then three more came over further down the wall. We shot them. They all came just like that. (77)

Or in Athens with the execution of Greek cabinet members:

> They shot the six cabinet ministers at half-past six in the morning against the wall of a hospital. There were pools of water in the courtyard. There were wet dead leaves on the paving of the courtyard. It rained hard. All the shutters of the hospital were nailed shut. One of the ministers was sick with typhoid. Two soldiers carried him downstairs and out into the rain. They tried to hold him up against the wall but he sat down in a puddle of water. The other five stood very quietly against the wall. Finally the officer told the soldiers it was no good trying to make him stand up. When they fired the first volley he was sitting down in the water with his head on his knees. (95)

Hemingway tried as a novelist to get rid of this terrible visionary imprint of the war, but the price of success was a crippling loss of artistic control. A single pure exception is his first novel, *The Sun Also Rises*, which endures because here Hemingway made his psychic wound physical and irreversible in the figure of Jake Barnes, thus ruling out any urge to cheat fate by some sleight of mind. "Well, it was a rotten way to get wounded," he says, "and flying on a joke front like the Italian" (31). Hemingway would say later that during his convalescence in Milan he talked with soldiers who had genital injuries, helping him to imagine a Jake Barnes, but his real research laboratory was his own mind. The point about Jake as a survivor of the war is that the experience of modern violence is an *unmanning* one. The compulsion to lie after the experience only demonstrates this. Jake can never forget, and forced to the sidelines of sexual competition, he can assess with a despairing fair-mindedness the spirit of a generation shattered by the war. To that generation the world now seems unreal. "All countries look just like the moving pictures" (10), Jake says, echoing the testimony of countless soldiers who returned home to what felt like a posthumous furlough. Language has been severed from a discredited cultural matrix, thus losing its restorative powers. "Talking's all bilge" (55). Jake is nominally a Catholic, but his session of prayer in an old cathedral his first day in Pamplona suggests that religion has become just an exercise of free associating back to terminal distress and self-pity. Such are the parameters of *nada* for those dubbed by Brett Ashley as "one of us."

All Jake and his expatriate pals who are also war veterans have left is a consuming regimen of drink, aimless travel, squalid pleasure-seeking, but we feel neither envy nor condescension. All of it is just a failing effort to cast off a shared nightmare that cannot be expunged. For these survivors a latent disgust inherited from the war is always breaking through the brain-numbing mists of absinthe. Even the fishing idyll in Burguete, Hemingway's version of pastoral, an attempt to rerun a movie of prewar innocence, is about as joyful as a romp of Bill Gorton's stuffed dogs. The witty exchanges between Bill and Jake allow Hemingway to express scorn for H.L. Mencken and mock the "irony and pity" that Gilbert Seldes had praised in a review of F. Scott Fitzgerald's *The Great Gatsby*. But when Bill turns with heavy irony to spell out the trouble with Jake, he actually touches on the truth: "You've lost touch with the soil. You get precious. Fake European standards have ruined you. You drink yourself to death. You become obsessed by sex. You spend all your time talking, not working. You are an expatriate, see?" (115) When Bill claims that detractors might call him impotent too, Jake replies, "No, I just had an accident," so his friend retreats and proposes: "That's what you ought to work up into a mystery. Like Henry's bicycle" (115). The reference is to Henry James' castrating injury which he euphemistically equated with Civil War America "rent with a thousand wounds."[30] Which is exactly what Hemingway has done in the novel, for Jake notes that James was not injured on a tricycle, but "a plane is sort of like a tricycle," and so is the bicycle that his creator rode to the front lines at Fossalta. What is left is only the code, among Jake and those grossly dichotomized by the war from a world of "superior, simpering composure," to avoid aggression and rivalry that might kindle war memories. "I did not care what it was all about," Jake admits. "All I wanted to know was how to live in it. Maybe if you found out how to live in it you learned from that what it was all about" (148).

But his posture of passive stoicism is very fragile. Robert Cohn, in Harvey Stone's words a case of "arrested development," partly because he missed the war, can easily move in to shatter it by unwittingly violating the code, forcing the group to recognize its lost options of physical prowess and romantic love. This is what sparks the anti-Semitism in Mike Campbell and Bill Gorton, and to a lesser degree in Jake. Cohn, we might guess, is an idealized version of the mediocre success young "Hemingstein" might have become minus his baptism in the war, and for this he is treated with the contemptuous pity one feels for old buoyant enthusiasms once they have been exploded by the shock of reality.[31] Cohn is made to feel that shock in his pathetic affair with Brett. "I hate his damned suffering," she says in dismissing him. "He can't believe it didn't mean anything" (181). Brett, already having lost her first lover to the war and Jake to the "bad joke" of his wound, got her title from a baronet who threatened to kill her and whose revolver she had to unload each night once he fell asleep. No wonder she can only experience sex as a mode of self-forgetfulness that parodies her real loss. By this order of compulsion she can only be a masculine force castrating real men (although removing the shells from a revolver, symbolically, is not castration so much as self-defense), but it hardly matters except to Cohn. His pugilistic revenge on Jake, Mike, and Romero seems more shameful than a vindication of manhood. Jake and his troops have already been unmanned by the war; Brett's promiscuity is only a spreading of the message, and she is always welcomed back into their solidarity of suffering.

As the action moves to Pamplona, Jake falls into the "wonderful nightmare" of the fiesta, for in the ritual of bullfighting he can witness a psychodrama of the war where manhood is commensurate with facing violent death. Betting on the bullfights, Jake explains, "would be like betting on the war. You don't need any economic interest" (99). Greeting the hotel owner Montoya, Jake thinks: "He always smiled as though bullfighting were a very special secret between the two of us; a rather shocking but really very deep secret that we know about" (131). But this secret can only clarify his own irremediable loss. Fireworks may burst "like shrapnel," the running of the corrida may evoke the terrors of trench assault to the crowd of "suicides" in the narrow streets, but Jake can only fade before it once again in a whirling blackout. The reaction of the waiter at the hotel to news about a young farmer running with the bulls that morning provides Jake with a sober perspective: "You hear? Muerto. Dead. He's dead. With a horn through him. All for morning fun. Es muy flamenco ... No fun in that for me" (198). Only Pedro Romero, the handsome nineteen-year-old Spanish matador, can earn the laurels of manhood, and Brett in the bargain, for he possesses what the expatriates lost to the war, "the old thing, the holding of his purity of line through the maximum of exposure" (168). Recovered from his beating by Cohn, he makes a perfect kill on the last day of the festival:

> He profiled directly in front of the bull, drew the sword out of the folds of the muleta and sighted along the blade. The bull watched him. Romero spoke to the bull and tapped one of his feet. The

bull charged and Romero waited for the charge, the muleta held low, sighting along the blade, his feet firm. Then without taking a step forward, he became one with the bull, the sword was in high between the shoulders, the bull had followed the low-swung flannel, that disappeared as Romero lurched clear to the left, and it was over. The bull tried to go forward, his legs commenced to settle, he swung from side to side, hesitated, then went down on his knees, and Romero's older brother leaned forward behind him and drove a short knife into the bull's neck at the base of the horns. The first time he missed. He drove the knife in again, and the bull went over, twitching and rigid. (220)

Hemingway didn't believe in "guts," something he said was of value only to violin makers, but rather in what Romero displays, "grace under pressure."[32] Once measured by this paragon, Gorton, Campbell, and Cohn easily fall into a state of stuporous self-pity and bellicosity. As long as Jake remains a peacemaker, in effect a "steer," he is able to maintain a bitter dignity. For like Belmonte, he has been gored by the war; now "life came only in flashes" (215). But the moment he rebels against this fate and tries vicariously to share some of Romero's manhood by pimping for Brett, he loses Montoya's respect and ultimately his own. "That was it. Send a girl off with one man. Introduce her to another to go off with him. Now go and bring her back. And sign the wire with love. That was it all right" (239). Finally it is Brett who has the honor to recognize that this deviancy has transpired in her sexual abduction of Romero and the decency to throw the young bullfighter back, thus sparing him his first goring (although her marrying him is impossible to imagine). She returns to Jake, her love and destiny so to speak, with the moral lesson that her abjuration is "what we have instead of God" (245). The declared shift from nymphomania to sainthood is a self-deception we can accept in such a sympathetic character. It is too barren of issue not to invite a wishful hedging. "Oh, Jake," she concludes in Madrid, "we could have had such a damned good time together" (247). But by now her man has regained his integrity. "Yes... Isn't it pretty to think so?" All that we have witnessed of the war's spiritual fallout tends to corroborate this pessimism, and the result is Hemingway's most flawless work of art.

But in *A Farewell to Arms*, a project that had been warily postponed for ten years, Hemingway ran into trouble, for he was forced to revive the war's terrible logic, a logic not formulated but suffered, and that he could get rid of only by rendering his art stillborn. It is revealing that the narrator of *A Farewell to Arms* is modeled after a dead man, Edward McKey, a Red Cross driver who was killed at Fossalta on June 16, 1918 (a date changed by Hemingway with devious accuracy to the night of his own wounding in a commemorative poem), and that the novel holds its "purity of line" only as long as Frederic Henry moves unerringly toward his fate.[33] Initially drawn to the front as a voyeur, bathing in its gentle homoerotic company, Henry is as yet unstamped by the war zone, which "did not have anything to do with me. It seemed no more dangerous to me myself than war in the movies" (37). Why he joined the ambulance corps escapes him, but as he tells Catherine Barkley: "There isn't always an explanation for everything" (18). He wavers between the gore-steeped cynicism of Rinaldi and the careworn transcendentalism of the Abruzzi priest, but devoid of affect he comprehends the experience of neither, so is emotionally unresponsive to their offers of true friendship. Nor can he accept the pacifism of Passini, who just before both are hit by a trench mortar tells him "there is nothing as bad as war," for most of all Henry "does not believe in defeat" — because he does not believe in his own death.

All this is altered by Henry's harrowing wound, which forges a subterranean bond with his dead comrades and enables him to grasp what was behind the priest's invitation to Abruzzi: "He had always known what I did not know and what, when I learned it, I was always able to forget" (14). Early on he spurned the priest for "the smoke of cafés and nights when the room whirled and you needed to look at the wall to make it stop, nights in bed, drunk, when you knew that that was all there was, and the strange excitement of waking and not knowing who was with you, and the world all unreal in the dark..." (13) However, taken from the front in an ambulance where the blood of a dead soldier streams down on him from the stretcher above, Henry has changed. He tells Rinaldi that he did nothing heroic, carried nobody on his back — "I was blown up while we were eating cheese" — as his creator disavows his own lies spread back in Oak Park, Illinois. Henry is able to forget while recuperating in a Milan hospital only by means of a love affair with Catherine that is so willed and sentimental that it feels like whistling in the dark. And of course it is, merely an actualized version of an earlier fantasized trip to Milan before his wounding, where Catherine "would pretend that I was her boy that was killed" at the Somme, which serves to shore up his manhood eroded when he escapes a similar death. Before his wounding, Henry's pursuit of Catherine is cynical and predatory, just a "chess game," but once in the hospital, "When I saw her I was in love with her" (91). Thus none of it rings true, neither Catherine's self-abnegation nor Henry's love, and especially not their embarrassing infantile double-talk with its sepulchral undertones, its endless protestations of love, its regressive slide into gender confusion and androgynous sexual play.[34] "There isn't any me," Catherine says at one point. "I'm you. Don't make up a separate me" (115). All of it operates as a bailing out of the war's logic made explicit by Nurse Ferguson when she predicts Henry's fate upon his return to the war: "You'll die then. Fight or die. That's what people do" (108).

And this fate seems assured when Henry, leaving Catherine pregnant and having been accused by Nurse Van Campen of contracting jaundice through excessive drinking to avoid a return to the front, rejoins his ambulance regiment armed with a dead officer's pistol. Casualties are terrible; morale has vanished; the British major at the club in Milan was right: "Everyone knew they were cooked" (134). The priest from Abruzzi is silenced by the extent of the slaughter. Rinaldi's spirit has been crushed, his body threatened with syphilis, and he reacts to the news of Henry's relationship with Catherine with the cynicism of a doomed man being told a palliating lie. But just before the Austrians and Germans break through at Caporetto, Henry regains a moral authority and has his revelation about the war:

> I did not say anything. I was always embarrassed by the words sacred, glorious, and sacrifice and the expression in vain. We had heard them, sometimes standing in the rain almost out of earshot,

so that only the shouted words came through, and had read them, on proclamations that were slapped up by billposters over other proclamations, now for a long time, and I had seen nothing sacred, and the things that were glorious had no glory and the sacrifices were like the stockyards at Chicago if nothing was done with the meat except to bury it. There were many words that you could not stand to hear and finally only the names of places had dignity. Certain numbers were the same way and certain dates and these with the names of places were all you could say and have them mean anything. Abstract words such as glory, honor, courage, or hallow were obscene beside the concrete names of villages, the numbers of roads, the names of rivers, the numbers of regiments and the dates. (184-85)

No words have captured with more brutal accuracy the fate of a generation of men sacrificed to the patriotic cant of Ezra Pound's "liars in public places."[35] Paul Fussell has suggested that the ironic discrepancy between the official euphemistic rhetoric used to prosecute the war and the actual fighting conditions in the trenches, which created a fog that concealed the truth from the home front, initiated a cultural devaluation of language that continues to this day.[36] Lynn rejects Henry's words as an expression of disillusionment with the war, pointing out that he begins "I was always embarrassed by the words sacred, glorious" and so forth, thereby proving the American's prejudice against abstract slogans existed before his entry into the war.[37] Perhaps, but the "always" might as reasonably extend back in time to precisely when Henry *did* enter the war. But does it matter? In either case the symbol or objective correlative of his words is clearly the Great War itself.

The retreat from Caporetto is a vividly drawn fast-moving panorama of deadly chaos. Their ambulance cars bogged down in the road, Henry shoots a sergeant who wanders off instead of obeying his order to help, and Bonello then finishes him off with his lieutenant's pistol. Aymo, a spirited socialist in the group, is mistaken for the enemy and shot dead in the darkness by Italian troops. Bonello soon wanders off. Henry suddenly finds himself detained by carabinieri who are summarily executing Italian officers as deserters or German agents on the banks of the Tagliamento. "We stood in the rain and were taken one at a time to be questioned and shot. So far they had shot every one they had questioned. The questioners had that beautiful detachment and devotion to stern justice of men dealing in death without being in any danger of it" (224). Henry escapes by leaping into the river and makes his "separate peace." Nor do we blame him. While hiding in a flat-car headed to Milan, he thinks: "You were out of it now. You had no more obligation . . . that ceased when the carabiniere put his hands on my collar" (232). Indeed every aspect of the retreat would seem to justify this position.

But as Hemingway wrote, then deleted from his manuscript, "*The position of the survivor of a great calamity is seldom admirable* (emphasis mine)" — and Henry is now in the same mental space upon his return to Catherine.[38] "In civilian clothes," he admits, "I felt like a masquerader" (221). And once again, as earlier in his hospital stay in Milan, he can partially deflect the war's claim on him only by means of a psychological regression: "But I did not have the feeling that it was really over. I had the feeling of a boy who thinks of what is happening at a certain hour at the schoolhouse from which he has played truant" (245). Obviously this transparent sleight of mind cannot be sustained. "I feel like a criminal," he says to Catherine. "I've deserted the army" (251). He may seek out in Count Greffi a father figure to sanction his flight from the war zone, one who equates wisdom with prudence and exalts love as a "religious feeling," but none of it assuages the uneasy tensions of survivor guilt that lurk under the surface. Henry might blister his hands rowing his lover to Switzerland, but adds derisively, "There's no hole in my side" (284), alluding to his own lapse from the prototype of the soldier as a crucified Christ at the heart of countless Great War poems.[39] As Hemingway was to observe later, Christ was "only successful because they killed him."[40] Henry's sense of manhood, then, is eroded once on neutral ground: he grows a beard, grows bored, drinks, and restlessly reads news accounts of the war. Catherine's death in childbirth is moving in isolation, but more a consequence of their leaving the war zone, it cannot serve adequately as a symbol of it.

Nothing is more revealing about Henry than his need to think so as he ruminates on his dead child:

> Poor little kid. I wished the hell I'd been choked like that. No I didn't. Still there would not be all this dying to go through. Now Catherine would die. That was what you did. You died. You did not know what it was about. You never had time to learn. They threw you in and told you the rules and the first time they caught you off base they killed you. Or they killed you gratuitously like Aymo. Or gave you the syphilis like Rinaldi. But they killed you in the end. You could count on that. Stay around and they would kill you. (327)

But this simply won't quite do. Catherine's death is the final stage of what Henry had called earlier a "biological trap," but the war certainly is not. By assigning a malevolent external cause to both, an unspecified *they*, Henry is simultaneously trying to recover his shattered self-esteem, blur human agency in the calamity that blew it up, and curtail his rising sense of *nada* and drift toward death. It was only after twenty-six revisions and the unappreciated aid of Fitzgerald that Hemingway was able to restore a measure of integrity. As Henry sits alone with Catherine's body, he tries to feel grief, feel anything, but "it wasn't any good. It was like saying good-by to a statue" (332). He walks out of the novel into the rain as if he owes the world a death: his own.

WE MIGHT SAY EXACTLY THE SAME of Hemingway as he moved into a new decade. He had his two best novels behind him, and his reputation was at a peak; yet he behaved as if his feats as a man and writer were secretly worthless. A world able to confront the legacy of the war, but unable to digest it completely, might respond to the strength of his art and be solaced by its flaws; yet he had discovered in the last half of *A Farewell to Arms* a compulsion to lie that must have sickened him and agitated even more the pull of death underlying it. Lynn shows clearly how this pull was strengthened by the suicide of Hemingway's father in 1930, a pistol shot through the temple, an action that the son felt was "cowardly," but which he still blamed on the castrating domination of his mother.[41] Thus, he is suddenly declaring in 1933 in *Death in the Afternoon* that all characters in fiction are "caricatures," a covert commentary on the masquerading identities of a Frederic Henry. And in order to avoid a repetition he will turn his literary credo of the 1920s upside-down: "A writer should create living people; people not characters," so that "his book will remain as a whole . . . as a novel" (191). In eschewing "characters," Hemingway was half-consciously admitting that he could only "make up" people who were marked for death, and that he was now prepared to write therapeutically of "living men" able to escape it with honor. Such a book would still be a "novel," since Hemingway would now "become" his living heroes, just as he was now using fame to efface his sense of unworthiness. His desperate rush into pure action from now on can also be understood as a terrified flight from a suicidal self. The obsession with bullring and hunting rifle, the risk-taking and accidents, the slide into alcoholism, the ugly competitiveness, the attacks on literary rivals, the bragging and bullying manner — all of this will contribute to the creation of the Hemingway legend, or, in Edmund Wilson's judgment, "the worst invented character to be found in the author's work."[42] The legend was widely embraced, but not by everyone. Hemingway's third wife, Martha Gellhorn, called him "the biggest liar since Munchhausen," while Zelda Fitzgerald dismissed his tough-guy image as "phony as a rubber check," defining him as "a pansy with hair on his chest."[43] Despite behavior that at its worst was truly despicable, it seems pointless to be censorious now. Through all of it Hemingway was only trying to witness or recreate the psychological coordinates of war, and in enduring blows, lend a momentary and resistant air of immortality to a more primary pursuit of death.

Death in the Afternoon is an uncanny investigation of these themes, an extended metaphor, and a series of visual double entendres that ritualized Hemingway's urgencies from the Great War and proposed a means of overcoming them. Steadied now by a prodigious feat of "natural" observation, he turned to the bullring not only because it was "the only place where you could see . . . violent death now that the wars were over" (2), but because that pivotal image of a bull charging an impassive matador dressed up for apparent sacrifice had to strike his inward eye as analogous to the murderous inter-penetration of opposing forces he felt on the battlefield, and the matador's most "ordinary wound," a castrating one that "comes oftenest between knee and groin" (255), analogous to his own war wound at Fossalta. Such subterranean connections can be made through the art of omission: "If a writer of prose knows enough about what he is writing about, he may omit things that he knows and the reader, if the writer is writing truly enough, will have a feeling of those things as strongly as though the writer had stated them. The dignity of movement of an ice-berg is due to only one-eighth of it being above water" (192).

What saves Hemingway's meditation from mere self-concern is the audacious, it unspoken, intuition that the postwar world was suffering from a similar trauma. Long before most of his contemporaries, Hemingway was able to sense its dread and distracting maneuvers, its moral vacuum, its infatuation with death, and from what we were to learn from Stalin, Franco, and Hitler, who can prove him wrong? In this light we can grasp his special scorn for the "self-called Humanists" of the 1930s, whose cultural decorum and pious optimism he saw as a blind denial of the world's persisting compulsion to do harm. This mode of amnesia is also embodied in the facile curiosity of the Old Lady, one who "liked to see the bulls hit the horses" (64), but will discuss these matters only in a "clean and wholesome" café. Again we might link the Old Lady up with Pound's "Hugh Selwyn Mauberley": "There died a myriad, / And of the best among them, / For an old bitch gone in the teeth, / For a botched civilization..." Lest we forget the legacy of death unleashed upon the world, Hemingway evokes with vindictive precision the carnage of the Austrian offensive of June 1918 in "A Natural History of the Dead":

> The color change in Caucasian races is from white to yellow, to yellow-green, to black. If left long enough in the heat the flesh comes to resemble coal-tar, especially where it has been broken or torn... The dead grow larger each day until sometimes they

become quite too big for their uniforms, filling these until they seem blown tight enough to burst. The individual members may increase in girth to an unbelievable extent and faces fill as taut and globular as balloons ... The heat, the flies, the indicative positions of the bodies in the grass and the amount of paper scattered are the impressions one retains. The smell of a battlefield in hot weather one cannot recall. (137-38)

Most striking about this is not its so-called morbidity, for it is naked fact, but that Hemingway has also projected upon these corpses a derisive portrait of himself as survivor: his flesh changing from "white to yellow," ego grown "quite too big" for his uniform, body evoking a smell "one cannot recall," only his own "scattered paper" speaking for the silent dead in solidarity. We can glimpse this eschatological bond also in the accompanying tale of a soldier who lies dying in a shelter, his head "broken as a flowerpot may be broken" (141), as his comrades plead with an army surgeon for an overdose of morphine. This is Hemingway's iceberg style with a vengeance, and it exposes with what stunning literalness he saw the Great War dead frozen under modern consciousness.

All that Hemingway could do as a tainted survivor, then, is find his morphine in the bullring, and the ingredients of salvation are there. Witnessing a faena, he says, "takes a man out of himself and makes him feel immortal while it is proceeding," indeed "gives him an ecstasy ... as profound as any religious ecstasy" (206). Deliverance lies in "that flash when man and bull form one figure as the sword goes all the way in" (247), for such a transformation of matador from impassive victim to potent killer held Hemingway spellbound as a sudden and uncanny transcendence of his own fate. Now he will turn to matadors like Maera in order to recast his identity in a heroic mold: "He was generous, humorous, proud, bitter, foul-mouthed and a great drinker. He neither sucked after intellectuals nor married money ... having no fear of death he preferred to burn out, not as an act of bravado, but from choice" (82-83). The Hemingway legend exactly, we say, but this will be no less a theatrical reflex than his fabricated rescue of a comrade that night at Fossalta. For "not being a bullfighter, and being much interested in suicides" (20), Hemingway turns his attention to matadors like Hernandorena, who falls inexplicably to his knees before the bull, without the training to fight from that position, and here suicide gleams like a hallucinatory rite of passage: "When he stood up, his face white and dirty and the silk of his breeches opened from waist to knee, it was the dirtiness of the rented breeches, the dirtiness of his slit underwear and the clean, clean, unbearably clean whiteness of the thigh bone that I had seen, and it was that which was important" (20). And yet a shameful image, too, for a matador can only increase his danger "within the rules provided for his protection" (21). This logic drives Hemingway at last to matadors like El Gallo, who "never admitted the idea of death" (159), thus corrupting the experience and initiating a modern period of decadence — "the decay of a complete art through a magnification of certain of its aspects" (70). Few words would apply with more accuracy and justice to Hemingway's own return to fiction, for in using it to assume his own "immortality," he would "magnify" just that aspect of bullfighting that provides such solace:

> Once you accept the rule of death thou shall not kill is an easily and a naturally obeyed commandment. But when a man is still in rebellion against death he has the pleasure in taking to himself one of the Godlike attributes; that of giving it. This is one of the most profound feelings in those men who enjoy killing. These things are done in pride and pride, of course, is a Christian sin, and a pagan virtue. But it is pride which makes the bullfight and true enjoyment of killing which makes the great matador. (233)

A terrible moral irony lurks in this "cure," for at last the moral gangrene that Hemingway had warned us about earlier is making inroads into his own soul. It is latent in the overbearing conceit of his new tone of voice in *Death in the Afternoon*, as his literary work is invaded by his own legend. When wounded, he had a glimpse of that soul leaving his body, but as a white handkerchief of surrender, not a red cape of provocation. Still tyrannized by that memory, he was now in danger of merging with the agency of his own oppression by exalting the therapy of killing. From now on his career will dramatize what Albert Camus, another war veteran, saw as the moral issue of our century: Will the victim be able to resist the role of executioner?[44] For Hemingway, at least, this proved to be only a passing intoxication. At one point in *Death in the Afternoon* he says sorrowfully of Maera that "he hoped for death in the ring but he would not cheat by looking for it" (82). Ultimately it is to his own credit that he would cheat for death rather than pursue such a morally repulsive triumph over it.

By the mid-30s, then, Hemingway's imaginative powers and mental health were in decline; yet two stories in a new collection, *Winner Take Nothing*, stand out as masterful and relevant here. In "A Clean, Well-Lighted Place," two waiters and a deaf old man who a week earlier had tried to hang himself sit in an Italian café. "He was in despair," one waiter says. "About what?" the other asks. "Nothing." A soldier and a girl walk down the street. "The guard will get him," a waiter says. The old man is asked to leave by the younger waiter who wants to close the café and go home to his wife, but when the older waiter objects, he is told: "You talk like an old man yourself." He replies, "I have never had confidence and I am not young . . . I am of those who like to stay late at the café. With all those who do not want to go to bed. With all those who need a light for the night" (290). He and the old man are both threatened with nothingness. And when the younger waiter leaves, he turns out the light and continues the conversation with himself that breaks into a prayer to the new deity:

> What did he fear? It was not fear or dread. It was a nothing that he knew too well. It was all a nothing and a man was nothing too. It was only that and light was all it needed and a certain cleanness and order. Some lived in it and never felt it but he knew it all was *nada y pues nada y nada y pues nada*. Our *nada* who art in *nada*, *nada* be thy name thy kingdom *nada* thy will be *nada* in *nada* as it is in *nada*. Give us this *nada* our daily *nada* and *nada* us our *nada* as we *nada* our *nada* and *nada* us not into *nada* but deliver us from *nada*; *pues nada*. Hail nothing full of nothing, nothing is with thee. (291)

In "A Way You'll Never Be," Nick Adams, having suffered a severe unspecified wound that leaves him unable to sleep "without a light of some sort," returns by bicycle through a landscape of bloated Austrian corpses to his battalion. It is as if Hemingway were imagining his own belated return to the front, now altered by all the "hurt" that life had dealt him. Nick is supposed to parade down the line in his fresh military uniform, to symbolize the immanent arrival of American forces and lift the morale of the Italian troops, but he refuses to wear a helmet because "they're absolutely no damn good. I remember when they were a comfort when we first had them, but I've seen them full of brains too many times" (313). He is haunted less by the front than a nightmare of a yellow house outside of Fossalta, "with willows all around it and a low stable and there was a canal, and he had been there a thousand times and never seen it, but there it was every night as plain as the hill, only it frightened him"(310). This image carries an eerie impenetrability as does much about the story. Indeed Nick's behavior, from his panicky free-associating to his bizarre lecture comparing the coming military forces to American grasshoppers, is recognized by his gentle and protective Italian comrades as evidence of madness, and even he verges toward this recognition. "It's a hell of a nuisance once they've had you certified as nutty," he says. "No one ever has any confidence in you again" (310). Sadly, this was more and more how Hemingway was being received by both friends and enemies alike.

In *Green Hills of Africa*, based on his trips to Kenya with his second wife, Pauline Pfeiffer, Hemingway leaps from the bullring into the wilderness with gun in hand, and this work is revealing of the slackening of performance as he turns with a rush to the therapy of killing. Moral drama is replaced by infantile rivalry between himself and his companion hunter, Karl; truth is trumped by a blustering self-confidence and adoration of Pauline while he was conducting an affair with Jane Mason; and tension is reduced to what it feels like to hunt big game. Of course the issue is not killing animals, but that Hemingway feels it all with too much relish, "that comic slap of the bullet and the hyena's agitated surprise to find death inside of him"

(37). It is as if he wants to get back, back to death, inside it looking out, as he gropes with necrophilic glee for the heart of a wounded roebuck: "I could feel it, hot and rubbery against my fingers, and feel the knife push it, but I felt around and cut the big artery and the blood came hot against my fingers" (53). As he is standing at last over his first slain kudu bull, "there was not a mark on him and he smelled sweet and lovely like the breath of cattle and the odor of thyme after rain" (231). It is easy to brand this version of pastoral as naked pathology, but Hemingway's compulsion to experience what he calls "the best elation of all, of certain action, action . . . in which you can kill and come out of it" (116), is merely a psychic replay of his war experience with himself emerging as victor. As long as he is stalking in trench-deep grass and the kill is "clean," this devious substitution seems to work, swelling him up with the "braggies." But mutilation, we can speculate, returned him in subliminal memory to his own wound and the Great War dead, and an air of bad conscience breaks forth when he gut-shoots a sable bull on the last hunt: "I was thinking about the bull and wishing to God I had never hit him . . . Tonight he would die and the hyenas would eat him, or, worse, they would get him before he died, hamstringing him and pulling his guts out while he was alive . . . It was my own lousy fault" (271-72). Of course this logic is hidden far from view in the narrative, but it is precisely in those dissociated leaps — the artistic equivalent of "not thinking about it" — that Hemingway reveals himself. His only allusion to the Great War emerges in this fashion, and revealingly, just as he has aired a rare empathy for a wounded elk that reminds him of his own pain:

> If you serve time for society, democracy, and the other things quite young, and declining any further enlistment make yourself responsible only to yourself, you exchange *the pleasant, comforting stench of comrades* (emphasis mine) for something that you can never feel in any other way than by yourself. (148)

But Hemingway could not hope to replace the legacy of the war by "something" else without extinguishing his own source of inspiration.

Early on he explains to his artistic conscience, Kandinsky, the need to forge a prose of "the fourth and fifth dimension" (27), but in reviewing the way writers are destroyed in America, he is only scoring his own fallen condition: "First economically. They make money . . . Then our writers when they have made some money increase their standard of living and they are caught. They have to write to keep up their establishments, their wives, and so on, and they write slop. It is slop not on purpose but because it is hurried. Because they write when there is nothing to say or no water in the well. Because they are ambitious. Then, once they have betrayed themselves, they justify it and you get more slop" (23). And most of *Green Hills of Africa* is slop — Hollywood natives, dead landscapes, literary gossip, with Hemingway stumbling through the brush like Huck Finn, a tripe knapsack on his shoulder and on the watch for snakes: "It's just like when we were kids and we heard about a river no one had ever fished out on the huckleberry plains . . ." (210). The reason he is able to pierce the mode of "cheating" in the last part of *Huckleberry Finn*, where Twain flinches from the psychic burden of exposing a murderous society, is that quite simply he is doing the same thing.[45]

When *Green Hills of Africa* was assailed by the critics, Hemingway wrote to John Dos Passos that "I felt that gigantic bloody emptiness and nothingness, like couldn't even fuck, fight, write and was all for death."[46] For the book was only designed to ward off another mode of cheating that he clarified soon afterward: "Since he was a young boy he has cared greatly for fishing; and shooting. If he had not spent so much time at them . . . he might have written more. On the other hand, he might have shot himself."[47] Indeed by 1936 suicide was beckoning. "Me I like life very much," he wrote to Archibald MacLeish. "So much it will be a big disgust when have to shoot myself. Maybe pretty soon I guess although will arrange to be shot in order not to have bad effect on kids."[48] Momentarily emancipated from his legend, and the therapy of killing, Hemingway was already taking indirect aim in two of his finest short stories from this period. In "The Snows of Kilimanjaro," Harry, a writer dying from gangrene in the African bush, awaits an evacuation plane with his wife Helen. Memories of Paris, Constantinople, and the war remind him of what he has failed to write about, and in particular a memory of a secret self hit by a German stick bomb coming in through the wire:

> He was a fat man, very brave and a good officer, although addicted to fantastic shows. But that night he was caught in the wire, with a flare lighting him up and his bowels spilled out into the wire, so when they brought him in, alive, they had to cut him loose. Shoot me, Harry. For Christ sake shoot me. They had had an argument one time about our Lord never sending you anything you could not bear and some one's theory had been that meant that at a certain time the pain passed you out automatically. But he had always remembered Williamson, that night. Nothing passed out Williamson until he gave him all his morphine tablets that he had always saved to use himself and then they did not work right away. (53)

Harry recognizes that his verbal hostility toward Helen, whom he has never loved and is guilty of nothing more than being concerned for her welfare, is baseless. "I don't know why I'm doing it," he says. "It's trying to kill to keep yourself alive, I imagine" (43). He has lied to his credulous wife from the beginning to make his "bread and butter," and in return, as the vultures gather, Helen shoots a Tommy ram to make him broth and tries to stop him from drinking alcohol that will inflame the gangrene. Nor can he blame her for destroying his talent. "Why should he blame this woman because she kept him well? He had destroyed his talent by not using it, by betrayals of himself and what he believed in, by drinking so much he blunted the edge of his perceptions, by laziness, by sloth, and by snobbery, by pride and by prejudice, by hook and by crook" (45). This pains him, not death, which "had obsessed him for years," and its arrival is a deliverance, giving Harry the sensation of flying a Puss Moth plane over the top of Kilimanjaro, "great, high, and unbelievably white in the sun," leaving Helen to deal with the rotting leg of her husband's corpse.[49]

In "The Short Happy Life of Francis Macomber," the hero, one of the "great American boy-men," seeks out a last desperate act of male assertiveness and is killed in the process. In a flashback we learn that the wealthy, yet sensitive Macomber ran away from a charging lion that he gut-shot in the African bush the previous day. For this he is scorned as a coward by his wife Margot, then cuckolded by Robert Wilson, their macho British hunting guide with a red face, "flat, blue, machine-gunner's eyes," and "a short, ugly, shockingly big-bored .505 Gibbs" (12). Macomber is both humiliated and furious, while Margot maintains a cold contempt for both her husband and Wilson, indeed for hunting big game. "You were lovely," she tells the guide after he shoots the lion. "That is if blowing things' heads off is lovely" (9). But the following day Macomber regains their respect on a buffalo hunt as he and Wilson shoot three bulls from a speeding car, causing Margot to exclaim to her husband: "You were marvelous, darling" (23). But one wounded bull wanders off into high brush, only now for Macomber "instead of fear he had a genuine elation" (24). Wilson quotes him the same Shakespeare passage that Eric Dorman-Smith quoted to Hemingway in that Milan hospital long ago, and in a redemptive replay of his moment of cowardice, Macomber now stands firm as the wounded bull charges from the brush into no-man's land toward him, "his rifle almost level with the on-coming head, nose out, and he could see the little wicked eyes and the head started to lower and he felt a sudden white-hot blinding flash explode inside his head and that was all he ever felt" (27). Trying to save him from the bull, Margot has accidentally shot and killed her husband with a 6.5 Mannlicher. This is the danger inherent in the pursuit of manliness, a danger Hemingway would try to disavow by misreading his own story, declaring to an interviewer in 1953 that "Francis's wife hates him because he's a coward. But when he gets his guts back, she fears him so much she has to kill him — shoots him in the back of the head."[50] This is the same false accusation that Wilson makes against Margot at the story's end, recasting a complex woman in a troubled marriage as a murderous bitch. Lynn suggests that Wilson embodies the Hemingway legend pitted against his true inner situation embodied in Macomber.[51] Certainly in his real life, Hemingway withdrew further into this legend of invincibility, became more pugnacious, spiteful, and paranoid. The bonds of friendship he had once so prized had been unraveling for a long time, but by 1936, Fitzgerald felt he had "completely lost his head" and was acting like "a punch-drunk pug fighting himself in the movies."[52] Obviously his scorn for Fitzgerald's moving confession in *The Crack-Up* only masked a terrified resolve not to follow him.

WHAT EMERGED FROM THIS ABYSMAL depression in his return to the novel was a new kind of hero, the he-man, a mere compensatory ideal that ironically the world came to accept as the real Hemingway. Such a hero, Harry Morgan, an ex-policeman with only his cojones to peddle for survival, is allowed a brief appearance amidst a volley of gunfire in *To Have and Have Not*. Often taken as Hemingway's turn to a new "social commitment" of the 1930s, this work is quite the opposite and makes excellent sense put next to what Charles Sorley wrote in a letter from the trenches as early as November 1914: "I should like so much to kill whoever was primarily responsible for the war."[53] Such an impulse seems to incite Morgan, and yet, while his escapades are superficially cast as a lawless response to the economic warfare of the Great Depression, his resort to violence is more reveled in than regretted. Early on he is drawn into a scheme to run "twelve Chinks" to the mainland, and to ward off an apparent double-cross and mass execution, he disposes of a nefarious Mr. Sing: "I took him by the throat with both hands, and brother, that Mr. Sing would flop just like a fish, true, his loose arms flailing. But I got him forward onto his knees and had both thumbs well in behind his talk-box, and I bent the whole thing back until she cracked. Don't think you can't hear it crack, either" (53-54). Such a mix of racism and pornographic violence runs through the action like gangrene. After losing his arm with devious justice in a bootlegging run, then allowing his wife, an ex-whore, to make insatiable love to his stump, Morgan is sunk into a more perilous scheme to run some blood-crazed revolutionaries into Batista's Cuba. "I didn't ask for any of this," he ruminates, "and if you've got to do it you've got to do it" (105). What Morgan does, however, is invite his friend Albert along without informing him of the risk, whereupon this genuine working-class victim is casually gunned down by the revolutionaries. Once held hostage on his own boat, Morgan has the unconscious hypocrisy to accuse them of betraying the working classes in slaying his friend. Again Morgan manages to thwart the double-cross with a Thompson automatic rifle; this time, however, he is fatally wounded in the process, and expires muttering: "No matter how a man alone ain't got no bloody fucking chance" (225).

We must resist, then, any temptation to see this despairing isolation of Hemingway's new "hero" as forced upon him by cold-blooded officialdom or depraved revolutionary politics. As his "nigger" friend, Wesley, says of him: "You ain't human . . . You ain't got human feelings" (86). Ultimately, Morgan is not fighting the establishment so much as mimicking it. The reasons lie deep in Hemingway's psyche, and they start floating up as derisive self-portraits, bobbing to the surface of an unraveling, quasi-confessional narrative. There is Robert Gordon, a commercial writer of immense personal opportunism whose works are regarded down at Freddie's place as "shit."[54] Branded as "selfish and conceited as a barnyard rooster" by his abused wife, Gordon is secretly impotent and wanders through the text looking for material to fan his sterile imagination. It is no accident that he is beaten up by the Vets as his reward. There are the exploiting and indolent rich, floating on their yachts through the insomniac night downing Luminal. Finally, and most important, there are the Vets, scorned stragglers from the Great War who are now punch-drunk rummies and learning to like it. These pitiful shades and their self-administered beatings down at Freddie's place make up the ugliest scenes in all of Hemingway: "We are the completely brutalized ones. We're worse than the stuff the original Spartacus worked with. But it's tough to try to do anything with because we have been beaten so far that the only solace is booze and the only pride is in being able to take it" (206). Trapped between these projections of himself, it is not surprising that Hemingway evokes a Harry Morgan, a virile "bad-dream man" whose urge to violence blends with the desolation of the Great Depression and at the same time masks a suicide pact with himself. *To Have and Have Not*, as the title suggests, is based on the nullity of any affirmation, the identity of disease and cure, success and nothingness, and it tails off with a concluding meditation on the consoling allure of self-harm:

> Some made the long drop from the apartment or the office window; some took it quietly in two-car garages with the motor running; some used the native tradition of the Colt or Smith and Wesson; those well-constructed implements that end insomnia, terminate remorse, cure cancer, avoid bankruptcy, and blast an exit from intolerable positions by the pressure of a finger; those admirable American instruments so easily carried, so sure of effect, so well designed to end the American dream when it becomes a nightmare, their only drawback the mess they leave for relatives to clean up. (237-38)

We might speculate that Hemingway was spared a more precipitous decline by the opening of a new theater of war in Spain in 1936, for as a correspondent there over the next two years he could give his oppression the more honorable dimensions it deserved. Still it was largely a matter of play-acting rather than a selfless commitment to the Loyalist cause, the need to project a personal heroism that might psychically cancel his fancied disgrace. He was inattentive to the internecine warfare between the Communists and the POUM, then aligned himself with the Stalinists even after they murdered Jose Robles, Dos Passos's friend and translator. Indeed, Hemingway's escapades as a correspondent in Spain in 1937 were marked by a boyish exuberance and reckless temerity while at the same time his political innocence was buttressing the Communist wing of the Loyalist side. As George Packer wrote in *The New Yorker* in 2005:

> The reasons for Hemingway's partisanship were entirely personal and literary. The imperative to hold the purity of his line through the maximum of exposure, which in 1931 made him an aficionado of bullfighting and in 1934 a crack shot in Kenya, in 1937 turned Hemingway into a willing tool of Stalin's secret police. It was a rough brand of radical chic that also created a new type: the war correspondent as habitué of a particularly exclusive night club, who knows how and how not to act under shelling, where to get the best

whiskey, what tone to use when drinking with killers. He's drawn to violence and power for their own sake; war and the politics of war simply provide the stage for his own display of sang-froid. The influence of this type helped to mar the work of successive generations of war writers up to our own.[55]

Hemingway exacted his revenge in 1940 with *For Whom the Bell Tolls*, a solid achievement with many of the virtues of *A Farewell to Arms*, yet vitiated to a degree by the operatic quality of the characters, the extensive use of archaisms and false cognates to convey the Spanish tongue, and the disconnect between the civil war and the romance ("la gloria") between Robert Jordan and Maria.[56] The novel's cinematic action — Pablo's guerilla band at large on the mountain, Pilar's astonishing account of the massacre of the Fascist officials in Avila, Sordo's destruction by Fascist cavalry and the "mechanized doom" of their bombers, Jordon's dynamiting of the bridge in the Sierra of Segovia — is vintage Hemingway. During three days with the partisans, Jordon reflects with deepening insight on the morality and tragedy of killing in war and on the corruption of leadership on the Loyalist side. Initially he is a robot of duty and has no problem with killing "when it is for the cause" (39), but Anselmo hates killing anyone and tells the Ingles upon returning from his sentry post: "I have watched them all day and they are the same men that we are" (192). Later Jordan shoots a cavalryman, and reading the boy's letters home makes him pause: "How many is that you have killed? he asked himself. I don't know. Do you think you have a right to kill any one? No. But I have to" (303). He resists such thoughts because "he would not think himself into any defeatism" (136), claims "my mind is in suspension until we win the war" (245), but the thoughts come anyway. Soon the abstract slogans of the Republican cause start to slip away. He accepts the Communists over the POUM because "they were the only party whose program and whose discipline he could respect," and yet:

> Enemies of the people. That was a phrase he might omit. That was a catch phrase he would skip . . . Any sort of clichés both revolutionary and patriotic. His mind employed them without

criticism. Of course they were true but it was too easy to be nimble about using them. But since last night and this afternoon (with Maria) his mind was much clearer and cleaner on that business. Bigotry is an odd thing. To be bigoted you have to be absolutely sure that you are right and nothing makes that surety and righteousness like continence. Continence is the foe of heresy. (164)

It is the mocking intelligence of the Russian journalist Karkov that helps dispel Jordan's hazy idealism and turns him into a disillusioned realist. The black-and-white depictions of Dolores Ibarruri ("La Pasionaria") as a romantic fraud and Andre Marty as a paranoid with a "mania for shooting people" did not win Hemingway any friends on the Left, but did reflect the simple dichotomizing of the world into "us" and "them" — in this case soldiers and staff — so common to survivors of the Great War.[57] The last night of his life, Jordon thinks about the politicization of the war that will defeat the Republican cause: "Muck them to death and hell . . . God pity the Spanish people . . . Muck all the insane, egotistical treacherous swine that have always governed Spain and ruled her armies. Muck everybody but the people and then be damned careful what they turn into when they have power" (369-70). As his anger abates, Jordan thinks "that he could no longer believe in it himself," yet those earlier affirmations, such as "a duty toward all of the oppressed of the world . . . an absolute brotherhood with the others who were engaged in it" (235), have acquired the weight of cliché.

Beneath the American's self-debate over the ethics of killing and his political education, however, lies the theme of self-destruction. Jordan's father committed suicide, and although the son thinks this was a cowardly act, that "you have to be awfully occupied with yourself to do a thing like that" (338), he appears to be seeking a heroic context in which to follow suit. Indeed all the partisans, because they risk unimaginable torture if captured, have made preparations for suicide. Jordan is replacing another demolition expert, Kashkin, whom he mercifully shot for this reason. Maria too has been instructed by Pilar how to commit suicide by deftly cutting her own throat, and tells Jordan "either one of us could shoot the other and himself, or herself, if one were wounded and it were necessary to avoid capture" (170). When the Fascists executed her parents, then gang-raped her on the couch of her father's mayoral office, Maria had hoped they would shoot her as well. Her romance with Jordan would seem to give him a reason to live, yet is best understood as a dream of escape from what he knows from the start to be a fatal mission. Maria's devotion is so extreme that Pilar asks: "Must you care for him as a sucking child?" (203) When not making the earth move, the two wish to merge into an androgynous whole and more. "Maria is my true love and wife," Jordan thinks. "She is also my sister, and I have never had a sister, and my daughter, and I never will have a daughter" (381). At some level he knows he is "slipping into make-believe again" (345), and it is only when he readies himself to die that Jordan dismisses "the gloria and all that nonsense that you had. You had wonderful ideas, didn't you? You had this world all taped, didn't you? The hell with all that" (386). Finally alone on the Sierra slope, his thigh bone broken yet clear of mind, Jordan takes aim at Fascist cavalry coming out of the timber line, embracing a circumstance that will bring him death without having to cheat for it.*

It was Hemingway's response to the outbreak of hostilities in Europe in 1939, however, that most clearly revealed his inner situation. For two years he contributed to the war effort by hatching a crackpot mission of cruising the Caribbean waters for German U-boats, ready to charge them in his heavily armed cabin cruiser, the *Pilar*, and drop grenades down the conning tower. He had to settle for blowing buoys out of the water and machine-gunning sharks

---

*It is ironically relevant that the cavalryman that Jordan takes aim at as he rides into the clearing is Lieutenant Berrendo, a sensitive, dignified, and religious figure who lost his friend Julian in the battle with Sordo's guerilla band. Berrendo felt that the beheading of Sordo and his men was a necessary but "barbarous business," that the use of bombers was excessive and "we could have done it all, without losses, with a Stokes mortar." While the ethics of killing during war has been mediated throughout by Anselmo and Jordon, it is revealing that Hemingway should give the issue such prominent play in the concluding moment of *For Whom the Bell Tolls*.

in petulant boredom. Finally he went to Europe for the real thing, and anyone reading Carlos Baker's account of Hemingway's war adventures in Europe in 1943-1944 must be struck by his boisterous and reckless designs against his own life.[58] At last he was back on the stage of 1914-1918 and would atone for his survivorship once and for all. Between RAF flying missions, a serious car accident in London that left him with a concussion, a second damaging concussion in a motorcycle accident during the Normandy invasion, and driving his jeep well in advance of the First Army in France, Hemingway was boorishly evoking the lost fraternity of the Great War, drinking and brawling in a way that reminded John Pudney, an RAF officer, of "a sentimental nineteenth-century actor called upon to act the part of a twentieth-century tough guy. Set beside . . . a crowd of young men who walked so modestly and stylishly with Death, he seemed a bizarre cardboard figure."[59] What was quite real, however, was the physical courage he displayed in "cheating" for death. During the fall of 1944 he fought side by side with Colonel "Buck" Lanham at Rambouillet, then the terrible ordeal of Huertgen Forest, where the regiment suffered 80 percent casualties, and if he survived it wasn't his fault. John Garth recalls visiting Hemingway and the regiment on the Siegfried line just as shells started to fall on their farmhouse:

> The meat had just been served, when an 88 crashed through the wall which Hemingway was facing. It went out the other side without exploding . . . The 88 traveled at almost exactly the speed of sound, so there was never any warning of its approach. In a matter of seconds my well-trained people had disappeared into a small potato cellar . . . I was the last one to get to the head of the stairs. I looked back. Hemingway was sitting there quietly, cutting his meat. I called to him to get his ass out of there into the cellar. He refused. I went back and we argued. Another shell came through the wall. He continued to eat. We renewed the argument. He would not budge.[60]

Hemingway always knew that heroism under the conditions of modern war was just a matter of luck, and this "cardboard" figure was just waiting for his to go bad. Yet when he wanted it least, he was plagued by his own stubborn invincibility.

Hemingway rallied the pieces of his fractured psyche for a last assault in *Across the River and into the Trees*, but it is more a clinical document of war psychosis than novel. If Colonel Cantwell, despite the obvious pun, is meant to be taken seriously, matters could hardly be nearer the breaking point. All that Cantwell has left at fifty, besides a bad heart and the experiences of two wars that have left him "so beat up . . . he's slug-nutty," are his wounds and bad conscience and infantile military rituals. Upon returning to Fossalta, Cantwell defecates on the exact spot of his wounding, then says with unconscious self-derision: "A poor effort . . . But my own" (18). All that he can leave as a monument to his fallen trench comrades is a hole filled with "*merd*, money, blood," a shocking glimpse of what his creator felt of his own life as a tribute to these dead. For the genesis of Cantwell's identity "goes back so damn far that it isn't funny," and he says of that experience long ago: "No one of his other wounds had ever done what the first big one did. I suppose it is just the loss of the immortality, he thought" (33). But now those modes so often used by Hemingway to reclaim that air of immortality have become piteous, a mix of transparent fantasy and nightmare breaking its seams. Returning to Venice, Cantwell is reduced to sitting in his favorite restaurant with his "flanks covered," pretending he is the war hero he no longer believes in. All he does hold to is nightmares of that "earlier stupid butchery" of the Great War, which earn him membership in the Order of Brusadelli, and it reeks of that mix of maudlin sentiment and utter sang-froid so common to survivors of that war. The fantasy, of course, is Renata, a lovely nineteen-year-old whose slavish devotion to Cantwell's wounds is an embarrassment. Yet as we have seen of Hemingway's regressive flights into adolescence in *A Farewell to Arms* and *For Whom the Bell Tolls*, this "love affair" of Cantwell's is needed to annul a more primary destiny with death: "I feel as though I were out on some bare-assed hill where it was too rocky to dig, and the rocks all solid, but with nothing jutting, and no bulges, and all of a sudden instead of being there naked, I was armoured" (128-29).

But there are piteous holes in the armor now. Cantwell may score three orgasms with Renata, but symbols of psychic castration litter the canals. Pledged to be the "best goddamed boy" to his "Daughter," he must be given tokens of manhood by Renata, a set of "jewels" that she drops into his pockets and that he then sits "rubbing" as he converses with her portrait in an empty hotel room. Soon more psychic wounds start to flow. Cantwell is moved by the "sexology and beautiful foods" in *Ladies Home Journal*, then furtive visits to the market where he eyes the butchered delectables. All of this is sad stuff, not comic, not absurd, but the disintegration of a man who has only his nightmares as a language of love, only a desire for death "loosening itself from the bomb rack, and falling with that strange curve" (220) that marked his creator thirty-two years earlier.[61] And lastly, there is the issue of survivor guilt. It is no accident that Renata, who in a more perfect dream would be "a soldier with your straight true brain" (231), conducts her inquiry into warfare in the form of an interrogation, for as a staff officer, Cantwell is eligible for that "Red Badge of Funk," a term so often on the lips of the Great War troops.[62] As David Jones put the issue in artistic terms forty-five years later:

> Ars is adamant about one thing: she compels you to do an infantryman's job. She insists on the tactile. The artist in man is the infantryman in man . . . all men are aboriginally of this infantry, though not all serve with this infantry. To pursue the analogy, this continued employment "away from the unit" has made habitual and widespread a "staff mentality."[63]

It is his contamination by this "staff mentality," and the subsequent loss of three regiments in obedience to some general with a "half-assed pointer," that haunts Cantwell. Initially there was the "massif" at Grappa "where I grew up," and he still wakes up "sweating, dreaming I would not be able to get them out of the trucks. They should not have gotten out, ever, of course" (121-122). Perhaps the classic ironic instance of this was the mud-drowned slaughter at Passchendaele in 1917.[64] Later Cantwell admits that he found World War II to be only "an emotional experience," but in trading on the ordeal of Huertgen Forest, where he lost a regiment in combat which was like "Passchendaele with tree bursts" (249), we can glimpse his creator's shame in acting out a legend of military assault and success that he knew from the Great War meant sending men to their doom. "It boils down, or distills, to the fact you stay in until you are hit badly or killed or go crazy and get section-eighted" (250). For this Cantwell owes his comrades a death and later tells Renata that he ought to be buried on the Grappa, "on the dead angle of any shell-pocked slope" (228). She might call him the "lionhearted," but he counters with swift scorn: "The crap-hearted" (229). *Across the River and into the Trees* ends with Cantwell's heart attack and a death that is not a delivery, or even atonement for his survivorship: "Death is a lot of shit . . . the one thing we do alone. Like going to the bathroom" (219). Only in this stink and horror that recalls the trenches in shame can Hemingway imagine his battle over at last.

ALTHOUGH NOW IN A CONDITION to be section-eighted, Hemingway carried on for another ten years. His friends (those he still had) could only stand by helplessly and watch him go mad. Socially he was drinking, bragging, picking fights for unknown reasons, spewing "Black Ass." There was one other novella, *The Old Man and the Sea*, a labored reworking of his anecdote about an old man fishing alone in the Gulf Stream that appeared in *Esquire* in 1936. While containing vivid descriptions of the sea and an arresting action sequence of Santiago capturing the giant marlin and battling with sharks, the novella as a whole is silly and tendentious, awash in sentimentality and contrived Biblical echoes. The boy Manolin treats the old man like a deity, reverently tending to his needs and listening to his talk about baseball: "Have faith in the Yankees, my son. Think of the great DiMaggio . . . They say his father was a fisherman" (21-22). Worse are the clunky crucifixion symbols that litter the text. When Santiago sees the first shark and utters *Ay*, we are told "there was no translation for this word and perhaps it is just a noise such as a man might make, involuntarily, feeling the nail go through his hands and into the wood" (107). Back from his voyage, he drags the mast up a hill like a cross on his shoulders, and once in bed in his shack "he pulled the blanket over his shoulders and then over his back and legs and he slept face down on the newspapers with his arms out straight and the palms of his hands up" (122). The novella may be an anguished rendering of Hemingway's struggles, of the danger inherent in going too far out, but it is stupefying to think that it won him both a Pulitzer Prize and the Nobel Prize for Literature in 1953. He must have secretly concurred, referring to his honor as the IgNoble Prize. His son Gregory, admittedly fueled by filial rages, might have been closer to the mark when he declared that *The Old Man and the Sea* "was as sickly a bucket of sentimental slop as was ever scrubbed off the bar-room floor."[65]

Hemingway's trajectory remained on a downward spiral. There were the plane crashes in Africa in 1954 that nearly killed him. He grew more and more paranoid, and thought the Feds were after him when not the critics. This mental darkness informed his memoir of Paris in the 1920s that appeared after his death, *A Moveable Feast*, in which he slandered most of those to whom he owed a literary debt. Ford Maddox Ford is a "heavy, wheezing, ignoble presence" (86), Wyndham Lewis has the eyes "of an unsuccessful rapist" (109), and Gertrude Stein is overheard begging to Alice B. Toklas, "Don't, please don't. I'll do anything, pussy, but please don't do it" (118). Death haunts the sketches of Hemingway's acquaintances. The debauched painter Pascin looks like a Broadway character of the Nineties "and afterwards, when he had hanged himself, I liked to remember him as he was that night at the Dome" (104); the poet Ernest Walsh uses his deathly consumption to elicit favors, but upon remarking that Hemingway is marked for life, he is told: "Give me time" (127). The portrait of Fitzgerald is cruel gratuitous caricature. The long-time supporter and editor of Hemingway's work has short legs, "whores" by dumbing down his fiction to increase sales, and passes out drunk in a flash: "The eyes sank and began to look dead and the lips were drawn tight and the color left the face so that it was the color of used candle wax. This was not my imagination. His face became a true death's head, or death mask, in front of my eyes" (152). This image reflects a fear that is self-referential, just as the fictional scene of Hemingway checking the adequacy of Fitzgerald's sexual equipment in a men's room reveals his own worries about impotence. On a trip to Lyon, Fitzgerald's hypochondria, alcoholism, and snobbery are calmly tolerated by his friend who explains: "You could not be angry with Scott any more than you could be angry with someone who was crazy" (166).

Ironically this is the only reasonable excuse for Hemingway's own performance in *A Moveable Feast*. The concluding, and sincerely felt vignette of himself and Hadley skiing in the mountain snows of Schruns in Austria during avalanche season seems ultimately an alluring death wish. In his own life Hemingway turned to the Mayo Clinic for electric shock therapy in 1958, but it did no good. He went back to Spain to recover the past, but that was no good either. By the end of the decade he was obviously suicidal, once forcibly restrained from leaping out of a plane onto the tarmac and running into its propellers. Finally, near the end of June 1961, he made his break from the hospital, back to Ketchum, Idaho, and in a last act of self-reliance moved to his double-barreled shotgun and killed himself.

Hemingway's madness and suicide should hardly shock us by now, but brief mention must be made of a novel, *Islands in the Stream*, he kept locked in a safety deposit box in Havana until it was posthumously published in 1970.[66] For here is the damnation of his legend, embodied in Thomas Hudson, a successful painter of declining productivity, and his sidekick, Roger Davis, a writer of "vicious" stories during the 1930s. Davis is drawn early on into a fistfight with a wealthy yachtsman, only to conclude after destroying him: "All fights are bad ... when you start taking pleasure in it you are awfully close to the thing you're fighting" (47-48). Hudson then invites his three sons down to Bimini for a vacation, but only to subject them to familiar trials of manhood: an attack by a hammerhead shark that eludes Hudson's rifle fire, then a six-hour duel with a giant broadbill that leaves the son bleeding and corpselike and Hudson ashamed: "I'm his father ... It was my fault" (153). The sons, whose courage is never in doubt, do recover, but two are "accidentally" killed in a car crash upon leaving Bimini, which serves only as a devious forecast of what Hudson has prepared for them as a paternal authority, and we might say the same of the third son's death flying RAF missions over Europe shortly afterward. It is this remorse, cause unacknowledged, that Hudson carries through the novel ("I'm in hell now . . ."), as the prose starts to bleed cats, menus, frozen daiquiris, fantasies . . . all that his creator shored up against his ruin. Now Hudson hangs around the Floridita telling lies about his sexual exploits to whores, until his first wife reappears, the ghost of Agnes von Kurowsky, only to reject him again. All Hudson can do now is start dreaming of his penis as a .357 Magnum and burst into the action of hunting Germans whose submarine has wrecked off the Cuban coast. Only now he has no heart for killing "Krauts," wants to avoid a massacre "for fuck-all nothing" (427), echoing a term, "The Great Fuck-Up," used by troops at the Somme for going over the top. But the big show must go on, and while admitting "I've never liked to kill, ever" (449), Hudson leads his irregulars into certain ambush and at the close lies dying of that old familiar wound in the leg his creator suffered years ago.

What, then, is Hemingway's significance to us today? The Great War, as Fussell says, was "perhaps the last to be conceived as taking place within a seamless, purposeful 'history' involving a coherent stream of time," and we are all living in the vacuum of that loss.[67] What is left to shape modern man, as Hemingway reminds us, are only the grooves of memory cut deep by fear.[68] For him the grooves were cut by the very catastrophe that has determined the quality of our despair. His sense of duty to what he knew, even if it were his own fancied disgrace, never wavered. He followed Wilfred Owen who wrote in a letter of February 1918: "I confess I bring on what few war dreams I now have, entirely by willingly considering war of an evening. I do so because I have my duty to perform towards War."[69] Hemingway's mission was a terrible one, and Yeats was quite right: he camped too close to death for too long to escape contamination. Still it was a luckless, brave, and deeply moral fate. If he appears never to have grown up, this was only recoil from the war, lest he become a killer or suicide beyond it. His career dramatizes the peril of morally engaging the unspeakable crimes of our century, but he never anesthetized himself from them. On the lower frequencies he scorned the legend our culture has made of him for its own unacknowledged reasons. His literary legacy is still viable and needed, for as an artist of the infantryman, he gave us that moment-to-moment feel of dread that is the air we breathe.[70] During his life the real Hemingway was quite "unknown," and he gave that life in loyalty to millions of other Unknown Soldiers. For this alone he merits an ad hoc epitaph found scrawled on a board over the trenches:

> *Sleep on. Beloved Brother*
> *Take thy Gentle Rest.*

NOTES

1 Quoted by Richard Ellman, *Yeats: The Man and the Masks* (New York: Dutton, 1948), 228.

2 Quoted by Paul Fussell, *The Great War and Modem Memory* (New York: Oxford University Press, 1975), 201. I am deeply indebted to Fussell's brilliant study, not for the train of thought on Hemingway in this essay, but certainly for the dramatic prominence he gives to World War I as an influence on modern consciousness, and for the wealth of literary testimony he has collected and analyzed in his study.

3 Dwight Macdonald, *Against the American Grain* (New York: Random House, 1962), 168.

4 Perhaps the best of the psychological studies on Hemingway remains Philip Young's *Ernest Hemingway: A Reconsideration* (University Park and London: Pennsylvania State University Press, 1966). Young finds a "traumatic neurosis" at the heart of Hemingway, resulting from his Great War wounds, a neurosis over which he tried to gain a belated mastery in his fiction by an incessant return to the theme of death. And yet one feels that Young, despite delivering many insights, is trapped in his own clinical terminology. It is doubtful whether terms like "trauma,"

"neurosis," "death wish," or "repetition-compulsion," oblivious as they are to historical or moral dimensions, can provide access to the real quality of Hemingway's vision. Young himself seems to wonder about this, when, before launching into Otto Fenichel to illuminate Hemingway, pauses to admit: "Actually it is not clear how any of these things work" (165). A more exhaustive use of psychological concepts on Hemingway's work can be found in Richard Hovey's *Hemingway: The Inward Terrain* (Seattle & London: University of Washington Press, 1968). This too is a useful, often very insightful book; yet one grows frustrated by the way Hovey routinely and often contemptuously catalogs Hemingway's "mental disorders," and the way he continuously berates his subject for not espousing a more "positive affirmation of life." Hovey has not imagined the Great War deeply enough.

5 Kenneth Lynn, *Hemingway* (Cambridge: Harvard University Press, 1987).

6 As early as October 1977, in an issue of *Esquire*, a board of writers and critics were asked to choose the most underrated and overrated modern American writers. It is interesting to see how many of these "experts" were ready to throw Hemingway to the wolves. Recent biographers of Hemingway, in particular Kenneth Lynn, have unearthed enough unattractive truths about the man — his betrayal of friends, mendacious promotion of his own legend, anti-Semitism, braggadocio, and mistreatment of women, just to name a few — to make it easy to dismiss him and overlook the thirty-year slide into madness that explains much of this behavior.

7 Carlos Baker, *Ernest Hemingway, A Life Story* (New York: Scribner, 1969), 5.

8 Ernest Hemingway, *A Moveable Feast* (New York: Scriber, 1964), 108. In this essay, all page references to the novels and nonfiction of Hemingway are to the Scribner editions. Page references to the short stories are to *The Complete Short Stories of Ernest Hemingway: The Finca Vigia Edition* (New York: Scribner, 2003).

9 Quoted by Baker, 38.

10 In his introduction to the Viking *Portable Hemingway* (1944), Cowley accepts Hemingway's account of his own heroism at Fossalta and sees his fiction as primarily a reflection of a wounded war veteran. See Lynn, 102-08.

11 Quoted by Fussell, 192.

12 *Ibid.*, 193.

13 For a more complete account of Hemingway's ordeal that night at Fossalta, see Baker (44-45) and Lynn (75-92).

14 Quoted by Baker, 48.

15 *Ibid.*, 52.

16 A single exception that I am aware of is Richard Drinnon's article, "In the American Heartland: Hemingway and Death," *Psychoanalytic Review*, 52 (1965), 5-31. Drinnon does not develop this line of thought, but does remark: "Try as they would — even to holding up shrapnel-riddled trousers for social approval — Hemingway and his heroes could not shake the feeling that these war wounds were somehow Red Badges of Shame."

17 Quoted by Lynn, 91.

18 Quoted by Fussell, 90.

19 *Ibid.*, 218-19.

20 Quoted by Baker, 57.

21 Jeffery Meyers, *Hemingway: A Biography* (New York: Harper, 1985), 35.

22 For a rigorous psychoanalytic reading of "Now I Lay Me," see Hovey, 47-53.

23 For an excellent account of the influence of Dr. Hemingway's suicide on his son, see Lynn, 378-81.

24 I am indebted here to John Thompson's brief but excellent set of remarks on Hemingway in his review of A.E. Hotchner's book, *Papa Hemingway*. See Thompson's "Poor Papa," *The New York Review of Books*, April 1966, 6-7.

25 Quoted by Lynn, 114.

26 *Ibid.*, 68.

27 *Ibid.*, 318.

28 See Fussell, 181.

29 Fussell shows that persisting literary habits of the modern world — ironic understatement, gross dichotomizing, exploded versions of pastoral, paranoia — are traceable to the actualities of the Great War. "Prolonged trench warfare," he writes, "with its collective isolation, its 'defensiveness,' and its nervous obsession with what 'the other side' is up to, establishes a model of modern political, social, artistic, and psychological polarization. Prolonged trench warfare, whether enacted or remembered, fosters paranoid melodrama, which I take to be a primary mode in modern writing. Mailer, Joseph Heller, and Thomas Pynchon are examples of what I mean." *The Great War and Modern Memory*, 76.

30 See Lynn, 327-28.

31 "Hemingstein" was Hemingway's favorite nickname as a young man among his friends, a nickname to which he took no offense. Cohn's pugilistic skills and his egregious romanticism also link him with his creator. A reader must decide whether or not this self-referential link distances Hemingway from the anti-Semitic strain in the novel.

32 Hemingway told Fitzgerald in a letter that something else was required besides guts to take the measure of a matador's bravery: "Grace under pressure." Guts, he pointed out, "never made money for anybody except violin manufacturers." See Lynn, 342-43.

33 Apparently McKey was killed the very week before Hemingway arrived at the front lines at Fossalta, as if the latter were taking the place of the dead American. For a full account of McKey as a real-life model for Frederic Henry, see Michael S. Reynolds's *Hemingway's First War* (Princeton: Princeton University Press, 1976), 147-49.

34 For an excellent discussion of the gender confusion in *A Farewell to Arms*, see Lynn, 384-90.

35 One can guess that Hemingway was deeply impressed by Ezra Pound's "Hugh Selwyn Mauberly," especially parts IV and V: "Died some, pro

patria / non 'duke' non 'et decor' / walked eye-deep in hell / believing in old men's lies, then unbelieving / came home, home to a lie / home to many deceits / home to old lies and new infamy / usury age-old and age-thick / and liars in public places."

36 "It would be going too far," Fussell writes, "to trace the impulse behind all modern official euphemism to the Great War alone. And yet there is a sense in which public euphemism as the special rhetorical sound of life in the latter third of the twentieth century can be said to originate in the years 1914-18. It was perhaps the first time in history that official policy produced events so shocking, bizarre, and stomach-turning that the events had to be tidied up for presentation to a highly literate mass population. Perhaps one would not be mistaken in finding in the official euphemisms of the Great War the ultimate progenitors of such later favorites as 'combat,' 'combat-fatigue,' 'mental illness,' 'nuclear device,' 'Department of Defense' (formerly 'War Department'), 'Free World,' 'homicide,' and 'fatality.' Americans have not too long ago heard an invasion conducted in their name termed an 'incursion,' bombing called 'protective reaction strikes,' and concentration camps called 'pacification centers.' Carelessly aimed or wildly dropped bombs are now 'incontinent ordnance.' There's little question that Great War communiqué-writers would admire that one and be proud to acknowledge it as their progeny." *The Great War and Modern Memory*, 178-79.

37 Lynn goes so far as to say *A Farewell to Arms* is not about the war or the disillusionment it fostered in those who fought in it and survived. Instead he traces the American's prejudice against moral slogans back to Hemingway's hatred for his mother, who, for instance, reacted to *The Sun Also Rises* by calling it "one of the filthiest books of the year," and asking her son: "What is the matter? Have you ceased to be interested in loyalty, nobility, honor and fineness of life?" While this may help us understand why Hemingway called his mother "that damn bitch" throughout his life, it has no definitive bearing on the fictional character, Frederick Henry. In a biography otherwise so rich with insight, Lynn seems too reluctant to grant catastrophic external events a place in influencing Hemingway's psyche, too ready to reduce his fiction to a shadow play with his parents.

38 Quoted by Reynolds, 60.

39 See Fussell, 115-120.

40 Quoted by Baker, 226.

41 In a deleted passage from *Green Hills of Africa*, Hemingway wrote: "My father was a coward. He shot himself without necessity. At least I thought so. I had gone through it myself until I figured it in my head. I know what it was to be a coward and what it was to cease being a coward. Now, truly, in actual danger I felt a clean feeling as in a shower. Of course it was easy now. That was because I no longer cared what happened. I knew it was better to live it so that if you died you had done everything that you could do about your work and your enjoyment of life up to that minute, reconciling the two, which is very difficult." Quoted by Lynn, 415. That his son thought Ed Hemingway committed suicide to escape the henpecking domination of his wife is conveyed in *For Whom the Bell Tolls* when Robert Jordan, with a dark irony that reaches beyond the plot, answers Pilar's question whether his father killed himself to avoid being tortured: "Yes . . . To avoid being tortured" (67).

42 See Edmund Wilson's "Hemingway: Gauge of Morale" in his *The Wound and the Bow* (New York: Oxford University Press, 1941).

43 Quoted by Frederick Crews, *The Critics Bear It Away* (New York: Random House, 1992), 92, 98.

44 See Albert Camus' introduction to *The Rebel* (New York: Knopf, 1957), 3-11.

45 "All modern American literature comes from one book by Mark Twain called *Huckleberry Finn*. If you read it you must stop where the Nigger Jim is stolen from the boys. That is the real end. The rest is just cheating . . ." (*GHA*, 22)

46 Quoted by Lynn, 427.

47 Ernest Hemingway, *Portraits and Self-Portraits* (Boston: Houghton Mifflin, 1936), 57.

48 Quoted by Lynn, 441.

49 It is noteworthy that at the time of his suicide, Ed Hemingway was worried about a leg infection that might lead to gangrene, and perhaps amputation. His son claimed the weapon that he used, a Civil War "Long John" revolver, and returned with it to Key West.

50 Quoted by Lynn, 432.

51 See Lynn, 436.

52 Quoted by Baker, 290.

53 Quoted by Fussell, 86.

54 The character Robert Gordon is intended as a vicious caricature of John Dos Passos, whose literary success with *1919*, the second volume of his trilogy *U.S.A.*, filled Hemingway with an insane jealousy. Yet as would be true with most of his caricatures, especially in *A Moveable Feast*, the hidden target is himself.

55 *The New Yorker*, October 31, 2005, 85.

56 Compare with *A Farewell to Arms* and the disconnect between the romance of Frederick Henry and Catherine Barkley and military action on the Italian front.

57 See Fussell, 79-82.

58 See Baker, 356-57.

59 Quoted by Baker, 393.

60 *Ibid.*, 427.

61 In this respect Cantwell calls to mind a Great War poet, Ivor Gurney, who was wounded and gassed in 1917, and who died in a mental hospital twenty years later, still writing about a war he was convinced was still going on. See Fussell, 74.

62 See Fussell, 83.

63 Quoted by Fussell, 85.

64 Cantwell's guilt over ordering troops into combat that consigned them to certain death mirrors the reaction of a Lieutenant General Sir Launcelot Kiggell, who, upon his first visit to the combat zone at Passchendaele, burst into tears and muttered: "Good God, did we really send men to fight in that?" Quoted by Fussell, 84.

65 Quoted by Lynn, 563.

66 There was a second posthumous novel, *Garden of Eden*, which was patched together by Scribner and bowdlerized by Hemingway's son, Patrick, then published in 1995. The novel is clumsily plotted, thematically vague, the characters flat caricatures, the bi-sexuality reminiscent of a clinical document. To publish an edited version of a manuscript that Hemingway labored for over fifteen years and then abandoned seems totally unjustified.

67 Fussell, 21.

68 I am indebted for this image to Oliver Lyttelton's account of his war memories: "Fear and its milder brothers, dread and anticipation, first soften the tablets of memory, so that the impressions which they bring are clearly and deeply cut, and when time cools them off the impressions are fixed like the grooves of a gramophone record, and remain with you as long as your faculties. I have been surprised how accurate my memory has proved about times and places where I was frightened..." Quoted by Fussell, 327.

69 Quoted by Fussell, 327.

70 It has been often said by critics that Hemingway is no longer a literary influence on the contemporary scene, but clearly those few writers with the courage to deal up close with the 1960s in America, another apocalyptic death-haunted era, writers such as Robert Stone, Joan Didion, and more recently Michael Herr, learned from him.

FRANZ KAFKA

Metamorphosis and the Holocaust

"I AM DIVIDED FROM ALL THINGS by a hollow space," Franz Kafka wrote in his diary in 1911, "and I don't even push myself to its boundaries."[1] And in another diary entry of 1913: "Everything appears to me to be an artificial construction of the mind. Every mark by someone else, every chance look throws everything in me over on the other side . . . I am more uncertain than I ever was, I feel only the power of life. And I am senselessly empty."[2] Such uncanny seizures of alienation are faithfully recorded in the diaries which Kafka clung to as a mode of self-rescue; for he experienced the new century as a "phantom state" in which the self and experiences were forever fluctuating under the exigencies of living. "How pathetically scant my self-knowledge is," he lamented. "Why? There is no such thing as observation of the inner world, as there is of the outer world. The inner world can only be experienced, not described."[3] Because this epistemological black hole cursed his own relationships with either bad faith or the danger of merging into the other, Kafka was to renounce them out of love.[4] But as a writer he would embrace this state of maximum uncertainty. "What one is," he wrote, "one cannot express, for one is just that; one can only communicate what one is not, that is to say falsehood."[5] From this level of submersion in reality, where the self was protean and beyond the reach of language, there was no rescue into meaning, least of all from psychology, which Kafka dismissed as "mirror-writing . . . the description of a reflection such as we, who have sucked ourselves full of earth, imagine; for no reflection actually appears — it is simply that we see earth wherever we turn."[6]

What both deepened and mirrored his inward exile was that the earth Kafka saw at every turn was Prague, "the little mother with claws," torn apart by virulent strains of German and Czech nationalism in the waning decades of the Hapsburg Empire. "The racial doctrines which an Austrian corporal was to translate into genocide half a century later," observes Ernst Pawel in *The Nightmare of Reason*, "were already sprouting in the subsoil of Austro-Hungarian politics."[7] In retrospect, Pawel notes that the Edict of Toleration issued in 1782 by Emperor Joseph II was calculated not to free the Jews so much as to obliterate their ethnic identity through assimilation. This was one of the primary tasks of the German educational institutions Kafka attended in Prague, which he accurately denounced as "a conspiracy of the grown-ups," and of the Hapsburg bureaucracy in which he later worked. Pawel observes that in 1883, the year of Kafka's birth, the first political manipulation of Jew-hatred surfaced as German, Czech, and Hungarian extremists joined ranks to form an abortive movement based solely on anti-Semitism. The ancient Jewish ghetto in the heart of Prague was torn down or "sanitized" at the turn of the century. In 1897, a pogrom struck the city that required the intervention of Austrian troops and martial law. Two years later erupted the infamous "blood libel" Hilsner case, in which a Jewish shoemaker from Polna was baselessly accused of murdering a Christian virgin — thereby freeing psychotic propagandists to spill their ancient mythological "constructions" of the Jew as Christ-killer, rapist, and usurer across Bohemia.[8] It was only the principled intervention of Jan Masaryk, who would become leader of an independent Czechoslovak republic after World War I, that cleared Leopold Hilsner's name.

This toxic turn-of-the-century anti-Semitism was fueled not only by the rise of nationalism in central Europe but by widespread poverty, rapid industrialization, and a new component of irrationality liberated by the weakening of age-old forces of repression. The Jewish middle class of Prague, comprising 85% of the 35,000 German speakers in a total population of 420,000, was caught in a no-man's land. Politically powerless, culturally and linguistically dispossessed, they were viewed as subhuman even by the ruling German minority whose culture and language they loyally supported as a matter of practical necessity. Ultimately, what would inspire Kafka's literary generation was the failure of assimilation, and perhaps even more insufferable, the familiar denial by the Jewish bourgeoisie of the very existence of anti-Semitism. "The ghetto walls had been razed," Pawel writes, "the age-old traditions were rapidly eroding, but the newly emancipated citizens of the nation-state still found themselves accused of being Jewish — and increasingly unable to understand the nature of the accusation. The harder they tried to defend themselves by being more Czech than the Czechs, more German than the Germans, the harsher the ultimate sentence."[9]

This was Kafka's earth, and it invaded his consciousness with an inexorable linking of accusation, guilt and punishment. "I have never been under the pressure of any responsibility," he wrote, "but that imposed upon me by the existence, the gaze, the judgment of other people."[10] And he was fully aware that he was registering the full pressure of his historical moment. "I have vigorously absorbed the negative element of the age in which I live," he wrote, "an age that is, of course, very close to me, which I have no right to even fight against, but as it were a right to represent . . . I have not been guided into life by the hand of Christianity — admittedly now slack and failing — as Kierkegaard was, and have not caught the hem of the Jewish prayer-mantle — now flying away from us — as the Zionists have. I am an end or a beginning."[11] Except for his last nine months with Dora Diamant in Berlin, Kafka lived out his entire life with his parents in Prague. He hardly ventured out of the inner city — except to leave town to calm his nerves in sanatoria whose faddish "nature therapy" at the time — consisting of nudism, hydrotherapy, mud packs, exercise drills, and vegetarianism — was ironically in harmony with the racist German myth of masculinity that would deliver the "ultimate sentence" twenty years later.

Already the way was being prepared by the elders of the tribe, whose feats of self-deception amounted on a spiritual level to collaboration in their own extinction. Kafka's own father, Hermann, the owner of a successful wholesale dry-goods store, treated his employees with a vulgar tyranny. His cash-register mentality fulfilled the very anti-Semitic stereotypes he was so eager to dismiss as a marginal phenomenon. Indeed those stereotypes could infect even his son. Kafka would urge his sister Elli to send her son to a boarding school so as to shield him from "the special mentality which is particularly virulent among wealthy Prague Jews and which cannot be kept away from children . . . this small, dirty, lukewarm, squinting spirit."[12] Yet here too he experienced another oscillation of consciousness. For whatever his private grievances, Kafka acknowledged in *Letter to His Father* that Hermann Kafka's desperate bid for assimilation was merely a reflection and escape from the racial prejudice and poverty of his own youth. Given the earth as it was, his betrayal of Judaism was inevitable.

> You really had brought some traces of Judaism from the ghetto-like village community; it was not much, and it dwindled a little more in the city and during your military service; but still, the impressions and memories of your youth did just about suffice for some sort of Jewish life, especially since you did not need much help of that kind but came of robust stock . . . At bottom the faith that ruled your life consisted in your believing in the unconditional rightness of the opinions of a certain class of Jewish society, and hence actually, since these opinions were part and parcel of your own nature, in believing in yourself. Even in this there was still Judaism enough, but it was too little to be handed on to the child; it all dribbled away while you were passing it on . . . The whole thing is, of course, no isolated phenomenon. It was much the same with a large section of this transitional generation of Jews, which had migrated from the still comparatively devout countryside to the cities.[13]

Granted the complexities of Kafka's own relations with a father who was a bullying arbiter of authority, such an objective grasp of reality became a paralysis, a form of bondage. "Perhaps the strangest of all my relationships with him," the son wrote about his father, "is that I am capable of feeling and suffering to the utmost not with him, but *within him.*"[14] Given this amazing power of sympathetic merging, even with his own opposite, no wonder Kafka clung to his "hovering nothingness" as a writer. At least it was a privileged position of espionage, offering momentary freedom from that place where the world of the fathers and the world of officialdom converged, from the weight of a new and threatening world where, as Walter Benjamin recognized, Kafka "could have defined organization as destiny."[15]

This mental turmoil appears without much secondary elaboration in 1912 in Kafka's first published work, "The Judgment," an astonishing piece of automatic writing that "came out of me like a real birth, covered with filth and slime . . ."[16] Kafka disclosed in his diaries that the son in the story, Georg Bendemann, is a transfiguration of his own name, that the name of Georg's fiancée is a transformation of Felice Bauer's, his future fiancée whom he had just met, and that the friend in St. Petersburg is "the link between father and son, the greatest commonality." Georg is seeking independence through marriage and assumption of the family business, a reasonable bourgeois aspiration, and one Sunday morning writes a letter about his hopeful prospects to his distant friend. But when he visits his father's room with the letter, a room "he had not visited for months," the narrative stays calm while the plot, invaded by violent passions, turns absurd. Though seemingly senile and sickly, when the father stands up at the window, his dressing gown falls open and the son thinks: "My father is still a giant of a man."[17] The father accuses Georg of lying about the friend in St. Petersburg, that he is a fiction, but Georg reminds him that the friend visited them three years ago, as he changes his woolen drawers and "carried his father to bed in his arms." At this instant Georg recognizes that the father must join him and his bride in their future accommodations, thus confirming that he is a captive in what Kafka called "the circle of blood relationship" that connects the two.[18]

Once Georg tucks his father in bed, this deceptively powerful figure springs up in rage, touching the ceiling in mythic disproportion, and becomes a Gatling gun of accusations. He distorts his son's care-giving attentions as wanting to "cover me up," of sticking "your father in bed so he can't move." He accuses Georg of having "disgraced Mother's memory" by getting engaged to a woman "because she lifted up her skirts" and promises to "sweep her from your side" (85-86). He charges his son with being a fraud, of "strutting through the world, finishing off deals that I had prepared for him, bursting with triumphant glee, and stalking away from his father with the closed face of a respectable businessman" (86). Suddenly the friend in St. Petersburg does exist, and the father too has been writing letters to him, Georg's double, clearly Jewish with a beard and "skin . . . so yellow as to indicate some latent disease" — but an unassimilated Jew in St. Petersburg who started his own business abroad, witnessed real revolution in Russia, that is, embraced the risk of real independence. The father shouts: "Of course I know your friend. He would have been a son after my own heart" (85). All Georg can do is cry out: "So you've been lying in wait for me!" (87) Finally, the predatory father passes judgment on his son: "An innocent child, yes . . . but still more truly have you been a devilish human being — I sentence you now to death by drowning" (87). Earlier Georg had wryly labeled his father a "comedian" for his irrational antics, but now he reacts in deadly earnest. There is no question of protesting his innocence because his father's judgment, as manic and arbitrary as it may be, has been irreversibly internalized. As he hangs from the bridge railing just before his suicide drop, Georg calls out: "Dear parents, I have always loved you, all the same" (88).

During this time Kafka was working on the first draft of a fragmentary novel that Max Brod would entitle *Amerika*. Kafka had relatives who immigrated to the New World and had read Arthur Holitscher's book of reportage, *Amerika Heute und Morgen*, to inform his creation of a mythological America. The novel recounts the adventures of Karl Rossman, a sixteen-year-old European cast away by his father for being seduced by a servant girl who became pregnant, thus disrupting the family business. Blessed with transparency, lucidity, a cheerful naiveté, pluck, a sense of justice, strength to withstand set-backs, and faith that managing situations is "just a matter of understanding the mechanism," Karl radiates an optimism that will not protect him from suffering a series of immigrant nightmares. Arriving in New York, he returns to the ship for his umbrella, finding "his way down endlessly recurring stairs, through corridors with countless turnings, through an empty room with a deserted writing-table," emblematic less of a ship than a new ambivalent literary world.[19] Back in his room Karl defends the summarily fired German stoker by appealing to "his rights," but his demand for justice is soon negated by the testimony of Schubal, the chief cashier and the captain — officials who alone can allow him to disembark within sight of a Statue of Liberty raising not a torch, but an "arm with a sword." This New World is not about liberty, but power.

Ultimately Karl is claimed by his Uncle Jacob, a wealthy senator who tells him the stoker's case "may be a question of justice, but at the same time it's a question of discipline" (33). Now groomed as an apprentice secretary in his uncle's business, Karl will soon learn that breaking the rules of business is the ultimate crime in America. He is allowed some liberties — playing the piano, horse-riding with Mack, learning English — but after being invited to the country house of Mr. Pollunder, he learns these liberties are commandments when his uncle requires his return the next morning. Karl is driven through the traffic-jammed streets of New York, "as if caught up in a whirlwind and roaring like some strange element quite unconnected with humanity," passing mounted police and a demonstration of steel workers on strike — so that "soon to be a welcome guest in a well-lighted country house surrounded by high walls and guarded by watch-dogs filled him with extravagant well-being" (53-54). But the country house metamorphoses into a prison as Karl spends the night wandering its dark corridors, struggling to ward off the treacherous Mr. Green and Pollunder's daughter, the flirtatious Miss Clara, who accuses him of "incivility," threatens to "box his ears," and throttles him with "wrestling holds" until he wants to leave. His departure for home is agonizingly delayed by Green, who instead delivers a letter from his uncle dismissing Karl for the seemingly petty offence of visiting the banker. "Against my wishes you decided this evening to leave me," Uncle Jacob writes, "stick, then to that decision all your life" (94-95). Indeed his "principles" are at stake, and he cannot "permit such a general assault upon me." Never mind that his uncle *had* given Karl approval to make the visit, or that the boy learns later that Uncle Jacob is "notorious" for his "fraudulent" employment practices.

Karl is now banished to the open road. Here he meets Robinson and Delamarche, two vagabonds who offer friendship, but will become a suffocating second skin, ensnaring him in a series of hopeless predicaments. Heading west they exploit Karl's naiveté, manage to steal his sausage, his suit, photographs of his family, and even money from his suitcase. He protests "you grudge me my few possessions and try to humiliate me because of them, and that I cannot endure" (127). When the vagabonds physically threaten him, Karl is led off by a waiter at the Hotel Occidental, where the Manageress offers him work as an elevator boy, but apparent success always creates a dark karma ready to bring him down. The Hotel Occidental is another complete social system with authorial hierarchy and strict rules. Robinson soon reappears, and when it is discovered that Karl left his elevator to help his friend, stashing the drunken Irishman in the boy employees' dormitory, he is brought to a "judicial hearing" and fired by the Head Waiter and associates. That Karl had broken the rules out of compassion, or throughout has treated employees like the typist Therese with kindness, carries no weight. Even the Manageress, who had been his protector, says, "When things are right, they look right, and I must confess that your actions don't" (190). Karl had worked for two months "certainly better than many of the other boys . . . but obviously such considerations were taken into account at the decisive moment in no part of the world, neither in Europe or America; the verdict was determined by the first words that happened to fall from the judge's lips in an impulse of fury" (176-77). He comes to a central realization that "it's impossible to defend oneself where there is no good will . . . that all he could say would appear quite different to the others, and that whether a good or a bad construction was to be put on his actions depended alone on the spirit in which he was judged" (188-89). The weight of any social system, its momentum, will punish any deviation from its rules, however unjust those rules may be, or innocent the accused may be, like an ocean covering a pebble.

Karl's fall from apprentice secretary to elevator boy to servant of the vagabonds and the macabre Brunelda is a spiraling descent into degradation and physical abuse. Karl's first attempt to flee them is checked by the ultimate uniformed judge, a policeman barking: "Show your identification papers" (213). Karl flees the law, but can find refuge only on the balcony of Brunelda's flat, where he is encouraged by the sickly Robinson to imitate him and be a servant of Brunelda — a lazy, obese, vain, unclean divorcee who spends most of her time sleeping or catching flies, but whom both men find sexually irresistible. "That's what you need to do if you don't want to starve," Robinson tells Karl. "And if you're always treated like a dog, you begin to think that you're actually one" (231). The boy declines the offer but remains a prisoner. Blocked from an exit door by Delamarche sleeping with his lover, he becomes Kafka's semi-private joke — a grotesque reference to the domestic entrapment that he endured in his parents' apartment in Prague.[20] When Karl tries to break open the door, Delamarche and Robinson beat him senseless while Brunelda looks on "with glittering eyes." The streets below are filled with noise and the seething crowds of opposing political forces colliding in indecipherable mayhem. A student with Talmudic habits on the neighboring balcony also hates Karl's three captors, but counsels him not to the leave without a job in hand. He falls asleep "comforted by the reflection that he was still young and that some day or other he was bound to get away from Delamarche: this household certainly did not look as if it was established for all eternity" (270).

Is this just incurable naiveté, an inability to learn from experience, or rather the wisdom of the mystic who awaits change with equanimity? In the uncompleted last chapter of the novel, Karl finds eventual employment in the Nature Theatre of Oklahoma, where "everyone is welcome" provided he plays himself. This society appears to be democratic, promises some utopian hope; yet the sign concludes: "Down with all those who do not believe in us!" (272) Recruitment for jobs takes place at a race-course where on a stage "hundreds of women dressed as angels in white robes with great wings on their shoulders were blowing on long trumpets that glittered like gold" (274). Many critics have held that the Theater points in a religious direction, but these are Hollywood angels.

As Kafka wrote in his diaries at the time: "Opened the Bible. The unjust Judges. Confirmed in my own opinion ... But otherwise there is no significance to this. I am never visibly guided in such things, the pages of the Bible don't flutter in my presence."[21] Karl eludes the demand for identification papers, but is able to sign up as an "actor" only by using the nickname Negro, an oppressed minority whose foreignness seems ineradicable. Kafka leaves his hero on a train heading through mountains toward an unknown destination, which, as Pawel remarks, became clear "some forty years later."[22] Or we might merely consider the genocidal fate of "the Red Indian" which inspired Kafka's bizarre fantasy of escape to the New World, a novel he abandoned because of the increasing pessimism of his vision. Kafka told Brod smilingly that Karl would find a profession and his freedom, but a fascinating diary entry in 1915 that compares his heroes in *Amerika* and *The Trial* suggests otherwise: "Rossman and K., the innocent and the guilty both executed without distinction in the end, the guilty one with a gentler hand, more pushed aside than struck down."[23]

As "The Judgment" and *Amerika* indicate too well, Kafka's self-exile into writing was no real escape, not necessarily the struggle for self-preservation he often claimed. For to free what he called "this tremendous world I have inside my head" risked being "torn to pieces," being martyred to his miraculous feats of attention to everything, both good and evil.[24] Yet "a thousand times rather be torn to pieces than retain it in me or bury it. That, indeed, is why I am here, that is quite clear to me." On a personal level, the act of writing for Kafka meant embracing and exploring these lower frequencies, an identity burdened by inextinguishable guilt, "only a particular form of the knowledge that, at least among the living, no one can rid himself of himself."[25] One proof of this is what Malcolm Pasley has brilliantly shown as a technique of "semi-private games" present in Kafka's work—the deliberate, often playful use of covert reference, ambiguous jokes, riddles, puns, and latent meanings that comment on his own life and art.[26] For instance, take the pun on "correspondence" between Georg and his distant friend in "The Judgment," or the scar on his father's thigh which relates to Hermann Kafka's scar picked up during military service in his youth. What is miraculous is that Kafka's writing, with its roots in autobiography, opens up onto vast eras of time. "The unity of mankind," he wrote in a diary entry in 1913, "now and then doubted, even if only emotionally, by everyone . . . on the other hand reveals itself to everyone, or seems to reveal itself, *in the complete harmony, discernible time and again, between the development of mankind as a whole and of the individual man* (emphasis mine). Even in the most secret emotions of the individual."[27]

KAFKA INVESTIGATED this existential condition by writings whose mark of integrity is their ability to both invite and resist interpretation. "Our art," he wrote, "consists of being dazzled by the Truth. The light which rests on its distorted mask as it shrinks from it is true, nothing else is."[28] Such an aesthetic was continuous with a fluctuating self in all its enigmatic purity. "We burrow through ourselves like a mole," he wrote to Brod, "and emerge blackened and velvet-haired from our sandy underground vaults, our poor little red feet stretched out for tender pity."[29] His art, far from neurotic, reflects a higher lucidity, the wisdom of a clairvoyant stutterer, due, as he says, to "introspection, which will suffer no idea to sink tranquilly to rest but must pursue each one into consciousness, only itself to become an idea, in turn to be pursued by renewed introspection."[30] There was no escape from this dialogue with the unknown. "Man's own frontal bone bars his way," as the present is perpetually invaded by a dizzy re-categorization of all those discarded "selves" receding into oblivion. Kafka's challenge as an artist, then, was to discover a means "of making possible the exchange of truthful words from person to person."[31] And what his inner dream life discovered was *metamorphosis*—a process that was commensurate with the opposite, yet integral modes of being that exist within a single mind. "I am here," he wrote drolly in an autobiographical aside, "giving a clear explanation: everything that is said about me is false, if it follows on the assumption that I, as a human being, was the bosom friend of a horse. How strange that this monstrous assertion is spread abroad and believed!"[32] Indeed such a process would be mirrored in his own writing, where Kafka wished to imagine a world "in which life, while still retaining its natural full-bodied rise and fall, would simultaneously be recognized no less clearly as a nothing, as a dream, as a hovering."[33]

Under this dispensation Kafka saw the act of forgetting as vital to survival in the new century, a way of editing a metamorphosing self for the sake of an expedient, if illusory wholeness of being. Memory was not a fixed record, but rather subject to laws of Darwinian selection within an unpredictable and threatening environment. Such a saving amnesia allowed one (momentarily) the sensation of being on firm ground, the "efficiency" that Kafka lacked and admired, for instance, in Felice Bauer, or the "endurance, will for living, for business, and for conquest" that he respected in his father. Indeed the entire process of assimilation of European Jews was a conscious and seemingly prudent exercise of forgetting. Again here one can see the utility of stupidity, the control of uncertainty by cutting it in half, the convergence of pretending or acting and being. Once sealed through repression, such lapses of memory performed on a personal level the task of ordering the psyche once reserved for a viable and interdictory tradition.

But this was no option for Kafka. "Lying is terrible," he told Milena Jesenska, "a worse spiritual torture does not exist."[34] Any learning for this soul-voyager was an act of recovery, a reversal of time into the past, and here again Kafka turned to his animals, which Walter Benjamin has aptly labeled "receptacles of the forgotten."[35] For Kafka, the private man, what had been forgotten was that alien territory that underlies his superb asceticism—his body or "animality." He writes in his diary during his early epistolary romance with Felice: "Coitus as punishment for the happiness of being together. Live as ascetically as possible, more ascetically than a bachelor, that is the only possible way for me to endure marriage."[36] Or remembering his sexual initiation with a shop-girl years later, Kafka is haunted by "something slightly disgusting, embarrassing, obscene . . . This urge had in it something of the eternal Jew, being senselessly drawn, wandering senselessly through a senselessly obscene world."[37] But the animal world is more than a source of droll metaphors for his feelings of inadequacy and self-loathing, or for that matter the plight of the urban European Jew. Speaking for mankind as a whole in the new century, Kafka felt what had been forgotten was an ancestral inheritance of Judeo-Christian values that once offered us wholeness of being and has now degenerated into a tradition in decay. "Either you conceal what you know about me, and do so with a definite motive," says the Hunter Gracchus, with his burden of ancient wisdom before the ordinary world, " . . . or you actually think that you can't remember me, because you confuse my story with someone else's" (*CS*, 233-34). As illustration of the decay of tradition operating in the secret emotions of the individual, we might consider Kafka's remark to Brod: "What do I have in common with Jews? I hardly have anything in common with myself and should stand very quietly in a corner, content that I can breathe."[38]

From this perspective, "A Hunger Artist" becomes not simply a semi-private joke, a wry spiritual autobiography, but a glimpse of what religious asceticism looks like to a world that has evolved beyond it. The hunger artist becomes comic in his devoutness, and denied martyrdom because he would devour food were there any he could tolerate. One might be licensed with the hindsight of history to see in the hunger artist a prescient *muselmann* neglected unto death as the crowd moves on to the panther.[39] One might say the same relation holds between the Mosaic Law and the first Commandant's torture machine in "In the Penal Colony." But one thing seems certain. Retreating from humankind for fresh air, Kafka found his own fallen secular state reflected in his animals, who have "forgotten" their sagacious ancestors of the Hasidic fables. By focusing upon their "earth," now a "distorted mask" of our own, Kafka evokes the feeling of endless reflection minus any clarifying doctrine that was to harrow the new century. Shorn of human wisdom, his animals emerge as some far pole of dispossession from ourselves and each other, and we stand in the same relation to them as God does to us. "We are nihilistic thoughts, suicidal thoughts that came from God's head," Kafka told Brod. "There is plenty of hope — for God — no end of hope — only not for us."[40]

What is suicidal about this inward nihilism is that Kafka experienced it as a departure from prevailing norms and hence a "failing to prove one's worth." Whether these tribunals took the form of his own family or secular institutions, Kafka found them stifling; yet out of some deeper integrity he had to breathe their polluted air. His father did not deliver physical abuse, but something worse — a slow ebbing away of his self-confidence and in its place a burden of boundless guilt. In *Letter to His Father* he admits: "My writing was all about you; all I did there, after all, was to bemoan what I could not bemoan upon your breast."[41] About his injured working-class clients who entered the official maze of the Workers' Accident Insurance Institute, where he was the only Jew among two hundred employees, Kafka remarked: "How modest these men are . . . They come to us and beg. Instead of storming the Institute and smashing it to little pieces, they come and beg."[42]

In both cases the supplicants have suffered an injustice, but they are under the bondage of a nostalgia, or mode of survivor guilt before an ancestral past, forgotten yet extending into the present in the form of what Kafka called "an artificial, miserable substitute for everything, for forebears, marriage, and heirs."[43] Clearly the diffidence of his injured working-class clients before the factory owners of Bohemia was an obsolete gesture. More ontological than psychological, Kafka's own guilt bore the weight of vast eras of time. "You think my sense of guilt is a crutch, a way out," he told Felix Weltsch. "No, I have a sense of guilt simply because for me it is the most perfect form of repentance, but you do not have to look very closely to discover that this sense of guilt is really only a longing for the past."[44] By this order of compulsion, to disavow this guilt with protestations of innocence is merely to confirm it. "Original sin," Kafka wrote, "the ancient wrong committed by man, consists in the complaint that man makes and never ceases making, that a wrong has been done to him, that it was upon him that original sin was committed."[45] Nowhere does Kafka say that this complaint is false, only that guilt and innocence are linked in an ongoing process of metamorphosis.

Living among the invisible realities of a lost tradition did not enable Kafka to "foresee" the Holocaust. Perhaps only an omniscient God whose omnipotence would confer moral bankruptcy could do that. But his writings can be seen to have anticipated it, for looking back gave him a visionary grasp of the wide margin of terror that surrounded a present in ruins. The streets of "the hygienic new town" of Prague were a "launching ramp for suicides." It is revealing that with only a few exceptions Kafka chose to suppress mention of his encounters with Jew-hatred in the diaries and his voluminous correspondence, encounters that extended from his early school days to the end of his life. But a letter to Milena in 1920, at a time when the streets of Prague were awash in racist violence, suggests that this moral darkness was a primary source of inspiration, indeed the amniotic fluid of his nightmare art:

> I've spent all afternoon in the streets, wallowing in the Jew baiting. "*Prašivé plemeno*" — "filthy rabble" — I heard someone call the Jews the other day. Isn't it the natural thing to leave the place where one is hated so much? (For this, Zionism or national feeling is not needed.) The heroism which consists of staying on in spite of it all is that of cockroaches, which also can't be exterminated from the bathroom.
>
> Just now I looked out of the window: Mounted police, *gendarmerie* ready for a bayonet charge, a screaming crowd dispersing, and up here in the window the loathsome disgrace of living all the time under protection.[46]

Kafka had already envisioned the heroism of the cockroach in "The Metamorphosis," written shortly after "The Judgment" in another genuine burst of automatic writing in 1912. In turning to his family, he most likely needed the animal world for fear of violating his own sense of wholesomeness while exploring under the rock of repression. Kafka told Brod that, for him, to write out of bad or perverted passions ("I have hundreds of wrong feelings — dreadful ones — the right ones won't come — or if they do, only in rags; absolutely weak") was to let them get the upper hand.[47] Prior to composition, he confessed to Felice that "when I didn't write, I was at once flat on the floor, fit for the dustbin."[48] This becomes the fate of his hero, Gregor Samsa, a vehicle for Kafka to exorcise his own "general load of fear, weakness, and self-contempt" before his father. Upon completing the story, at one level a semi-private joke at his own expense, he is reported to have buoyantly asked of a friend on the streets of Prague, "What do you think of the terrible things that go on in our family?"[49]

What went on in Kafka's family was the projected fate of his entire "post-transitional generation" being groomed for a role that invariably led from obedient son to vermin, the cockroach a droll image of his self-loathing that would later be seized by Nazi propaganda to dehumanize the Jews. Gregor's metamorphosis into his own "troubled dreams" is less a tragedy than a naked clarification of all his relations to the world, a telescoped restoration of Truth — in particular, the hidden rage of his father who has been battening on *him* like an insect.[50] So has the chief clerk who, waiting for Gregor to emerge from his bedroom, warns him that "your position in the firm is not so unassailable . . . for some time your work has been most unsatisfactory" (CS, 97). Yet he is as far removed from such recognitions as the gap between his consciousness and his numerous waving legs. This son and servant of officialdom now feels "guilt and shame" that his father must work, even after learning that the elder has been hoarding secret funds, for he has no existence apart from his filial loyalty. For Gregor and for his creator, metamorphosis is a kind of secret rescue from the loss of self into others, the attending alienation a form of liberation even if it does no good.

Gregor's only real pleasures and resentments — what we might call his real or hidden self — arise out of that despicable, forgotten, yet indestructible side of being: his body or animality. A promise of deliverance comes when he abandons human postures and falls onto his legs: "Hardly was he down when he experienced for the first time this morning a sense of physical comfort; his legs had firm ground under them . . . and he was inclined to believe that a final relief from all his sufferings was at hand" (102-03). But Gregor's relish for garbage, his discovery of the autoerotic freedom of hanging from the ceiling, his possessive gaze at an innocently lewd picture of a lady with a muff on his wall, these are also the freakish and regressive antics of a sexuality too long deferred. What we witness is a kind of trans-Freudian comedy as Gregor breaks free on three different occasions into the domain of his mother, only to be repelled with increasing violence by his father, by "the enormous size of his shoe soles" (pun intended). Such humor is not psychological, but rather ontological: "The noise in his rear sounded no longer like the force of one single father" (104). Indeed, these primal scenes take us back to the dawn of creation. At one point Gregor is trapped between his mother, who has fainted in his room in a swamp of petticoats, and the stalking wrath of his father, and suffers a bombardment of apples for bumbling into this tableau that suggests and parodies the Biblical Fall. Under this cosmic burden, Gregor might very well choose to forget his animal nature and embrace his human consciousness.

But it isn't easy. Gregor touches on reality only when he acknowledges his pain and its causes through his body, a result of the social reorganization of the household. The evolution of Grete's emotions from shock to grudging ministration, from churlish possessiveness to annoyed indifference, soon oppresses him. Still he listens devoutly to her playing the violin, feels "as if the way were opening before him to the unknown nourishment he craved," and daydreams that upon sending his sister to the Conservatorium "she would burst into tears, and Gregor would then raise himself to her shoulder and kiss her on the neck." (131). Instead she soon wishes he were dead, and is replaced by the derisive attentions of the bony charwoman. Gregor grows more rebellious as he moves toward starvation. Hunger is real. And yet his father's obsequiousness before the three lodgers, followed by his violent purging of them, only anticipates his son's urgencies and then extinguishes them. At last Gregor accepts the family verdict placed upon him, cooperates with their desire he be gotten rid of, and (like Georg Bendemann) expires "thinking of his family with tenderness and love" (135). We are left with a concluding glimpse of the metamorphosis of Grete into an attractive young woman. There is no resistance to fate here, for what else could have happened given this family and this metamorphosis?

In the ensuing four years, none of Kafka's animal stories would entertain a metamorphosis from human to animal worlds — instead the two worlds converse across an abyss. "Far, far away world history takes its course," he muses in his diary, "the world history of your soul."[51] We might surmise two matters intervened now to rarefy Kafka's personal experience into an empty mirror, to lead him beyond his own family to its equivalent in the world at large: tradition in decay. First, there was the failure of his long and tortured relationship with Felice, his yearning for marriage that would only have put him in paralyzing competition with his father, threatening his destiny as a writer. "She was an excellent girl, but utterly bourgeois," Dora Diamant told an interviewer. "Kafka felt that marrying her would mean marrying the whole lie that was Europe."[52] The second matter that likely turned his attention from personal experience to larger vistas was the presence of World War I on his mind, the atavistic slaughter conducted in 475 miles of trenches that criss-crossed the earth of a once-proud Europe. Equipped with new technology, the machine gun and high explosives, World War I was the first "death factory," producing ten million corpses over four years, the flower of Europe's younger generation. Kafka maintained a pregnant silence about the war in his diaries, except to muse that "it would be a great good fortune to become a soldier"; yet no event more clearly suggested that a whole tradition was committing suicide, and he would be ceaselessly involved in measuring the consequences.

It is tempting, if audacious, to see such a trench warfare with a defunct past at the heart of Kafka's unpublished story of 1914, "The Village Schoolmaster (The Giant Mole)," an investigation of the obstacles in communicating the "forgotten" element in the new century. Once again that element, unspecified, "related to fundamental axioms of whose existence we don't even know"(CS, 180), takes an animal form, a giant mole that was seen in a village by an obscure old schoolmaster in the district, whose firsthand account has been dismissed as a rumor by the public and a joke by the scholarly community. The narrator, a man of business with mild curiosity, comes to the aid of the schoolmaster by duplicating his original research — but this provokes hostility in the old man, a pamphlet which competes with his own labors and, as it were, eclipses them. Once alarmed that the narrator "wanted to rob him of the fame of being the first man publicly to vindicate the mole" (171), the schoolmaster is devoured by an ambitious narcissism, as his discovery starts to fade into oblivion, not "completely forgotten," yet outside the radius of "trivial interest that had originally existed." Not much can be salvaged from this realm: the narrator's pamphlet is fated to be wryly disregarded by a prestigious journal as a re-circulation of the schoolmaster's — "An unpardonable confusion of identity" (174).

Now the old man takes refuge in a childish daydream of his metamorphosis from rustic obscurity to tawdry public acclaim in the city. About the urban world, however, only the narrator can speak with authority, and he warns the schoolmaster of what he will lose under the weight of modern institutions: "Every new discovery is assumed at once into the sum total of knowledge, and with that ceases in a sense to be a discovery; it dissolves into the whole and disappears, and one must have a trained scientific eye to recognize it" (180). For Kafka, it is ultimately the way work and life are set up in a new urban system that confers destiny. "After all," he wrote to Weltsch, "our nervous system does take in the entire city."[53] In this droll way he anticipates the entropic effects of information flow in our era, in which, devoid of any mediating authority, a public response of inert uniformity can be expected even in the face of the miraculous.

One earthly reflection of this vision was the war itself, sending off a generation to be sacrificed to patriotic lies, returning "elements of the forgotten" in the steady stream of destitute refugees from Eastern Europe and trainloads of wounded soldiers into Prague. At first Kafka wished evil on all the participants, but he admitted in 1915, "I mostly suffer from the war because I am not taking part in it."[54] Deemed indispensable at the Institute, he assumed responsibility for medical benefits for disabled war veterans, working with amazing dedication to establish neurological clinics for shell-shocked survivors of the trenches. Kafka had displayed a similar identification with the underdog through his "sneak attacks" on conditions in Bohemian factories before the war, producing meticulous reports on the death and mutilation of workers by machinery. Those reports he shared with Brod exhibit a Chaplinesque playfulness, a trait that would be so often overlooked in his fiction: "In my four districts — apart from all my other jobs — people fall off the scaffolds as if they all were drunk, or fall into the machines, all the beams topple, all embankments give way, all ladders slide, whatever people carry up falls down, and whatever they hand down they stumble over. And I have a headache from all these girls in porcelain factories who incessantly throw themselves down the stairs with mounds of dishware."[55]

Written in 1914, "In the Penal Colony" suggests what the idolatry of the machine held for the future. Kafka wrote to his publisher Kurt Wolff that "not merely is the story itself painful, but rather that our times in general — and my own times in particular — have been, and still are, very painful indeed . . . "[56] For Kafka personally, the pain was his own body and the old Commandant an embodiment of the dominant father. "I am nothing but a mass of spikes going through me," he wrote to Brod in 1910. "If I try to defend myself and use force, the spikes only press in the deeper . . ."[57] As for the times in general, the old Commandant suggests a tradition of guilt and punishment leading to redemption being replaced by an era of secular pragmatism and liberal reform. While visiting the penal colony on a tropical island, a distinguished Western explorer is witness to an execution, but more particularly the presiding officer's worship of the torture machine. The prisoner's crime is insignificant — he was sleeping, not disobedient; he is a "stupidlooking, widemouthed creature" who acts "like a submissive dog" (CS, 140); he "doesn't know the sentence passed on him," has been denied a defense because "guilt is never to be doubted" (145). In these respects the prisoner is a pawn in a semi-private game, another degraded image of an assimilated Jew his creator would place throughout his fiction. It is also possible that Kafka, besides his personal experience, related his penal colony to the famous Dreyfus case, in which in 1894 Captain Alfred Dreyfus, the only Jewish member of the French general staff, was falsely accused of betraying his country and banished to Devil's

Island until his eventual pardon in 1906.[58]

But the officer is now presiding over a sick tradition, a mere stand-in for the old Commandant, a demigod who had been "soldier, judge, mechanic, chemist, and draughtsman" of the penal colony and its torture machine (144). The new Commandant is modern and wants to be done with the penal code, wants the approval of foreigners, and the officer complains that now "resources for maintaining the machine are now very much reduced," that the policy is "mostly harbor works, nothing but harbor works!" (158) The guiding plans of the torture machine, drawn by the former Commandant, its Holy Writ, are an inscrutable "labyrinth of lines crossing and recrossing each other" (148). Once the Western explorer, witnessing the execution, declares of the process that "the inhumanity is undeniable," that he cannot help the official defend the practice, the official places himself in the Harrow, now set to write "Be Just" into his body, and is mutilated by the malfunctioning apparatus. And on his face "no sign was visible of the promising redemption" (166). But the story ends with menace. The explorer visits the grave of the old Commandant in the Tea House, and reads an inscription: "There is a prophecy that after a certain number of years the Commandant will rise again and lead his adherents from this house to recover the colony. Have faith and wait!" (167) How secure, then, is the emancipation from this tradition? And why does the explorer hastily leave the island, leaving the soldier and prisoner behind in fear? Pawel sees in the amorality of the old Commandant a "prescient portrait of Adolf Eichmann" — although Eichmann fainted when he made a visit to the Nazi death camps.[59] Kurt Tucholsky was one of the few contemporaries to recognize the full implications of what Kafka's called his "dirty" story:

> This officer is no torturer, let alone a sadist. His delight in the manifestations of the victim's six-hour agony merely demonstrates his boundless, slavish worship of the machine, which he calls justice and which in fact is power. Power without limits. To be able for once to exercise power without any constraints — do you still remember the sexual fantasies of early adolescence? What stimulated them was not just sex but the absence of restraints. To be able to impose one's will, without any limits . . . the torture is eventually cut short not

because society, the state, or the law indignantly rise up in protest and put a stop to it but because the spare parts for the machine turn out to be defective; the apparatus, though still tolerated by the higher echelons of bureaucracy, no long enjoys full support at the top . . . Don't ask what it means. It means nothing. The book may not even be of our time. It is completely harmless. As harmless as Kleist.[60]

AT THIS TIME KAFKA was also completing *The Trial*, which again was rooted in personal experience as it illuminated a cultural development. The personal experience was the termination of his first engagement with Felice in Berlin in 1914, what Kafka called a "tribunal in a hotel" where he was found guilty because in him were "two selves wrestling with each other."[61] The two had met in 1912, for one hour, and before meeting again seven months later, Kafka had bombarded Felice with over 300 lengthy letters that would grow into the most stressful, egregiously exogamous epistolary romance on record. Kafka seemed to want marriage and fatherhood as much as he feared these conventions would suffocate him. He warned Felice she could look forward only to a "monastic life at the side of a man who is peevish, miserable, silent, discontented, and sickly . . ."[62] Yet such feats of self-deprecation, designed to discourage her and preserve his creative solitude, would metamorphose into verbal love-making that kept her involved. "I am frightened when you tell me that you love me," he wrote, "and if you don't tell me, I should die."[63] This pattern of manipulation through slick and at times meretricious paradox pervades the correspondence. Kafka had every reason to feel guilty about his treatment of Felice, and as John Winkelman has shown, details of this struggle are deeply embedded in the novel.[64]

But *The Trial* is memorable not as veiled confession but as a symbolic and dreamlike vision of the abuse of power. Unlike Karl Rossman, Joseph K. is a successful native son, a banker whose arbitrary arrest by some nameless malignant authority or Law leads him into foreign labyrinthine proceedings that will provide no exit. Ignorant of the charges against him, at first K. is dismissive of the guards and the inspector. Yet that he wakes up with the guards devouring his breakfast and confiscating his undergarments, thereby stripping him of all authority, already signifies that symbolically he is a dead man. "Committing suicide would be so irrational that even had he wished to," we are told, "the irrationality of the act would have prevented him."[65] The burden of the novel now becomes to establish the rationality of such an act. K. may reenact his arrest as a comic farce to entertain the typist in his lodgings, Fräulein Bürstner, but his sudden sexual hunger for her reveals a new desperate need. At his initial inquiry held in a shabby suburban tenement, K. denounces the court behind his arrest to a gallery of onlookers with incisive eloquence:

> An organization that not only engages corrupt guards, inane inspectors, and examining magistrates who are at best mediocre, but that supports as well a system of judges of all ranks, including the highest, with their inevitable innumerable entourage of assistants, scribes, gendarmes, and other aides, perhaps even hangmen, I won't shy away from the word. And the purpose of this extensive organization, gentlemen? It consists of arresting innocent people and introducing senseless proceedings against them, which for the most part, as in my case, go nowhere. (50)

But declarations of virtue or denunciations of injustice are always nugatory in Kafka. This speech is wasted on the gallery, for K. sees all of them are wearing the badges of officials. Perhaps his words are even hurtful to his purpose, for the examining magistrate informs him "that you have today deprived yourself . . . of the advantage that an interrogation offers to the arrested man in each case" (52-53). The stale air, the gloomy corridors, the dirty attics that collect forgotten things, the fog-like haze permeating the tenement, everything signals a new realm of enervation and paranoia. Indeed when K. returns the next week to discover a filthy courtroom laden with pornography instead of law books, and debauchery rampant among the officials, they "thought he was about to undergo some profound metamorphosis at any moment, one they didn't want to miss" (73). Now feeling "seasick," K. escapes from the tenement. But a few evenings later, when he discovers Franz and Willem, the two guards who arrested him, being flogged in a junk room *at his bank*, apparently because he had complained about them to the examining magistrate, the accused learns not only that ordinary life might be a mere front for the world of the court but that he shares with that world a baffling and arbitrary complicity in guilt. K. is clarifying his own metamorphosis when he tells his assistants: "Clean out that junk room once and for all. We're drowning in filth" (87).

As in *Amerika*, the hero is offered dubious help from a relative, Uncle Karl, who recognizes the metamorphosis and leads his nephew to Huld, a defense lawyer with heart trouble whose nurse, Leni, tells the new client prophetically that "you can't defend yourself against this court, all you can do is confess . . . That's the only chance you have to escape" (106). While he waits for Huld's interminable contacts with court officials to bear results, K. is still determined to "stand up for his rights" (126). Yet his spontaneous liaison with Leni, ignited when he kisses her webbed hand, signals a slide toward degeneracy: "Hastily, with an open mouth, she climbed up his lap on her knees . . . an exciting, almost bitter odor, like pepper, rose from her; she pulled his head to her and bent over it, biting and kissing his neck, even biting his hair" (108). Ultimately Leni, who is sexually attracted to the guilt of all defendants, who is "drawn to all of them, loves them all, and seems to be loved by them in return" (184), affords K. no help. She is a servant of the court who distracts and disarms the accused, then will return to tell Huld of all her promiscuous affairs "to entertain him." Or perhaps she is a mere cover for the lawyer's pontifical procrastinations.

To gain more influence with his judges, K. visits a court painter, but art offers no answer. Indeed art can serve tyranny. Titorelli's vacuous heathscapes and his flattering, indeed mythologizing portraits of vain court judges, created in accordance to "secret" rules for the purpose of intimidating defendants, are both mendacious versions of reality. But Titorelli does know the court, and despite K.'s mistrust, the painter proceeds to explain the defendant's three possibilities. *Actual acquittal* doesn't require the painter's help, because it is unknown, "forgotten" except in the realm of ancient legends, the verdicts "not published" (154). If legends tell of judgments that are inaccessible, they can't be utilized. Titorelli can provide *apparent acquittal* with a certificate of innocence that buys temporary freedom, but the charge and proceedings remain "alive," able to be reactivated at any time, causing ongoing anxiety. K. sees in this case that the court "serves no purpose" since it is "firmly convinced of the defendant's guilt." And *protraction* can extend the trial constantly at a lower stage, leaving K. free yet forever a defendant of the court. These possibilities leave the accused with "only a hair's difference between the advantages and disadvantages" (162). Under this dispensation, there are no acquittals, no convictions, no innocence, just the assumption of guilt and dawning punishment — which leaves K. "totally cut off from air." Perhaps his shocking insight goes to the heart of the matter: "A single executioner could take the place of the entire court" (154).

Joseph K. returns to dismiss Huld as his lawyer because he feels "the trial is closing in on me" and must invest everything in his own legal defense, thus yielding to an impatience that all those familiar with or connected to the court have warned him to control. At the lawyer's apartment K. and Leni take condescending notice of another client, the merchant Block, "a scrawny little man with a full beard, a candle in his hand" (167). Block gains more attention when the merchant shares his knowledge of the courts gained during his five-year trial. "Waiting isn't pointless," he counsels, "the only thing that's pointless is independent action" (176). Once K. is summoned to Huld and proceeds to release him, the lawyer, as if to make him retract, calls in Block, in his words "that miserable worm," and subjects the merchant to a series of humiliations — kneeling, crawling, kissing the lawyer's hand — that are a travesty of religious ritual. Suddenly K. realizes that Block "was no longer a client, he was the lawyer's dog. If the lawyer had ordered him to crawl under the bed, as into a kennel, and bark, he would have done so gladly" (195). As Roberto Calasso has brilliantly pointed out, this pitiful merchant is his creator's most abject portrait of an assimilated urban Jew, and a foreshadowing of what K. might become in the future.[66] As Block fires back at the supercilious banker:

> Why are you insulting me? And in front of the lawyer, who tolerates

both you and me merely out of compassion? You're no better a person than I am, for you're a defendant too and also on trial. But if you remain a gentleman in spite of that, then I'm as much a gentleman as you, if not a greater one . . . But if you think you're privileged because you're allowed to sit here quietly and listen while I, as you put it, crawl around on all fours, then let me remind you of the old legal maxim: a suspect is better off moving than at rest, for one at rest may be on the scales without knowing it, being weighed with all his sins. (192-93)

Still K. rebels against the court right up to the end. His job now threatened by the vice president, he is assigned to show an Italian businessman the art treasures in the town cathedral. As K. leaves the office Leni phones him: "They're hounding you" (205). But the businessman never appears, and instead K. is summoned by a prison priest in the cathedral pulpit to whom he still protests his innocence. "That's right," says the priest, "but that's how guilty people always talk" (213). Then he tells K. the parable of the man from the country seeking admittance to the Law, but blocked for a lifetime by a doorkeeper who roars at him near his end: "No one else could gain admittance here, because this entrance was meant solely for you. I'm going to go and shut it now" (217). In a travesty of critical exegesis, the priest offers interpretations of the parable that are so ingenious he is able to cast the doorkeeper as conscientious, self-deceived, simple-minded, compassionate, or perhaps just a loyal servant of the Law that remains beyond human judgment. "I'm just pointing out the various opinions that exist on the matter," the priest says, adding that "the correct understanding of a matter and misunderstanding the matter are not mutually exclusive" (219). K. balks at this notion of epistemological metamorphosis, which dissolves all meaning into ambiguity. "No, you don't have to consider everything true," the priest says, "you just have to consider it necessary" (223). "A depressing opinion," K. replies. "Lies are made into a universal system."

The last chapter, though confusing and somewhat inconsistent with K.'s behavior so far, still represents such a metamorphosis. Although his guilt is never established, nor the charge even revealed,

K. cooperates in every step of his execution. There is a touch of burlesque theater in the two executioners with their top hats, black coats and double chins, and social sanction conferred as their walk out of the city is observed by people from windows, several policemen, and possibly even Fräulein Bürstner. At the quarry K. is calm and resigned, for he "knew clearly now that it was his duty to seize the knife as it floated from hand to hand above him and plunge it into himself" (230). But instead he reaches out towards a human figure atop a nearby building, a friend maybe, or a judge, until an executioner delivers the verdict. "Like a dog," K. says, dying in shame. Of course the simile links him with Block, or his creator, who also wrote in a startling diary entry: "This morning, for the first time in a long time, the joy again of imagining a knife twisted in my heart."[67] Kafka's burden of guilt in relation to his father, or a guilty conscience regarding his treatment of Felice, such realities may have partially informed Joseph K.'s fate, but his trial was instigated by slander, by false testimony, which can only bring to mind the Dreyfus Affair again or the Hilsner "blood libel" case that symbolized the general plight of European Jews in a rising tide of anti-Semitism.

Any attempt, then, to read *The Trial* as the allegory of a religious quest or successful search for God must be resisted, for He has been replaced by venal and corrupt judges who inculcate guilt by the sheer weight of their system. Nowhere is there any evidence that Kafka believed in a deity. Not that he wasn't preoccupied with religion, and in particular the history of Judaism, for another "forgotten element" that Kafka had encountered now was Eastern European Jewry, first with the arrival in Prague in 1911 of a Yiddish troupe of actors led by Yitzhak Lowy, then during the war as impoverished Polish Jews poured into refugee camps in Prague. Their roots and sense of communal strength were exactly what he lacked in his "inner emigration" — while their strident contempt for the city's middle-class assimilated Jews mirrored his own. Kafka's reunion and second engagement with Felice in 1916 seems linked to her work as a volunteer at the Jewish People's Home in Berlin, set up to aid the refugee children of Ostjuden. "I am desperately eager for you to participate," he wrote her, "... to let the dark complexity of Judaism as a whole, so pregnant with impenetrable mystery do its work."[68] But for him memory was fate. "The synagogue is not something you sneak up on. I could not do this today any more than I could as a child; I still remember how I literally drowned in the terrifying boredom and pointlessness of the temple services. They were hell's way of staging a preview of my later office career."[69] Nor was Kafka approving of the god of Soren Kierkegaard, who could accept Abraham's sacrifice of his son Isaac as, in his words, a "teleological suspension of the ethical." For Kafka there was never a leap of faith or a suspension of the ethical. When Hermine Beck, who helped him with his Hebrew, once swatted a fly in his presence, he exclaimed angrily, "Why don't you leave the poor fly in peace, what has he done to you?"[70]

Spiritually, then, Kafka was still banished to the animal kingdom. He did not idealize the primitive, for there were the war and the blood-and-sex ideologies swirling in the streets of Prague. But he did investigate the impulse with devilish innocence. Brod tells us that Kafka was fond of quoting Kierkegaard's perception that "as soon as a man appears who brings something of the primitive along with him ... a metamorphosis takes place in the whole of nature."[71] What the primitive does is to stir traces of theological crisis, now replayed in terms of secular magic and fairytale — but by itself is no theology at all. Kafka's strict vegetarianism, for instance, a rite he always associated with the early Christians and their persecutions, was merely double-edged spiritual mimicry — a respect for the primitive and a refusal to be polluted by it. Once at a Berlin aquarium, his companion Ludwig Hardt heard Kafka murmur to the fish in their illuminated tanks: "Now I can look into your eyes with a clean conscience. I don't eat you anymore."[72]

This remark offers a clue to what lies behind the "distorted mask" of Kafka's magical tale, "Jackals and Arabs," written in a sudden release from war depression in 1916. Here a man "from the North" is visited by a swarm of jackals as he falls asleep at an oasis. They have awaited him for "endless years" so that he might be recruited as a messiah to deliver them from Arabs. These vile nomads "kill animals for food," and their meat-eating ways have cleared the desert of carrion. Kafka would seem to suggest that jackals are like European Jews looking for divine intervention, but whose present plight is equivalent to the humiliation of eating dead and putrefying flesh. Speaking with aggrieved dignity, the jackals seem to have natural justice on their side — until suddenly the man from the North finds "two young beasts behind me had locked their teeth through my coat and shirt" (CS, 409). He protests only to be told this cannot be helped: "We are poor creatures, and we have nothing but our teeth; whatever we want to do, good or bad, we can tackle it only with our teeth" (409). So much for primitive adaptability. The head jackal tries to allay our uneasiness by delivering a speech which is ecologically superb — "We want to be troubled no more by Arabs; room to breathe; a skyline cleaned of them; no more bleating of sheep knifed by an Arab: every beast to die a natural death" — but humanly repulsive — "no interference till we have drained the carcass empty and picked its bones clean" (409).

This sardonic complement to the dream of Jewish deliverance, possible only with the help of others without the militancy of Zionism, recurs moments later as visual pun when the man from the North is offered a pair of sewing scissors that the jackals have adopted for the purpose of cutting the throats of Arabs. Such a confusion of realms, however, only exposes their impotence (jackals are boastful, stupid, and cowardly fighters), and suddenly an Arab appears to crush the conspiracy with a crack of his whip (the oppressor regains through sadism what he has lost as carrion). "So long as Arabs exist," he explains, "that pair of scissors goes wandering through the desert and will wander with us to the end of our days. Every European is offered it for the great work; every European is just the man that Fate has chosen for them. They have the most lunatic hopes, these beasts; they're just fools, utter fools. That's why we like them; they are our dogs; finer dogs than any of yours" (410). The canine species, so often in Kafka a reference to the humiliations of the Jews, is replayed here, with the suggested "deliverance" through assimilation offered by Europeans no less degrading than treatment by the Arabs. We are left gazing awe-struck at what was forgotten as the jackals, once thrown the carcass of a camel, forget their hatred of Arabs before this "stinking carrion," then lash themselves into ecstasy in pursuit of primitive cleanliness.

But apes are another matter, as Kafka starts to reduce the evolutionary gap between his animals and the human world, and sharpen the antagonism between them. In "A Report to an Academy," a performing ape reports to a learned body of mankind on his former life, now reduced to a fleeting nostalgia, "only a gentle puff of air that plays around my heels" (CS, 250). In imagining how he learned to forget his origins, Kafka gives us a humorous replay of the assimilation process of European Jews, compressed into five years, that has enabled the ape to "reach the cultural level of an average European" (258). Once a native of the Gold Coast, the ape was bushwhacked by technology (hunters with guns) at a watering hole, and the nature of his wounds, one in the cheek and the other "below the hip," suggests that access to the European world is experienced as a sexual wounding — as the ape is willing to demonstrate by pulling down his trousers to expose "well-groomed fur and the scar made . . . by a wanton shot" (252). His trauma sealed by amnesia and the wall of language, the ape is now locked up where he can only squat, miming the act of human defecation. He experiences only one feeling — "no way out . . . I had to find a way out or die" — and reaches one conclusion: "Well, then, I had to stop being an ape" (253). To achieve this, he must renounce the heaven of his former freedom for its laughable equivalent in the human world: "self-controlled movement" or acting. Over vast eras of time mankind has learned this as part of the Darwinian drama; in particular the Jews of Europe have learned it after centuries of persecution. Now that a fluctuating self-consciousness had turned action into acting and all human gestures were losing their traditional supports, Kafka saw his present by a wide curve of irony beginning once more to approximate the ape's. That the first human gesture he learns is a handshake is likely to fill us with the same wonder that led Kafka to describe his encounter with daily life in Prague as "a seasickness on dry land."[73]

The breaking of the ape begins at sea by a sailor who acts out the process of drinking schnapps, even though the ape is disgusted by schnapps. "After theory came practice" (256). But torture, a burning pipe held against his fur, simply a necessary cauterization "against the nature of apes," at last enables him to break into the human world "as an artistic performer" by getting drunk and blurting out a brief but unmistakable "Hallo!" This dismal triumph for mankind is merely a matter of survival to the ape: "I repeat: there was no attraction for me in imitating human beings; I imitated them because I needed a way out, and for no other reason" (257). Set in motion by guns and then torture, the process of assimilation ends in a state of alienation. Unlike all those invited to join the Nature Theater of Oklahoma provided they play themselves, the ape must play man and graduates to performing in variety shows as his teachers file into mental hospitals. Yet imitation is only the pragmatics of the void: "There was nothing else for me to do, provided always that freedom was not to be my choice" (258). A wistful sadness remains for what has been lost, as when the ape returns from successful performances to a little half-trained chimpanzee awaiting him in his room: "By day I cannot bear to see her; for she has the insane look of the bewildered half-broken animal in her eyes; no one else sees it, but I do, and I cannot bear it" (259). Indeed Kafka would not sacrifice that freedom in his art or life ever again.

"MY MALTREATED BLOOD finally burst out," Kafka said of his massive hemorrhage on August 9, 1917, diagnosed as tuberculosis of the lungs, which he experienced with relief as freedom from his commitment of marriage to Felice. At the same time he recognized that he had caused her great pain in his long and futile prolongation of their ordeal. "As you know," he wrote to her in breaking off their second engagement, "there are two of me at war with each other... one is good, the other evil. At times they switch masks, which further confuses the already confused struggle . . . The blood shed by the good one on your behalf has served the enemy... I don't believe this illness to be primarily tuberculosis, but my all-around bankruptcy

... I shall never get well again."[74] But if it seemed that marital happiness was to elude him, Kafka now saw an opportunity to commit himself completely to his literary aspirations. As he wrote in a diary entry: "You have the chance, as far as it is at all possible, to make a new beginning. Don't throw it away ... If the infection in your lungs is only a symbol, as you say, a symbol of the infection whose inflammation is F ... then the medical advice (light, air, sun, rest) is also a symbol. Lay hold of this symbol."[75]

Of course insomnia, splitting headaches, stomach disorders (as well as general hypochondria) had plagued Kafka for many years. He had no doubt that these were psychosomatic ailments, brought on by his writing, his work at the Institute, and his bid for normalcy with Felice. Like a prisoner strapped in the Harrow, he felt that his sins were written on his body. To his sister Ottla he described the tuberculosis as "this mental disease." But as a matter of fact, starting in 1916 Europe had experienced a stunning rise in cases of tuberculosis, especially among Jews, who according to anti-Semitic propaganda were resistant to it.[76] Contributing factors were the harsh winter of 1916, food shortages, and the flood of indigent Jewish refugees into urban areas from Poland and Russia. Nevertheless, with more luck Kafka might have been mistaken in the dark prediction he made to Felice about his illness. Living in Prague for periods, then retreating to Ottla's cottage in Zurau, his health actually improved during 1918. Then on October 14, a month before the armistice, he caught the Spanish influenza. This viral infection devastated his body — and soon became a pandemic that killed somewhere between 20 and 40 million people. Kafka's early desire for battlefield oblivion may have eluded him, yet he was ultimately the casualty of a disease whose outbreak was made possible by the devastated earth of World War I.

In 1919 Kafka started a correspondence with Melina Jesenska, the Czech journalist and translator of his writing, who soon became his lover. The affair at last joined him to a woman who was vibrant, sensual, and intelligent — a Gentile who understood and revered him. "She is a living fire," he told Brod, "of a kind I have never seen before."⁷⁷ At first Kafka was stunned when Melina asked him if he were Jewish:

> You ask me if I'm a Jew. Perhaps this is only a joke, perhaps you're only asking me if I belong to those anxious Jews. In any case as a native of Prague, you can't be as innocent in this respect as Mathilde, Heine's wife . . . You may reproach the Jews for their specific anxiousness, although such a general reproach shows more theoretical than practical knowledge of human nature . . . The strangest thing is that, in general, the reproach does not fit. The insecure position of the Jews, insecure within themselves, insecure among people, would make it above all comprehensible that they consider themselves to be allowed to own only what they can hold with their hands or between their teeth, that furthermore only tangible possessions give them the right to live, and that they will never again acquire what they once have lost . . . From the most improbable sides Jews are threatened with danger, or let us, to be more exact, leave the dangers aside, they are threatened with threats.⁷⁸

He told Melina he was in most respects a typical European Jew: "This means, expressed with exaggeration, that not one calm second is granted me, everything has to be earned, not only the present and future, but the past too, something after all which every human being has inherited, this too must be earned, it is perhaps the hardest work."⁷⁹ He also told her of the Jew-baiting he witnessed regularly in the violent streets of Prague. Shortly afterwards, Kafka wrote again to say he intended no reproach.

> . . . I could reproach you for having much too high an opinion of the Jews whom you know (myself included); there are, of course, others. Sometimes I'd like to cram them all as Jews (including myself) into the drawer of the laundry chest, wait a while, then open the drawer a little to see whether all have already suffocated, and if not, close the drawer again, and so on like this to the end.⁸⁰

Fueled by all his parricidal and cosmic rages, Kafka's concluding metamorphosis of mind is not Jewish self-hatred, but rather a private, cleansing "holocaust" directed at the assimilated Jew, someone who was not Jewish enough. Yet the vision of extermination is there, and directed against himself as well. If such a moral being could entertain such a vision, anything was possible. And in view of the earth he saw at every turn, clearly all was permissible.

In 1922, over a period of several months, Kafka wrote a last unfinished novel, *The Castle*. While more complex and rich in characters than *The Trial*, both novels are about what Roberto Calasso has called "the mystery of election — its impenetrable obscurity," for Joseph K. his struggle to escape conviction by the court, for K. his struggle to be chosen as land surveyor.[81] Like Karl Rossman, K. is a foreigner from a distant land who must struggle against a secret and latently hostile social network of officials to fulfill a mission to "stay here." A novel of infinite suggestibility that is woven together by long roaming conversations and monologues, often metamorphosing into self-contradiction, from both guardians and rebels of the prevailing system, *The Castle* has elicited what Kafka (probably with an ironic smile) expected — a flood of allegorical or supernatural interpretations. But given what was on his mind in 1922, that the novel is on the lower frequencies about the European Jew seeking acceptance in a Gentile world cannot be ignored.[82]

Arriving without an official letter of appointment, K. is regarded with mistrust by the village ("there is no custom of hospitality here") as he starts to penetrate the fog of mystification surrounding the authorities. The first sight of the Castle is not encouraging:

> The tower up here — it was the only one in sight — the tower of a residence, as now became evident, possibly of the main Castle, was a monotonous round building, in part mercifully hidden by ivy, with little windows that glinted in the sun — there was something crazy about this — and ending in a kind of terrace, whose battlements, uncertain, irregular, brittle, as if drawn by the anxious or careless hand of a child, zigzagged into the blue sky. It was as if some melancholy resident, who by rights ought to have kept himself locked up in the most out-of-the-way room in the house, had broken through the roof and stood up in order to show himself to the world.[83]

Neither Klamm's personal letter to K. nor the telephone call with "the singing of the most distant, of the most utterly distant, voices" provide connection to the Castle. The land surveyor represents a threat because as he tells the council chairman "what I want from the Castle is not charity, but my rights" (74). This assumption of individual freedom stirs the hostility of Gardena, landlady of the Bridge Inn. "Wherever you go, keep in mind that you're the most ignorant person here," she tells K., "and be careful" (55). Although officials of the Castle prove to be corrupt, sexually predatory, and all but inaccessible, the village peasants are given to mute submission, aware of the consequences. K. is pushed into a "non-official, completely uncontrollable, murky, strange life," and marginally aware that pushing too hard against custom will alert a police mentality that is ultimately in charge: "The authorities, gentle and friendly as ever, would have had to intervene, as if against their will, yet in the name of some public ordinance unknown to him, in order to haul him away."

It is to women that K. turns for knowledge of the officials, officials who prey upon them, and his flaunting of the rules is his appeal. Frieda has risen from chambermaid to Klamm's lover in the Gentlemen's Inn, but she becomes K.'s lover within minutes of meeting him, will wish they "had gone away at once that very night," and confesses to him that "believe me, your closeness is the only dream that I dream, none other" (254). But in the village this remains just a dream. According to Pepi, K. is attracted to Frieda only because of her "connections that no one else knows about" with Castle officials. When Erlanger asks him to return his fiancée to Klamm since "the slightest change on Klamm's desk, the removal of a stain that was there forever, all of these things can disturb him" (273), it will become Pepi's turn to fall in love. Again K. becomes "a hero, a rescuer of maidens" who would himself be attracted if he knew that Pepi had some kind of connection with the Castle. She too associates K. with freedom, and "anyone who had the strength to set the entire Gentlemen's Inn on fire and burn it down, without leaving a trace, to burn it up like a sheet of paper in a stove, today would be Pepi's chosen one" (291). Both these women may dream of liberation, yet they are inextricably bound to the system they wish to destroy. Frieda returns to Jeremias through Klamm, whom K. will get no closer to than tasting the cognac in his empty sleigh. Pepi offers K. refuge in her quarters, a parenthetical paradise, but he is looking for acceptance, not secret sanctuary. And invisibly orchestrating everything is Klamm — revered, lascivious, dreaming, forgetful, given to vulgar utterances and smoking Virginia cigars, a fat demigod because a man "who is so often the object of yearning and yet so rarely attained, easily takes on a variety of shapes in the imagination of people" (181).

The story of Barnabas's family makes clear that the Castle hardly needs terror to maintain control when the influence of custom is so decisive. K.'s young assistant is recovering from the ostracism that fell upon his once-respected family following his sister Amalia's encounter with Sortini at the Firemen's Festival. Olga, another sister now forced to prostitute herself with stable boys to support the family, tells of how the sternly beautiful Amalia, "with a desire for solitude that overpowered every other feeling," was spotted by a "tiny, weak, brooding" official, and passed a coarse letter demanding a meeting, which she scornfully shredded. Olga explains that "women cannot help loving officials when the officials approach them, and indeed even beforehand they're in love with the officials, no matter how strongly they attempt to deny it . . ." (197) Amalia's rejection of Sortini, however, demonstrates how completely she rejects the rule of the Castle, how boldly she remains "face to face with the truth," how imperiously she now stands "quietly in the background, observing the devastation." And the devastation is considerable. Her parents are dishonored and shunned, especially her father the shoemaker, who is guilty of nothing but begs the Castle to inform him of his crime so he can attempt through bribery to obtain a pardon. Again Calasso has revealed one of Kafka's semi-private games by astutely linking the shoemaker's self-humiliation, like Block's, to the fate of the assimilated Jews of Central Europe.[84] K. is drawn to Barnabas's family because they "were at least outwardly more or less in the same situation as he himself and with whom he could therefore ally himself" (177), but the purity of Amalia's rebellion mocks his own, and she tells him a fable that scornfully bears upon his own case: "I once heard of a young man whose mind was taken up day and night with thoughts of the Castle, he neglected everything else . . . but in the end it turned out that it wasn't actually the Castle he was thinking of but only the daughter of a scullery maid at the offices, he got her, and then all was fine again" (205).

At four in the morning in the Gentlemen's Inn, searching for Erlanger, K. wearily wanders by mistake into secretary Burgel's room and listens to another interminable monologue, this one revealing more details about the Castle's connection with the petitioning parties than ever before. Burgel is sympathetic, sees K. is suffering because "you are a surveyor, but you have no surveying work," holds out that "sometimes opportunities do arise that aren't altogether in keeping with the situation in general" (261). These opportunities arise during night interrogations, which secretaries object to because at night "one involuntarily inclines to judge matters from a more private point of view, the presentations of the parties are given more weight than should be the case . . . their sorrows and their fears interfere with the judgment, the necessary barrier between parties and officials, even if outwardly still intact, begins to crumble . . ." (262-63) K. has fallen asleep, and his dream of a victory celebration debunks any claim of divine status for the Castle as he wins a comic battle with the secretary, now "naked, very like the statue of a Greek god" but one who "squeaked like a girl being tickled" (265). Burgel regards the Castle as "a great living organization" whose order would be threatened by a party surprising a secretary in a night interrogation: "What a strange, precisely shaped, small, clever little grain such a party would have to be in order to slip through that incomparable sieve. You think this can never happen. You're right, it can never happen. But one night — who can vouch for everything? — it does happen" (268). Burgel explains how it might happen:

> Sitting there is the party whom one has never seen, always awaited, awaited with genuine thirst, and always quite wisely considered unreachable. Through his silent presence alone, he invites one to invade his poor life, to look about as though one were surrounded

> by one's own possessions, and to suffer along with him from the futile demands that he makes. On a quiet night an invitation like that is enchanting. One accepts it and has then actually ceased to be an official. The situation then is such that it soon becomes impossible to turn down a request. Speaking strictly, one is desperate, and speaking even more strictly, quite happy. Desperate, for the vulnerability with which one sits there waiting for the party's plea, knowing that one must grant it as soon as it is uttered, even if it should, at any rate insofar as one can perceive this oneself, literally tear apart the official system — this vulnerability must surely be the worst thing that can befall one in the course of one's duty. (269)

Ordinarily this would be called compassion, but for a secretary it is dereliction of duty that brings down the system. His reaction of "suicidal happiness" seems the perfect term. The party's behavior would ordinarily be called the demand for justice, but to Burgel, "at night, like a robber in the woods, the party forces from us sacrifices that we would never have been capable of otherwise" (269). A petitioning party in desperate need of these disclosures, K. has been fast asleep, "cut off from everything around him" (270).

Finally, K.'s illegal witnessing of the distribution of files at the Gentlemen's Inn offers an image of the organization's modus operandi that verges on sinister slap-stick comedy. Servants, pushing carts loaded with files, pursue the officials hidden behind half-shut doors as the two argue over who gets what bundle:

> Those negotiations took a long time, occasionally they came to an agreement, the gentleman gave up a portion of the files, or as compensation received another file since there had merely been a mix-up, but there were also times when somebody had to give up all the requested files without any fuss, either because the servant's evidence had driven him into a corner or because he had grown tired of the continual negotiations, but then he didn't hand the files to the servant, and threw them instead on a sudden decision along the corridor, so that the strings came loose and the sheets went flying and the servants had great difficulty putting everything back in order again. (276-77)

At least this can be concluded about the Castle, where "official decisions are as shy as young girls" (173). First of all, proceedings are meant to be secret, knowledge about them proscribed, and the ignorance of the petitioners an enabling condition of order. Second, petitioners and their personal histories are reduced to paper, to files, subject to being lost or destroyed, being handled by exhausted, forgetful, or corrupt officials. Third, the organization appears to be nowhere, yet is everywhere, indistinguishable from ordinary life. Finally, the world of the Castle is as drab and amoral as it is inescapable. *The Castle* ends in mid-sentence, as if still unfolding, both a reflection of the collapsing Hapsburg Empire that oppressed its Jews inside legalistic barbed wire, and a harbinger of the Nazi terror that would rise up in its place.

KAFKA RETURNED TO THE ANIMAL world late in 1922. By now Milena had passed through his life as a lost possibility for personal happiness. He had written that he loved her "as the sea loves a pebble in its depths, this is just how my love engulfs you . . ."[85] When she could not break from her husband, he was devastated. "I am too far away, am banished," he wrote to Brod, thus echoing what he had said upon the final breakup with Felice in 1917: "What I have to do, I can do only alone. Become clear about the ultimate things."[86] This impulse was only more urgent now, for Kafka was clearly dying of tuberculosis, moving from institution to institution, haunted by rampant *angst*. His cough he called the "animal" in him, and he was ready to write from entirely inside the animal world, abjuring metamorphosis between realms for the disembodied isolation of writing, "a sleep deeper than that of death."[87]

A year earlier he had written to Brod that most Jewish writers "who started to write in German wanted to get away from their Jewishness, usually with their fathers' vague consent (the vagueness of it was what made it outrageous). They wanted to get away, but their hind legs still stuck to the fathers' Jewishness, while the forelegs found no firm ground. And the resulting despair served as their inspiration."[88] But personally Kafka allied himself with the wild visionaries and legendary Talmudic scholars on his mother's side:

All such writing is an assault on the frontiers; if Zionism had not intervened, it might easily have developed into a new secret doctrine, a Kabbalah. There are intimations of this. Though of course it would require genius of an unimaginable kind to strike root again in the old centuries, or create the old centuries anew and not spend itself withal, but only then begin to flower forth.[89]

Kafka assumed this impossible burden and measured his failure in "Investigations of a Dog," among other things a "distorted mask" of his own contribution to the state of Jewish letters. Kafka's mute and gazing dog has his own fate, the expansion of a "little maladjustment" into a full-fledged metaphysical riddle, soon divorcing him from the legendary community of dogdom ("All in one heap!") and setting him on his investigations. A traumatic episode out of childhood started it, naturally, an encounter with seven dogs conjuring music from the air and walking on hind legs, "uncovering their nakedness, blatantly making a show of their nakedness" (CS, 284). The dog retreats into asceticism, the conversion of sexual fear into an investigation of "what the canine race nourished itself upon," what has crumbled away "like a neglected ancestral inheritance" (286-87). This inquiry pursues the unknowable, generating pedantry and headaches — yet the dog is pledged to "lap up the marrow" of life even if it might be poison. Others along the way only parody real spiritual pursuit, for instance the "soaring dogs," whom he finds "self-complacently floating high up in the air," whose "dumb senselessness" has "no relation whatever to the general life of the community," and who violate the silence with "an almost unendurable volubility" (294-95). So much for contemporary gurus, whether fractious Zionists or Jewish revivalists. His real colleagues remain "everywhere and nowhere" — that is, in the collective domain of lapsed memory, and this leads the dog to his pivotal insight: "Our generation is lost, it may be, but it is more blameless than those earlier ones. I can understand the hesitation of my generation . . . it is the thousandth forgetting of a dream dreamt a thousand times and forgotten a thousand times: and who can damn us merely for forgetting for the thousandth time" (300).

Amid this uncertainty, the dog can only improvise his own religious practices. "God can only be comprehended personally,"

Kafka warned Gustav Janouch. "Each man has his own life and his own God. His protector and judge. Priests and rituals are only crutches for the crippled life of the soul."[90] Science can only offer food in abundance: it begs the question. Traditional rituals seem tempting, but the dog finds singing ancient incantations with "faces turned upwards" to be mere escapism, an effort to "take flight from it (the earth) forever" (304). At last the dog resorts to fasting, but he can conquer neither physical hunger nor the ensuing guilt that aligns him with a past beyond his reach. Even his asceticism is an empty gesture, for traditions change and sages now find fasting too absurd to require prohibition, so that "only a dog lay here helplessly snapping at the empty air" (311). Polluted by false hope, he starts to vomit blood. At last his investigations return to music, the "ultimate science" that prizes "freedom higher than anything else" (316). The dog ends by coming full circle, with a pledge that seals his isolation as it confirms his campaign of self-transcendence. Kafka often called himself "Chinese," and never was his genius for illuminating the central axiom of these spiritual ancestors more clear: the mind is a monkey.

In an extraordinary letter to Brod in 1922 that recasts these issues, Kafka accused himself as a writer of "devil worship," of creating "a whole planetary system of vanity" as a surrogate for living, of having "not fanned the spark of life to a flame but simply used it to illuminate my corpse."[91] Never was a genius more sensitive to the modern urge toward idolatry of self. It is the basis for Kafka's elevation of life over art, what enabled him to declare, "I have no literary interests, but am made of literature, I am nothing else, and cannot be anything else."[92] He concludes that letter by imagining a "nonexistent" writer who might yield up his corpse to the grave: "Although it will never happen now, I am writer enough to . . . tell this story . . . completely forgetting my self, for in the final analysis writing depends not on vigilance but on the ability to forget one's self."[93]

This literary credo finds a pure manifestation in Kafka's last animal story, "Josephine the Singer, or the Mouse Folk." For here he vanishes into his own creation, evoking an entire world devoid of human wisdom, a "distorted mask" of the human world losing its old supports. "I shall never grow up to be a man," Kafka lamented to Brod. "From being a child I shall immediately become a white-haired ancient."[94] This, as we are told, is exactly the path of spiritual growth among the Mouse Folk, and one need not gaze too long and self-forgetfully (mouselike) upon the present to recognize this metamorphosis as a reflection of our common destiny.

A sympathetic "opponent" of Mouse culture, yet able to "sink in the feeling of the mass," the narrator proceeds with a patient and wondrous analysis of the power that Josephine holds over the nation. This power resides in her "piping," what remains of a decayed tradition of singing, the voice of music, always in Kafka an intimation of undivided being. But what might have been the dividend of a viable tradition is reduced now among the Mouse Folk to mere daily speech. Piping is "one of our thoughtless habits," but Josephine's audience "sits in mouselike stillness" (*CS*, 362). She makes "a ceremonial performance out of doing the usual thing"; indeed, "we admire in her what we do not at all admire in ourselves" (362). In the absence of God the miraculous takes up residence in the commonplace — and this is mirrored in Josephine's personality. She is vulgar ("She actually bites"), vain ("She believes . . . she is singing to deaf ears"), clearly an idiot; but under the modern dispensation, in which all of us are holding counsel in empty space, only an idiot might offer spiritual help, though worthless help. "All advice seems to me to be at bottom a betrayal," Kafka told Janouch. "It is a cowardly retreat in the face of the future, which is the touchstone of our present."[95] But this does not deter Josephine. Blinded by her own conceit, she makes large claims for her art and herself as a savior; in national emergencies she rises up "like a shepherd before a thunderstorm" to rally the Mouse Folk. The narrator dismisses these messianic claims by noting that the Mouse Folk "save themselves, although at the cost of sacrifices which make historians — generally speaking we ignore historical research entirely — quite horrorstruck" (366). What, then, is the ground for Josephine's appeal? Her piping is "a message from the whole people to each individual," allowing the Mouse Folk merely respite from an existence that threatens extinction, an occasion to "dream . . . at ease in the great warm bed of the community" (370).

"For this, doubtless," the narrator says, "our way of life is mainly responsible" (368). A tragically brief childhood, incessant work, over-population, the bloody depredations of enemies, a sudden and premature agedness of spirit — under these conditions, we are told, "a little piping here and there, that is enough for us" (369). Too great a gap exists between the "unexpended, ineradicable childishness" of the Mouse Folk that indulges Josephine, and their "infallible practical common sense" that ultimately dismisses her, to permit any real musical talent to unfold. What eludes Josephine, any "unconditional devotion" or "permanent recognition of her art," reflects only an absence of tradition among the Mouse Folk and a resulting fall into the quotidian that makes her appeal possible.* She is merely the present, mere rumor and folly — a comic reference to Jewish assimilation — and she can vanish at the end and "be forgotten like all her brothers" (376). Josephine, then, enters the only heaven available to the Mouse Folk and perhaps to all of us: the redemptive depths of oblivion.

We must take seriously, then, Kafka's choice of just such a heaven for himself when he willed that all his unpublished works be destroyed at his death. Impelled as an artist with a messianic urge to "raise the world into the pure, the true, the immutable," he fell wondrously short of his goal. "If I were to define the writer,"

---

*Only in the degree to which conditions of the human world start to approximate those of the Mouse Folk might we draw a parallel between the two. Yet consider our state of constant warfare, our eschewal of history, our early loss of innocence, our collapse of tradition into mass culture, our hunger for massive doses of nostalgia to retain a sense of continuity. Kafka's generation possessed at least a vestigial piety, but much avant-garde art today — that which sardonically brackets and inflates the dreck of mundane existence, as in the work of Andy Warhol or Donald Barthelme — might be viewed as human "piping." A part of its appeal can be discerned in what we are told of Josephine's art: "Something of our poor brief childhood is in it, something of lost happiness that can never be found again, but also something of active daily life, of its small gaieties, unaccountable and yet springing up and not to be obliterated." (*CS*, 370) he wrote in 1922, "I would say: he is a scapegoat for humanity, he enables people to enjoy sin without — or almost without — a sense of guilt."[96] Kafka's experience of sin was a radical empiricism, with the earth his only sacred text, the historical present his only realm of interest. His animal stories, born of metamorphosis, offered him an opportunity for endless reflection on that present without presuming to grasp it. Language will never be more than a lurching probe of life, and Kafka's led into the far recesses of negativity of his era — both private alienation and coercion by emerging social norms that are the beneficiaries of our guilt under the evacuated heavens. For this saintly genius, all was a temptation to despair that made his own works suspect. If writing was an "act of prayer," all of Kafka's work reduces to a serene and secular act of attention: he regarded himself as a failure, and everything else followed as if he were a banished animal dreaming of home.

"The experience which corresponds to that of Kafka, the private individual," Benjamin wrote, "will probably not become accessible to the masses until such time as they are being done away with."[97] That was observed in 1936, four years before Benjamin himself committed suicide while fleeing the Nazis. Janouch tells us that Kafka, as the two were passing the Old Synagogue in Prague, declared that men "will try to grind the synagogue to dust by destroying the Jews themselves."[98] All of Kafka's three sisters were killed in German death camps. Ottla, his favorite, renounced her protection as a wife of a German non-Jew in 1942, and after her divorce was deported to the Terezin ghetto and then to Auschwitz. Yitzhak Lowy, the Yiddish actor and friend of Kafka, gave his final performance in the Warsaw ghetto and was killed at Treblinka. Milena joined the underground, was arrested by the Gestapo in 1939, and died at Ravensbruck. All of them in their own unimaginable circumstances might have echoed Kafka's last outcry of pain on his deathbed: "Kill me, or else you are a murderer!"

NOTES

1 *The Diaries of Franz Kafka 1910-1913*, edited by Max Brod, translated by Joseph Kesh (New York: Schocken, 1948), 180.

2 *Ibid.*, 309.

3 Franz Kafka, *Wedding Preparations in the Country and Other Posthumous Prose Writings*, translated by Ernst Kaiser and Eithne Wilkins (London: Secker & Warburg, 1954), 72.

4 "He who renounces the world," Kafka wrote, "must love all men, for he renounces their world too. He begins from that point to divine the true nature of mankind, which cannot but be loved, provided that one is capable of it." *The Great Wall of China: Stories and Reflections*, translated by Willa and Edwin Muir (New York: Schocken, 1949), 292.

5 Quoted by William Emrich, *Franz Kafka*, translated by Sheema Zeban Buehne (New York: Frederick Ungar, 1968), 43.

6 *Ibid.*, 221.

7 Ernst Pawel, *The Nightmare of Reason* (New York: Farrar, Straus and Giroux, 1984), 31.

8 "The heart of the myth itself has remained inviolate," Pawel writes, "and can be fully understood only by those able to understand how an unremarkably ordinary, respectable, and conscientious family man, fond of his wife and children, can smash the skull of a six-year-old little girl, dump the body into a lime pit, and pride himself on having done his duty as a patriot and soldier." *The Nightmare of Reason*, 40.

9 *Ibid.*, 40-41.

10 Franz Kafka, *I Am a Memory Come Alive: Autobiographical Writings*, edited by Nahum Glatzer (New York: Schocken, 1974), 192.

11 *Wedding Preparations in the Country and Other Posthumous Prose Writings*, 113-14.

12 Franz Kafka, *Letters to Friends, Family and Editors*, translated by Richard and Clara Winston (New York: Schocken, 1978), 290.

13 Franz Kafka, *Letter to His Father*, translated by Ernst Kaiser and Eithne Wilkins (New York: Schocken, 1953), 79-81.

14 *I Am a Memory Come Alive*, 93.

15 Walter Benjamin, *Illuminations* (New York: Schocken, 1968), 123. I am indebted throughout my essay to the many insights found in Benjamin's two articles, "Franz Kafka: On the Tenth Anniversary of His Death" and "Some Reflections on Kafka," collected in this volume. See 111-145.

16 *The Diaries of Franz Kafka 1910-1913*, 278.

17 Franz Kafka, *The Complete Stories* (New York: Schocken, 1971), 81. The page references in my discussion of Kafka's short stories are to this edition.

18 "Georg is left with nothing; the bride, who lives in the story only in relation to the friend, that is, to what father and son have in common, is easily driven away by the father since no marriage has yet taken place, and so she cannot penetrate the circle of blood relationship that is drawn around father and son." *The Diaries of Franz Kafka 1910-1913*, 279.

19 Franz Kafka, *Amerika*, translated by Willa and Edwin Muir (New York: Schocken, 1946), 4. The page references in my discussion of the novel are to this edition.

20 "There is only one episode in the early years of which I have a direct memory. You may remember it, too. One night I kept on whimpering for water, not, I am certain, because I was thirsty, but probably partly to be annoying, partly to amuse myself. After several vigorous threats had failed to have any effect, you took me out of bed, carried me out onto the *pavlatche*, and left me there alone for a while in my nightshirt, outside the shut door. I am not going to say that this was wrong — perhaps there was really no other way of getting peace and quiet that night — but I mention it as typical of your methods of bringing up a child and their effect on me. I dare say I was quite obedient afterwards at that period, but it did me inner harm." *Letter to His Father*, 17.

21 *The Diaries of Franz Kafka 1914-1923*, edited by Max Brod; translated by Martin Greenberg (New York; Schocken, 1949), 130.

22 Pawel, 278.

23 *The Diaries of Franz Kafka 1914-1923*, 132.

24 *The Diaries of Franz Kafka 1910-1913*, 288.

25 Quoted by Roberto Calasso, *K.*, translated by Geoffrey Brock (New York: Alfred A. Knopf, 2005), 214.

26 See Malcolm Pasley's "Semi-private Games" in *The Kafka Debate*, edited by Angel Flores (New York: Gordian Press, 1977), 188-205.

27 *The Diaries of Franz Kafka 1910-1913*, 316-17.

28 *The Great Wall of China: Stories and Reflections*, 151.

29 *Letters to Friends, Family, and Editors*, 17.

30 *The Diaries of Franz Kafka 1914-1923*, 202.

31 *Letters to Friends, Family, and Editors*, 387.

32 Quoted by Emrich, 167.

33 Franz Kafka, *Shorter Works, Volume I*, edited and translated by Malcolm Pasley (London: Secker & Warburg, 1973), 114.

34 *Letters to Milena*, edited by Willy Hass and translated by Tania and James Stern (New York: Schocken, 1953), 221.

35 I am indebted to Walter Benjamin's brilliant train of thought on the theme of "forgetting" in Kafka. See *Illuminations*, 127-34.

36 *The Diaries of Franz Kafka 1910-1913*, 296.

37 *Letters to Milena*, 198.

38 *The Diaries of Franz Kafka 1914-1923*, 11.

39 Compare Kafka's panther with W.B. Yeats' "rough beast slouching toward Bethlehem to be born" in his poem "The Second Coming."

40 Quoted by Max Brod, *Franz Kafka: A Biography* (New York: Schocken, 1947), 75.

41 *Letter to His Father*, 87.

42 Quoted by Brod, 82.

43 *The Diaries of Franz Kafka 1914-1923*, 207.

44 *I Am a Memory Come Alive*, 96.

45 *Shorter Works, Volume I*, 116.

46 *Letters to Milena*, 213.

47 Brod, 75.

48 *I Am a Memory Come Alive*, 55.

49 Quoted by Erich Heller, *Franz Kafka* (Modern Masters Series, New York: Fontana/Collins 1974), 1.

50 At the conclusion of *Letter to His Father*, Kafka imagines what his father's answer will be to his complaints: "You have put it into your head to live entirely off me. I admit that we fight with each other, but there are two kinds of combat. The chivalrous combat, in which independent opponents pit their strength against each other, each on his own, each losing on his own, each winning on his own. And there is the combat of the vermin, which not only sting but, on top of it, suck your blood in order to sustain their own life. That's what the real professional soldier is, and that's what you are." (123).

51 *I Am a Memory Come Alive*, 202.

52 Dora Diamant in *Recollections of Kafka*, edited by Hans-Gerd Koch (Berlin: Klaus Wagenbach, 1995), 183.

53 *Letters to Friends, Family, and Editors*, 40.

54 Franz Kafka, *Letters to Felice*, edited by Erich Heller and Jurgen Born; translated by James Stern and Elizabeth Duckworth (New York: Vintage, 1992), 449.

55 *Letters to Friends, Family, and Editors*, 58.

56 *Ibid.*, 113.

57 *The Diaries of Franz Kafka 1910-1913*, 11.

58 For an excellent analysis of the influence of the Dreyfus Affair on Kafka's "In the Penal Colony," see Sander L. Gilman's *Franz Kafka* (London: Reaktion Books, 2005), 80-83.

59 Pawel, 328.

60 Quoted by Pawel, 328-29.

61 *Letters to Felice*, 438.

62 *Ibid.*, 308.

63 *Ibid.*, 67.

64 See John Winkelman's "Felice Bauer and *The Trial*," collected in *The Kafka Debate*, 311-334.

65 Franz Kafka, *The Trial*, translated by Breon Mitchell (New York: Schocken, 1998), 11. The page references in my discussion of the novel are to this edition.

66 See Calasso, 254-65.

67 *The Diaries of Franz Kafka 1910-1913*, 129.

68 *Letters to Felice*, 502.

69 *Ibid.*, 502.

70 Quoted by Nicholas Murray, *Kafka* (Yale University Press, New Haven, 2004), 279.

71 Quoted by Brod, 171.

72 Ludwig Hardt in *Recollections of Kafka*, 187.

73 "I have experience," Kafka wrote in an early note, "and I am not joking when I say that it is a seasickness on dry land." Quoted by Benjamin, 130.

74 *Letters to Felice*, 544-46.

75 *The Diaries of Franz Kafka 1914-1923*, 182.

76 See Gilman, 97-101.

77 *Letters to Friends, Family, and Editors*, 237.

78 *Letters to Milena*, 49-51.

79 *Ibid.*, 219.

80 *Ibid.*, 59.

81 Calasso, 4.

82 Brod's comments are relevant here: "The riddle as to why K. cannot make himself at home is not solved. He is a stranger, and has struck a village in which strangers are looked upon with suspicion. More is not said. One feels at once that this is the general feeling of strangeness among men, only it has just been made concrete in this one special case. 'Nobody can be the companion of anyone here.' One can take this making-concrete a step further. It is the special feeling of a Jew who would like to take root in foreign surroundings, who tries with all the powers of his soul to get nearer to the strangers, to become one of them entirely — but who does not succeed in thus assimilating himself... On all sides the Jew comes up against the old customs — he becomes a nuisance without wishing to be one — at the same time he has the feeling he knows everything better than the people on the spot, he would like to make the whole thing simple, more practical than they do, but they, in their incredible self-will, remain unapproachable... In the long history of the sufferings of Jewry, we have heard all these notes before. K. comes to grief in the most pitifully ridiculous way, despite the fact that he went at everything so earnestly and conscientiously. He remains alone." *Franz Kafka: A Biography*, 186-90.

83 Franz Kafka, *The Castle*, translated by Mark Harman (New York: Schocken, 1998), 8. The page references in my discussion of the novel are to this edition.

84 Calasso, 93-95.

85 *Letters to Milena*, 50.

86 *I Am a Memory Come Alive*, 168.

87 *Ibid.*, 140.

88 *Letters to Friends, Family, and Editors*, 287.

89 *The Diaries of Franz Kafka 1914-1923*, 202-03.

90 Gustav Janouch, *Conversations with Kafka: Notes and Reminiscences*, translated by Goronwy Rees (New York: New Directions, 1968), 166.

91 *I Am a Memory Come Alive*, 223-24.

92 *Letters to Felice*, 304.

93 *I Am a Memory Come Alive*, 224.

94 Quoted by Brod, 37.

95 Janouch, 83.

96 *I Am a Memory Come Alive*, 225.

97 Benjamin, 143.

98 Janouch, 139.

JOSEPH CONRAD

Survivor Guilt and the Politics of Duplicity

"THE POSITION OF THE SURVIVOR of a great calamity is seldom admirable," Hemingway wrote, then deleted from his final draft of *A Farewell to Arms*.[1] Few writers knew of this malaise or suffered its far-ranging effects more abysmally than Joseph Conrad. He was preferred reading in the Great War trenches, for his best work spoke to the common fate of men trapped in the ironic anguish of a new, if momentary, lease on life in the aftermath of disaster that had claimed their fellow-men. For Conrad, the great calamity was the Polish Insurrection of 1863, a doomed and quixotic effort to throw off a century of occupation by czarist Russia. Both his parents were martyred to this cause which was to command his lifelong respect. At sixteen, Conrad may have departed from Poland to escape a similar fate, but it was his misfortune, one might say his claim to modernity, to find belief in nothing except the permanence of memory.[2] The lineaments of his personality and sense of manhood were forged in the graveyard of Poland, and his heart remained true: the survivor guilt he suffered in exile became the wellspring of his narrative art.[3]

It is necessary in fathoming this turmoil to grasp Conrad's spiritual bondage to his father, to whom all his fiction is secretly addressed.[4] Apollo Korzeniowski was a brave and talented, if unresourceful member of the Polish gentry, a man of letters who held to a blurred democratic ideal of racial fraternity. According to Zdzislaw Najder, his family members were "ardent patriots and soldiers to a man" who had lost practically all of their estates in the anti-Russian insurrections of 1797 and 1830.[5] A disciple of the pan-Slav mystic, Adam Mickiewicz, and leader of the extreme "Red" faction of the Polish liberation movement of 1863, Korzeniowski saw occupied Poland as akin to the crucified body of Christ, and left no doubt about his son's intended destiny. "My child, my son," he wrote at Conrad's baptism in 1858, "if the enemy calls you a nobleman and a Christian — tell yourself that you are a pagan and that your nobility is rot... My child, my son — tell yourself that you are without land, without love, without Fatherland, without humanity — as long as Poland, our Mother, is enslaved."[6]

Within three years this bold and reckless utopian commitment ignited an onslaught of calamities that left young Conrad the sole survivor. In 1861, Korzeniowski and his wife were imprisoned by the Russian authorities for their subversive activities, and soon thereafter the entire family exiled to Vologda, Russia. About this czarist version of the Gulag, Korzeniowski wrote home: "During the whole winter the frost remains at 25-30 (30 degrees below zero Fahrenheit) while the wind from the White Sea, held up by nothing, brings constant news from the polar bears . . . The population is a nightmare: disease-ridden corpses."[7] Within a year Conrad's mother died under the strain, ostensibly of tuberculosis. For Apollo and his son there lay ahead four more years of wandering exile, first in Chernikov, then Lwow, where young Conrad, suffering from poor health and possibly epilepsy, read aloud the works of Mickiewicz with his father and wrote patriotic plays. "My dear little boy looks after me — there are only two of us here," Korzeniowski wrote home. "I shall not be ashamed of his heart; he has his Mother's talents — but a head not to be envied: mine."[8] This would prove to be prophetic. It was during this period that his son devoured the romantic travelogues of Captain Marryat and Mungo Park in order, as he admitted later, to avoid going mad. Upon being released from exile, a grief-stricken Korzeniowski died in 1869, also of tuberculosis, and at his funeral the eleven-year-old orphan marched at the head of a patriotic procession through the streets of Cracow.

These memories of irremediable loss marked Conrad for life and, exacerbated by the revolutionary injunctions bequeathed by his father, were to shape his political vision. They also unlock the riddle of his abrupt decision in 1874 to quit Poland for a life at sea. "After reading so many romances," Conrad wrote in *A Personal Record*, "he desired naively to escape with his very body from the intolerable reality of things."[9] Naïve is right, for in exchanging either conscription in the Russian army or a death warrant as a Polish revolutionary for expectations of heroic adventure as a sailor, he was only replacing his own selfhood with a daydream, the claims of conscience with "a feeling of complete identification, a very vivid comprehension that *if I wasn't one of them I was nothing at all* (emphasis mine)."[10]

That this romantic stratagem failed Conrad will be obvious to any reader of his fiction. In his life, we need only ponder his suicide attempt in Marseilles in 1878, when, upon losing all his money in a failed smuggling scheme, the homeless twenty-year-old sailor fired a bullet through his chest, just missing his heart.[11] A *szlachcic* or member of Poland's privileged class, Conrad believed that suicide was an "unpardonable sin," and so passed a lifetime trying to conceal this ignominious incident, fostering the legend that he was wounded in a duel. Yet the shattered self-esteem evident in such a move can be traced back to a submerged vein of survivor guilt — borne of pursuing a vainglorious and false identity far away from a national struggle that had claimed his spiritual kith and kin. Only a need for self-exculpation can explain Conrad's embarrassing disclaimer once in exile that Apollo Korzeniowski was not a "revolutionist": "No epithet could be more inapplicable to a man with such a strong sense of responsibility in the region of ideas and action and so indifferent to the promptings of personal ambition as my father."[12] Conrad may have quit Poland feeling the need, in his words, to "redeem a tacit moral pledge," but the case was hopeless, for he was condemned (in his own eyes) in his very pursuit of atonement outside Poland. The depressive temper, indeed death wish that pursued him instead can best be grasped as both a devious act of loyalty to a doomed cause and punishment for surviving beyond it.[13] "One must drag the ball and chain of one's selfhood to the end," he wrote with grim clairvoyance to Marguerite Poradowska at the start of his literary career. "It is the price one pays for the divine and devilish privilege of thought... Which would you rather be: *convict or idiot* (emphasis mine)?"[14]

To rescue himself from these terrible urgencies, Conrad had an abiding need to recast his early psychic history, even if it required unstable feats of self-deception. To this end he found a perfect mentor in his uncle and guardian, Tadeusz Bobrowski, who spared no ink in trying over nineteen years to erase the defects of Apollo Korzeniowski that he found in his nephew.[15] A vigorous opponent of the 1863 insurrection, Bobrowski was stubbornly inclined to regard all those involved in revolutionary movements as impulsive, dishonest, or mad.[16] As a successful lawyer, he believed in "possessing for every problem of life a ready formula obtained by abstract reasoning."[17] Against his brother-in-law's extreme views, he counseled patience, a facade of wise reasonableness, and an appeal to evolutionary laws of progress, which, in the context of Poland's occupation, must have struck young Conrad as an uncourageous resignation to czarist oppression. Yet given his own survivor guilt, and given the blame he placed upon his father's high-minded fanaticism for the loss of his mother, Conrad was sorely susceptible to his uncle's influence. Najder, Conrad's finest biographer, puts the matter clearly:

> His father's heritage was for Conrad a cause of strong internal conflict. On one hand he could not escape the powerful appeal of Apollo's fascinating personality and of the heroic fidelity with which he had served to the tragic end the ideals of patriotism as he conceived them. On the other hand he was by no means sure if these ideals had any reasonable basis. Conrad's father must have seemed to him at once awe-inspiring and absurd; his attitude towards him was a mixture of admiration and contemptuous pity. And he could never forgive his father the death of his mother.[18]

This tortured internal conflict with his Polish origins left Conrad adrift in a realm of unconscious guilt and private grievance. "I think the proper wisdom is to will what the gods will," he wrote in *A Personal Record*, echoing Bobrowski's garbled belief in Providence, "without, perhaps, being certain what their will is — or even if they have a will of their own."[19] That is, if not a *convict*, then an *idiot*, and although Bobrowski may have influenced Conrad's emergence in his fiction as an irascible denouncer of revolution, there was no way to repress the revolutionary imperatives that tyrannize his plots.

One can detect exactly this submerged modus operandi in Conrad's letters on politics written prior to the so-called "Hueffer decade" of 1899-1909, the period of his greatest creativity. To his relative Spiridion Kilszczewski in 1885, after announcing that home was now "the hospitable shores of Great Britain," Conrad goes on to welcome the breach between England and Russia which gave him reason for "expecting great things" for Poland, an expectation that could only inflame his sense of dereliction from the national cause. This personal anxiety is projected onto contemporary events that suggest "the lurid light of battlefields," leaving Conrad in "a state of despairing indifference," and a month later he took the offensive before Kilszczewski by blaming the "infernal doctrines" of socialism:

> Where's the man to stop the rush of social-democratic ideas? The opportunity and the day have come and are gone! . . . The destiny of this nation and of all nations is to be accomplished in darkness amidst much weeping and gnashing of teeth, to pass through robbery, equality, anarchy and misery under the iron rule of a military despotism! Such is the lesson of common sense logic . . . Socialism must inevitably end in Caesarism . . . Disestablishment, Land Reform, Universal Brotherhood are but like milestones on the road to ruin . . . Still there is no earthly remedy for these earthly misfortunes, and from above, I fear, we may obtain consolation but no remedy. "All is vanity."[20]

Hardly a piece of dispassionate analysis, this eruption is more "the conversion of nervous energy into phrases" which Conrad admitted to H.G. Wells was his only mode of writing.[21] The equation of socialism with ruin harkens back to his Polish memories, and the reduction of all human motivation to vanity has more bearing on his makeshift identities in exile than anything else.[22] Behind the veil of fiction, in "Prince Roman," Conrad would admit: "But fanaticism is human. Man has adored ferocious divinities . . . It is only to vain men that all is vanity; and all is deception only to those who have never been sincere with themselves."[23] Most likely what unnerved him about socialism was its spiritual affiliation with his father's ideals which he would rather consign to oblivion. One cannot be engulfed by or accused of deserting a dead cause, and while unable to speak this way about Poland, Conrad was driven to discredit the revival of hope embodied in socialism by impugning its motives and prophesying its ruin.

Conrad remained silent on politics for the next ten years, but his letters to Marguerite Poradowska offer a fearful glimpse of the nihilism he was engaging in trying to sever his ideological ties with Poland. For in descending from the "stilts of one's principles," as he put it, this "castaway" in need of "pardon" found nothing else there. One can detect this oscillation between nihilism and the bewildered guilt of exile in Conrad's admission to Marguerite in 1894: "I am in the midst of a struggle to the death ... All is chaos, but slowly, the apparition changes into living flesh, the shimmering mists take shape, and — who knows — something may come from the clash of nebulous ideas."[24] It is tempting to see this "clash of nebulous ideas" as a hidden allusion to the Korzeniowski/Bobrowski split in his psyche that greeted Conrad upon emerging from the depths. His last resort, then, was to cast corrosive doubt on the springs of all action, which alone might make his case pardonable. This is what underlies Conrad's attack on even Christian abnegation, which, "carried to an extreme is not only profoundly immoral but dangerous, in that it sharpens the appetite for evil in the malevolent and develops (perhaps unconsciously) that latent human tendency toward hypocrisy in the ... let us say, benevolent."[25] Put beside Conrad's remark to Marguerite that "with us (Poles) religion and patriotism are closely akin," we cannot dismiss this as shallow cynicism, nor ignore its psychological insight for that matter, but rather recognize another effort to shake the posthumous grip of the father. After all, it was Korzeniowski's "dangerous" abnegation that cost Conrad his mother (for whom Marguerite was a surrogate), developed in his son "a latent tendency toward hypocrisy," and whose damning example must be extirpated. And yet in casting overboard a faith in the most selfless of motives, Conrad was only undermining his own ground for existence.

This tendency reached a peak in Conrad's series of letters to Cunningham Graham, a "secret sharer" with whom he could review under the auspices of friendship the censored self-debate to be later projected into his fiction. Indeed the Englishman, as an adventurer, writer, horseman, eccentric, and militant socialist, bears an uncanny resemblance to Apollo Korzeniowski, and while expressing sympathy for his ideals, Conrad was driven to entertain an absurd universe in order to eschew them. In 1897, he characterized that universe to Graham as a huge knitting machine that "has knitted time, space, pain, death, corruption, despair and all the illusions — and nothing matters."[26] By now we can recognize this as a metaphor for Conrad's own plight as an exile, and it was climaxed by another revelation to Graham a year later:

> The machine is thinner than air and as evanescent as a flash of lightning. The attitude of cold unconcern is the only reasonable one. Of course reason is hateful — but why? Because it demonstrates (to those who have the courage) that we, living, are out of life — utterly out of it. The mysteries of a universe made of drops of fire and clods of mud do not concern us in the least. The fate of a humanity condemned ultimately to perish from the cold is not worth troubling about. If you take it to heart it becomes an unendurable tragedy. If you believe in improvement you must weep, for the attained perfection must end in cold, darkness and silence. In a dispassionate view the ardor for reform, improvement, for virtue, for knowledge and even for beauty is only a vain sticking up for appearances, as though one were anxious about the cut of one's clothes in a community of blind men.
>
> Life knows us not and we do not know life — we don't know even our own thoughts. Half the words we use have no meaning whatever and of the other half man understands each word after the fashion of his own folly and conceit. Faith is a myth and beliefs shift like mists on the shore: thoughts vanish: words, once pronounced, die: and the memory of yesterday is as shadowy as the hope of tomorrow — only the string of my platitudes seems to have no end. As our peasants say: "Pray brother, forgive me for the love of God." And we don't know what forgiveness is, nor what love, nor where God is. Assez![27]

This outpouring of despair with its flash of tragic insight is deeply felt, but the way Conrad twists his stoical urgings into the "cold unconcern" of political quietism is not convincing. That the "ardor for reform" might be more than a "vain sticking up for appearances" is obvious, and perhaps even more suspect, it makes little sense to pray for "forgiveness" to a knitting machine. Indeed, one of the luxuries of being a helpless cog in such a mechanism is that one can't blaspheme against it, and Conrad's sense of having done so suggests

175

he was using this "string of platitudes" to conceal a more painful and deep-rooted reality.

By implication that reality was a more open universe where even ideals of human improvement might be viable and responsibility for their lapse be incurred. A month later, Graham pressed Conrad on the place of idealism in his scheme, but the bleak reply was not likely to relieve his bewilderment:

> You and your ideals of sincerity and courage and truth are strangely out of place in this epoch of material preoccupations. What does it bring? What's the profit? What do we get by it? Those questions are the root of every moral, intellectual or political movement. Into the noblest causes, men manage to put something of their baseness: and sometimes when I think of you here, quietly, you seem to me tragic with your courage, with your beliefs and your hopes. Every cause is tainted: and you reject this one, espouse that other one as if one were evil and the other good, while the same evil you hate is in both, but disguised in different words. I am more in sympathy with you than words can express, yet if I had a grain of belief left in me I would believe you misguided. You are misguided by the desire of the Impossible, — and I envy you. Alas! what you want to reform are not institutions — it is human nature. Your faith will never move that mountain. Not that I think mankind intrinsically bad. It is only silly and cowardly. Now you know that in cowardice is every evil — especially that cruelty so characteristic of our civilization. But, without it, mankind would perish. No great matter truly. But will you persuade humanity to throw away the sword and shield? Can you persuade even me — who writes these words in the fullness of an irresistible conviction? No, I belong to the wretched gang. We all belong to it. We are born initiated, and succeeding generations clutch their inheritance, in the name of God.[28]

After resisting Graham with a series of irrelevancies ("What's the profit?" etc.), Conrad yields to the same bracing defeatism as before, except that now it is base "human nature" rather than an absurd "universe" evoked to shore up his case. What should arrest us even more, however, is his emerging genius for double entendre, the quasi-confessional vein of reference to "cowardice" in man that leaves all causes "tainted" and their pursuit hopeless. While warning against self-righteousness, Conrad is simultaneously informing on his own fallen condition and then universalizing it into a pose of sanity. Such an "irresistible conviction" survives only on the level of hollow conscious avowal, and must be assessed in the light of Conrad's astonishing admission to Edward Garnett two years earlier: "Things get themselves into shape — and they are tolerable. But when I want to write — when I do consciously try to write or try to construct, then my ignorance has full play and the quality of my miserable and benighted intelligence is disclosed to the scandalized gaze of my literary father ... I always told you I was a kind of inspired humbug."[29]

Conrad's turn to politics, then, was wary yet inevitable. The theme of betrayal that pervades his early "sea-stuff" was misplaced aboard ship. "I am writing — it is true," he wrote to Garnett in 1897, "but this is only piling crime upon crime; every line is odious like a bad action. I mean odious to me — because I still have some pretenses to the possession of a conscience."[30] The crime was one of omission, a failure to deal at close range with his revolutionary legacy. The traditional values of the maritime service that Conrad endorsed — such as fidelity, discipline, and efficiency — that threaten to normalize his fiction with his own cooperation are, upon inspection, just thin dilutions of that same revolutionary legacy. Conrad's best critics have thrown the maritime platitudes overboard, focusing instead on the uneasiness and anxiety that precede his withdrawal into moral or political "views." Marvin Mudrick refers to Conrad's "suppressed ... nightmares," and detects a "sense of obstruction and deadlock, an opposition of matched and mutually paralyzed energies."[31] Frederick Crews finds Conrad's "most significant level of discourse is the unconscious level, where inadmissible wishes are entertained, blocked and allowed a choked and guarded expression."[32] Long ago T. E. Lawrence noticed that Conrad's style was "not built on the rhythm of ordinary prose, but on something existing only in his head, and as he never says what it is he wants to say, all his things end in a kind of hunger, a suggestion of something he can't say or do or think."[33] The blend of irritating unspecificity and sheer doubletalk that invades Conrad's prose when these inadmissible wishes and hungers are related to sexuality is well known.[34] Fortunately, Conrad was able to exercise more artistic control when they were political in nature, perhaps because politics issued from a more conscious level of his mind.

That Conrad was able to confront politics at all, given its psychic volatility and his depressive temperament, was quite heroic. Given the economy of "matched and mutually paralyzed energies" he was engaging, it is little wonder that his political critics have reached no agreement as the whether he was "conservative," "liberal," or "revolutionary." For instance, Leo Gurko sees Conrad as a staunch conservative, "acutely distrustful of democracy" and "rooted in the landed gentry," a counter-revolutionary who "did not believe in the reform of institutions as long as the human heart remained unaltered."[35] Avrom Fleishman argues that Conrad started out prejudiced against the liberal-democratic ideologies of the West, but worked himself free to entertain more positive ideals of social cohesion, indeed the "achievement of a grand vision of social community."[36] And Irving Howe, a far more sophisticated political observer, adopts a modified version of Gustov Morf's thesis that Conrad's political novels are efforts, by symbolic indirection, to justify his desertion of the Polish national cause, concluding that he was "a Tory with repressed affinities for anarchism."[37] Ultimately such traditional categories savor too much of self-assurance and salvation to be applicable to his disturbed vision.

In his major political novels, Conrad's conscience would again be engaged and at a terrible price to himself. This was no Lawrencian exercise of shedding one's sickness in fiction — his very fragile sense of identity was at risk and his fancied disgrace was too enormous for confession to be purgative. Whatever else, *Nostromo*, *The Secret Agent*, and *Under Western Eyes* are agitated, insightful, often warped, yet deeply logical works of anxiety that conceal their own deepest political truths. They expose a far more tortured and compromised mind than we might have guessed. All these novels, with uncanny political acumen, unveil modes of social oppression that form a mandate for revolution; yet all of them feature men who flinch before the fatal challenge, only then to adopt what we recognize as Conrad's own "official" reactionary views to assuage a survivor guilt that leads them in the end to suicide or retributive acts of self-destruction. To grant a redemptive weight to these views, which are pitted against his more enduring sense of social injustice and human failure, is to do Conrad a disservice.[38] He himself did not formulate this crisis of conscience — he lived and suffered it — and it was his courageous pursuit of the "moral discovery at the heart of every tale" that led to his own nervous collapse upon the completion of *Under Western Eyes* in 1910.

CONRAD INAUGURATED his long trial against himself with *Lord Jim* in 1900, and it is instructive to penetrate its symbolic disguises. Many critics and biographers have traced the parallel between Jim's leap from the *Patna* and his creator's youthful escape from Poland, which Conrad too must have recognized.[39] "I verily believe mine was the only case," he wrote in *A Personal Record*, "of a boy of my nationality and antecedents to take a, so to speak, *standing jump* out of his racial surroundings . . ."[40] Far more inadmissible, however, was that the "shadowy ideal of conduct" that Jim is convicted of violating at the Court of Inquiry has its antecedent in the political idealism of Conrad's martyred parents, and that we can draw the link between Jim's "desertion" of the *Patna* and his passively accepted "punishment" in Patusan. "I admit that I stood for a great triumph," he wrote to Garnett upon completing the novel, "and I have only succeeded in giving myself away. Nobody'll see it . . . That is the effect of the book upon me, the intimate and personal effect. Humiliation. Not extinction. Not yet . . . "[41]

This same blend of subterfuge and morbidity afflicts Jim, whose case is both simple and excusable, and his nobility obvious, but not to him.[42] Dowsed in heroic fantasies born of reading "light holiday literature," he early on exhibits natural impulses by failing to rescue two sailors while aboard a "training ship for officers."[43] This recurs when the *Patna*, carrying 800 Muslims, is stricken, and Jim, helpless to do anything, yields to a half-conscious instinct for self-preservation ("I jumped — it seems") and abandons ship. As the respectable Marlow, Conrad's alter ego, reflects upon his romantic young friend:

> He was not afraid of death perhaps, but I'll tell you what, he was afraid of the emergency. His confounded imagination had evoked for him all the horrors of panic, the trampling rush, the pitiful screams, boats swamped — all the appalling incidents of a disaster at sea he had ever heard of. He might have been resigned to die, but I suspect he wanted to die without added terrors, quietly, in a sort of peaceful trance. A certain readiness to perish is not so very rare, but it is seldom that you meet men whose souls, steeled in the impenetrable armour of resolution, are ready to fight a losing battle to the last, the desire of peace waxes stronger as hope declines, till at last it conquers the very desire of life. (80)

The first half of *Lord Jim*, in a taut and hypnotic crossfire of testimonies, pursues how this incident will be interpreted by Marlow, who, as Jim's sympathetic and unofficial attorney during the Court of Inquiry, resists his "artful dodges to escape from the grim shadow of self-knowledge."[44] Against Jim's tendency to blame external forces for his lapse, Marlow insists that character is fate; yet gradually the more he absorbs and recognizes in this young reprobate his own arrested potentialities, the more he needs to reclaim Jim as "one of us" by unconsciously looking for "some convincing shadow of an excuse" (48). But since Marlow will not admit fear as a mitigating circumstance (i.e. witness his hospital visit to the crazed engineer of the *Patna* who thinks the ship was "full of reptiles"), he cannot side with Jim without losing faith in that code of conduct upon which his sanity, and Conrad's, depend. "It seemed to me," Marlow says, "I was made to comprehend the Inconceivable . . . made to look at the convention that lurks in all truth and on the essential sincerity of falsehood . . . He swayed me, I own up" (85-86). Soon this is exactly what happens to Captain Brierly, who, upon hearing Jim out at the Court of Inquiry, finds his own impeccable credentials erased by nihilism and vicarious guilt, and later commits suicide. For as the French lieutenant, whose lack of introspection enables him to save the *Patna*, says afterwards: "The fear, the fear — look you — it is always there . . . But the honour — the honour, monsieur . . . that is real — that is!" (134) Once the verdict comes in, then, Marlow can only spare Jim "the mere detail of a formal execution" and arrange his "burial" in Patusan, far away from the spirit of the cliffs of Dover that might "ask me what I — returning with no bones broken, so to speak — had done with my very young brother" (201).

The second half of *Lord Jim*, then, which Conrad called the novel's "plague spot," can best be grasped as the farthest reach of that "everlasting deep hole" of survivor guilt from which Jim tries to salvage his shattered self-esteem.[45] Once established in the "unreality" of Patusan, stocked with exotic props and nihilistic undercurrents, Jim is free to fulfill in vivid action all the delusions of grandeur that he took aboard the *Patna*. As such, Patusan is a striking and melodramatic re-creation of that world of "light holiday literature" which has been exposed earlier as a mode of repression and denial. Thus Jim is now afforded a second "jump," this time not into infamy but into the trusting community of the Bugis, who install him as a demigod endowed with "supernatural powers." Yet none of this is convincing, least of all to Jim, who, while he "loved the land and the people with a sort of fierce egotism," is unable to shake off his latent depression. Indeed the very heroic deeds and martial campaigns that earn him his coveted acclaim in Patusan are conducted in a desperate fashion that borders on the suicidal.[46] When Marlow offers to take news home, he can only mutter sadly, "Tell them . . . No — nothing." And when the brigand Gentleman Brown, the first white man from "out there" to reach Patusan, arrives, he immediately erodes Jim's mythic self and paralyzes him with "a sickening suggestion of common guilt, of secret knowledge that was like a bond of their minds and of their hearts" (349). All Jim can do is treat Brown like himself, as a victim of circumstance, one who must be allowed a way out, a "clean slate," and when Brown rewards this fatal generosity by murdering his "brother," Dain Waris, Jim's real identity is hammered home once again. "Time to finish this," he mutters, and then allows himself to be executed by his "father," Doramin, in a gesture that is tantamount to suicide.

While Jim unerringly confirms his identity as a *convict* in Patusan, Marlow simultaneously slides toward *idiocy* in his need to exonerate him. Initially Marlow searches out the authoritative Stein, an unstained revolutionary in his youth, only to be told that Jim's case is "altogether hopeless," but that one must still immerse oneself in the "destructive element" and "follow the dream, and again to follow the dream — and so — *ewig — usque ad finem*" (193). Both Stein and the "privileged man" of Marlow's correspondence, who has a "firm conviction in the truth of ideas racially our own" and believes "we must fight in the ranks or our lives don't count," appear to echo the words of Apollo Korzeniowski (that "invisible personality" that possesses Jim's conscience), and these voices now drive Marlow to transparent feats of duplicity. Thus, while attesting to Jim's "constancy" to docile listeners back home, Marlow's confidence turns to willfulness in Patusan: "Nothing mattered, *since I had made up my mind* (emphasis mine) that Jim, for whom alone I cared, had at last mastered his fate" (292). And to make sure, Marlow now swaps his earlier ethic of responsibility for a metaphysic of chance that invites us to see Jim as simply a victim of bad luck: "It is not Justice the servant of man, but accident, hazard, fortune — the ally of patient Time, that holds an even and scrupulous balance" (288). Indeed Marlow keeps whistling in the dark right to the end — reinterpreting Jim's suicide as an "extraordinary success," a vindication of his "exalted egotism," a "victory in which I have taken my part" (374). It should hardly surprise us, then, that Conrad's declared politics at this time, as expressed to Graham, was based on "l'egoisme qui sauve tout, — absolument — tout ce que nous abhorrons, tout ce que nous aimons."[47] *Lord Jim* ends with a glimpse of the sententious Stein silenced, abandoned without an "heir," and adrift in a mood of terminal dejection.[48]

"Heart of Darkness" was composed simultaneously with *Lord Jim*, and the novella allows us to see how Marlow behaves in a milieu that is for the first time explicitly political. Based on Conrad's own trip to Africa nine years earlier, the novella is justly admired as a scathing indictment of Belgian King Leopold II's colonization of the Congo.⁴⁹ Conrad admitted that "before the Congo I was a mere animal," and reported elsewhere that he had witnessed "the vilest scramble for booty that ever disfigured the history of human conscience and geographical exploration."⁵⁰ Early on Marlow dismisses as "humbug" the claim to the "civilizing work" being done by the white Europeans, "faithless pilgrims" of Leopold II in a scramble for ivory and rubber that would ultimately kill an estimated ten million Africans.⁵¹ But Marlow discovers more than a political holocaust in progress. For as everyone recognizes, "Heart of Darkness" is also an uncanny descent into the self, a daring attempt in Marlow's words "to find yourself . . . your own reality . . . what no man can ever know." What is arresting for our purposes, however, is that Marlow is able to manage some control over his psychic secrets only by clinging to political "views" that it seems the very moral purpose of the novella to subvert. As Conrad warned Graham, the novella was "so wrapped up in secondary notions that you — even you — may miss it . . ."⁵²

Early on Marlow's vision of the colonization of England forecasts his dilemma in the Congo, which is one of political equivocation. He makes it quite clear that the Roman invasion was unjustified, "just robbery with violence, aggravated murder on a great scale," yet an instant later can gloss over this reality with a pious burst of epigrammatic doubletalk: "What redeems it is the idea only . . . not a sentimental pretence but an idea, and an unselfish belief in the idea."⁵³ This need for a redemptive idea grows more personally urgent once Marlow is assailed by the sordid farce of imperialism as he descends into the sub-continent. Initially there is the French man-of-war shelling an unseen "enemy" in the bush, then the terrible concentration camp of shackled natives used as slave labor to build a railroad, now retiring to a "grove of death" at the Outer Station:

> Black shapes crouched, lay, sat between the trees, leaning against the trunks, clinging to the earth, half coming out, half effaced within the dim light, in all the attitudes of pain, abandonment, and despair. Another mine on the cliff went off, followed by a slight shudder of the soil under my feet. The work was going on. The work! And

> this was the place where some of the helpers had withdrawn to die. They were dying slowly — it was very clear. They were not enemies, they were not criminals, they were nothing earthly now... Brought from all the recesses of the coast in all the legality of time contracts, lost in uncongenial surroundings, fed on unfamiliar food, they sickened, became inefficient, and were then allowed to crawl away and rest. (108)

There is the corpse of another Congolese with a bullet through his forehead, then the brutality and rapacious greed of the Eldorado Exploring Expedition; yet Marlow is driven to "strike and fend off" these damning visual indictments, for, as he admits derisively, "I also was a part of the great cause of these high and just proceedings." Instead his thoughts go out in obnoxious tribute to the chief accountant, whose starched tidiness amidst such demoralization is "backbone," whose determination to make "correct entries" in his ledger had led him to "hate these savages — hate them to the death" (120). This air of imbecile rapacity grows more extreme when Marlow is grilled by the manager at the Central Station, the "papier-mâché Mephistopheles" who thinks Kurtz's policy toward the natives should be replaced by repression: "Trangression — punishment — bang! Pitiless, pitiless... this will prevent all conflagrations for the future" (128).[54] All that Marlow has to maintain his distance from this "spy" is the "European power" behind him: "And there was nothing behind me!" Eavesdropping on the "uncle of our manager" who wants to usurp Kurtz's influence over the natives, all he can do is insanely "caper on the deck" of his sunken steamship.[55] Indeed no conception of conscious art can decipher these garbled exchanges, for as Marlow warns us, "I am trying to... convey... that commingling of absurdity, surprise, and bewilderment in a tremor of struggling revolt, that notion of being captured by the incredible which is the very essence of dreams... " (129)[56]

Approaching the Inner Station, Marlow becomes "scientifically interesting," feels the atavistic appeal of the wilderness, a "remote kinship" with the bedlam of cries along the bank (139). Only his work ethic keeps him from going ashore: "Fine sentiments, you say?

Fine sentiments be hanged! I had no time. I had to mess about with white-lead and strips of woolen blanket helping to put bandages on those leaky steam-pipes — I tell you" (140). But such expedients fail him when at "the farthest point of my experience," Marlow detects through binoculars the severed heads on stakes surrounding Kurtz's hut, and meets this charismatic agent — now wasted away by illness, lust for ivory, and his indulgence in "unspeakable rites." Already Marlow has learned from the Russian harlequin below the Inner Station of Kurtz's grandiloquent ideals and exalted reputation, and so without equivocation pronounces him "hollow at the core" (165). But once Marlow has this melodramatically overdrawn villain aboard the steamboat, he admits that "I had no clear perception of what I wanted." Now Kurtz's "voice" ultimately wins over his listener's "unconscious loyalty," and he becomes for Marlow the "nightmare of my choice."

But what does this mean?[57]

The swollen and muddled conclusion to "Heart of Darkness" arises because Kurtz is an over-determined dream figure. On one level he is a composite of several men Conrad met in the Congo, among them Leon Rom, known for displaying a row of severed African heads around his garden.[58] As the Company's prize agent, created by "all of Europe," Kurtz is a "shameless prevaricator," a criminal at large in the Congo whose lofty idealism toward Africans, expressed in his report to the International Society for the Suppression of Savage Customs, is trumped by a genocidal postscript: "Exterminate all the brutes!" (155) Marlow is all too ready to disavow this dissipated spectre and see him callously buried "in a muddy hole." But Kurtz also stands in *opposition* to Belgian officials, a man of "unsound method," a "political extremist," a writer, a "voice" of "burning noble words," a messianic figure adored by the natives and unwilling to desert them, a rebel accused by the Central Station of disrupting their domination of an enslaved territory — in these respects he is a dream representation of Apollo Korzeniowski — the "original" Kurtz that Conrad's alter ego was "ordered I should never betray."[59] The dying exhortation of *this* Kurtz — "live rightly, die, die . . . for the fulfilling of my ideas ... It's a duty" — echoes Apollo's speech at the baptism of his son, and for Marlow to obey is to find himself in the same peril as the Russian harlequin: "I saw the time approaching when I would be left alone of the party of unsound method ... I was, so to speak, numbered with the dead" (176).[60]

Immobilized by these deadlocked energies, then, Marlow has no firm ground from which to assess his experience, and must resort to mendacities to elude the burden of self-knowledge: "I would not have gone so far as to fight for Kurtz, but I went for him near enough to a lie. You know I hate, detest, and can't bear a lie ... " (129) What this means politically becomes clear when, upon returning to Europe, Marlow proceeds to protect Kurtz's reputation, support his Intended's idealization of him, censor out his lapse into depravity, and even deliver his report to the International Society for the Suppression of Savage Customs with the postscript *torn off*. For Marlow, the management of his own incipient morbidity overrides political truth, and finally he must lie on behalf of imperialism by sustaining the illusion of Europe's "civilizing work" in the African wilderness.

Of course it is the visual evidence of the criminality of imperialism, rather than any hidden vein of autobiographical reference, that has earned "Heart of Darkness" its reputation. The feverish disintegration of a "decent" European face to face with the white man's burden in Africa, resulting in Marlow's "monkey tricks" to retain his sanity, constitute the novella's most sober political warning. Yet Marlow's suggestion that Kurtz's dying recognition of his own complicity in the rape of the Congo ("The horror! The horror!") is proper atonement, somehow a "victory," is both obnoxious and puzzling to an ingenuous reader. And certainly Conrad remained an ardent imperialist as far as his adopted England was concerned. When Roger Casement, whom he had met and admired in the Congo, asked for his support for the Congo Reform movement, Conrad refused to join this international crusade. Still he wrote to Casement with moving humanity: "It is an extraordinary thing that the conscience of Europe which seventy years ago has put down the slave trade on humanitarian grounds tolerates the Congo State today. It is as if the moral clock had been put back many hours."⁶¹ And his empathy with the victims of the Leopold II's policy of slave labor is impressive. The black man, Conrad wrote, "shares with us the consciousness of the universe in which we live — no small burden. Barbarism per se is no crime ... and the Belgians are worse than the seven plagues of Egypt insomuch that in that case it was a punishment sent for a definite transgression; but in this the ... man is not aware of any transgression, and therefore can see no end to the infliction. It must appear to him very awful and mysterious; and I confess it appears so to me too."⁶²

The political equivocation at the core of "Heart of Darkness" was mirrored in Conrad's pronouncements to friends at the time. Take, for instance, his response to the Boer War which broke out in 1899. "The whole business is inexpressibly stupid," he wrote to Graham. "If I am to believe Kipling this was a war undertaken for the cause of democracy. *C'est a crever de rire!*"⁶³ Yet this was as close as he ever came to denouncing English imperialism, since, like Marlow in the novella, Conrad had been deprived of a "European power" (Poland) and needed a surrogate to recast his identity. Thus shortly afterwards he was leaping to the defense of British policy against the criticism of Aniela Zagorska:

> My feelings are very complex — as you may guess. That they — the Boers — are struggling in good faith for their independence cannot be doubted; but it is also a fact that they have no idea of liberty, which can only be found under the English flag all over the world. *C'est un people essentiellment despotique*, as all the Dutch. This war is not so much a war against the Transvaal as a struggle against the doings of German influence. It is the Germans who have compelled the issue.⁶⁴

Yet parallel to Marlow's baffling response to Kurtz, these remarks cut in opposite ways. At first glance they seem an embarrassed defense of English imperialism, a part of Conrad's need to bury his allegiance to his native land by adopting the national sentiment of his adopted one, thus lending support to Ford Maddox Ford's wry judgment that "if it was a question of his private principles against any honor he could show the English State, his private principles must go by the board."⁶⁵ Still, like Marlow's "unconscious loyalty" to Kurtz, Conrad's principles do deviously survive, since the reason for this apparent defense of English policy is the desired erosion of the might of Germany — the arch foe of Poland's hope for national revival. In the ensuing decade, it would be this revolutionary energy breaking the seams of uneasy accommodations that lay in ambush for Conrad.

WITH *NOSTROMO*, IN 1904, Conrad turned at last to a panoramic treatment of politics in a nation embroiled in revolutionary upheaval. Both Morf and Jocelyn Baines have shown how the novel is in part a transplanted depiction of the politics and intrigue of his own native land.⁶⁶ In his Author's Note, Conrad cites as his "principal authority" for the history of Costaguana a "venerated friend," Don Jose Avellanos, and there is a devious truthfulness in granting him a real existence, for Avellanos' eloquent "Fifty Years of Misrule" seems to echo Tadeusz Bobrowski, whose own scornful commentary on Polish politics appeared in his *Memoirs* in 1900.⁶⁷ But opposed to this demoralization is seemingly Giorgio Viola, the leonine shade of Conrad's father, whose "simple devotion to a humanitarian idea" verges on the "puritanism of religion" and leaves him marooned amidst a clash of social forces that "cared nothing for the wrongs of downtrodden nations."⁶⁸ Beneath the broad mediation in *Nostromo*, then, between political idealism and skepticism, Conrad was reviving that feud with his revolutionary origins from which he would emerge this time as if from a dangerous illness.

Because of his explosive material (Costaguana means bird excrement, used in the manufacture of dynamite), Conrad had to adopt literary strategies that afforded him psychic distance — what he called elsewhere "that saving callousness" which "reconciles us to the conditions of our existence" and *"will assert itself under the guise of assent to fatal necessity, or in the enthusiasm of a purely esthetic rendering"* (emphasis mine).⁶⁹ There is fatal necessity, for instance, in Conrad's treatment of motivation. "The novel recognizes unconscious motives and self-deceptions," Albert Guerard observes, "but its treatment of theme — its psychology, in a word — is classical rather than Freudian."[70] That is, ideals (or the lack of them) are allowed to serve as sole motives for action, thus enabling Conrad to expound a fable of "fatal necessity" by leading all his representative political types to ruin, thereby eschewing what is personal and complicated about their character. His broadly "esthetic" or "melodramatic" treatment of them also serves this end. Charles Gould, conspicuously reticent and usually engaged at the San Tome mine, remains a vivid presence by virtue of his flaming mustache, leather leggings, guns, and sabers. Dona Emilia, his wife, encircled in a somber brocade of muslin and lace, dispensing charity to the poor and adrift in loneliness, remains to the bitter end an imprisoned fairy. Nostromo, when not away on some mission, is realized by a yellowish match in the dusk, his silhouette on a silver-gray mare, fierce black whiskers, and silver spurs. This use of elements of moral fable and a selective superfluity of cinematic detail for characterization is what accounts for critical dismay over the "dramatic impenetrability" and "hollow" reverberations of *Nostromo*, but to begrudge Conrad these maneuvers is to underrate the emergent vein of self-incrimination in his material.[71]

Conrad's control of the narrative is not just aesthetic and psychological, but metaphysical as well. Time itself seems to be static in Costaguana, its history a grim cycle of eternal verities: exploitation and misrule, revolution and ensuing social anarchy. This sense is augmented by the splintering of time-sequence, a heavy reliance on flashback, fragmented action, adroit juxtaposition of opposing views, abrupt shifts in place, scenes whose outcome we already know that fill up with irony, and personal anecdote. We are left, like Captain Mitchell's privileged listener, often "stunned and as it were annihilated mentally by the sudden surfeit of sights, sounds, names, facts and complicated information imperfectly apprehended . . . " (458) Such ruptures in the narrative impressively capture the disruption and anarchy of civil war; but they also allow Conrad to withdraw from and obfuscate the revolutionary veering of his plot, while forcing us to feel history as failing to make sense, just a blind repetitive mechanism. The political contestants in Costaguana are just helpless cogs whose lives are tragically nullified in the void of time.[72]

The objective correlative of this metaphysic is the San Tome mine itself, which in the eyes of Emilia Gould, for instance, is an active and malevolent agency, a "monstrous and crushing weight" which "had left her heart to turn into a wall of silver bricks, erected by the silent work of evil spirits, between her and her husband" (209). Indeed in his obsession with the mine, Gould has become guilty of "a subtle conjugal infidelity." By such personification and arrogation of motive, the San Tome mine operates in the plot as a separate character, its giant maw thundering by torchlight in the night, warping and devouring all who come within its radius of power — both exploited Indian laborers and arrogant overlords alike.[73] With remarkable clairvoyance, Conrad sees the mine as attracting the apostles of Manifest Destiny, embodied in the American millionaire Holroyd, a man with "the temperament of a Puritan and an insatiable imagination of conquest" who sees the relentless march and triumph of U.S. imperialism as inevitable:

> We in this country know just about enough to keep indoors when it rains. We can sit and watch. Of course, some day we shall step in. We are bound to. But there's no hurry. Time itself has got to wait on the greatest country in the whole of God's Universe. We shall be giving the word for everything: industry, trade, law, journalism, art, politics, and religion, from Cape Horn clear over to Smith's Sound, and beyond, too, if anything worth taking hold of turns up at the North Pole. And then we shall have the leisure to take in hand the outlying islands and continents of the earth. We shall run the world's business whether the world likes it or not. The world can't help it — and neither can we, I guess. (73-74)

So far as it bears out what Marx called the "fetishism of commodities," Conrad's mystification of the San Tome mine deepens his penetration of imperialism, for as Martin Decoud rightly anguishes: "The whole land is like a treasure-house, and all these people are breaking into it, while we are cutting each other's throats... We are a wonderful people, but it has always been our fate to be" — he did not say "robbed," but added, after a pause — "exploited!" (164) But to the degree the exploiters, both foreign and native-born, become merely passive victims of its "evil" magnetism, the mine serves Conrad's need to project human iniquity onto a non-human mechanism, thus blurring the issue of personal responsibility and ensuring the ruin of any political idealism in Costaguana.

By these strategies Conrad was able to channel his political anxieties into an ambitious expose of imperialism. As the dashing "King of Sulaco," Charles Gould may scorn political theorizing and wish only to rescue his native land from chaos; but his fatal error is a blind faith in material interests:

> What is wanted here is law, good faith, order, security. Any one can declaim about these things, but I pin my faith to material interests. Only let the material interests once get a firm footing, and they are bound to impose the conditions on which alone they can continue to exist. That's how your money-making is justified here in the face of lawlessness and disorder. It is justified because the security which it demands must be shared with an oppressed people. A better justice will come afterwards. That's your ray of hope. (80)

The novel admits no equivocation on this matter. Far from securing the virtues of stability and justice, the Gould Concession subverts them and plunges Costaguana into a new and more insidious brand of misrule. Amidst the social chaos following the collapse of the Guzman Bento tyranny, the wealthy *Hidalgo* landowners, through the Blanco party, back a conservative "democratic" revolt by bribing off the political opposition with monies from the Concession. Despite his "mandate for reform," the regime of Don Vincente Ribiera is little more than the official arm of the Blancos, and themselves the unofficial pawns of Gould's sponsor, the American millionaire, Holroyd. The regime cannot seize the popular imagination, indeed is deeply resented by Costaguana's declassed majority of Indians, for as Howe has brilliantly reasoned, it is trapped in the contradictions of a "client" imperial operation.[74] The Ribierists cannot initiate genuine land reform to meet the needs of the poor without incurring the resistance of the haughty Blancos, nor engage the dormant energies of nationalism without scaring off its foreign investors like Holroyd, and so must turn to the military for stability.

Soon civil war is ignited when General Montero launches a barracks revolt to seize the whole Concession, but its deeper and more muted causes are "rooted in the political immaturity of the people, in the indolence of the upper classes and the mental darkness of the lower" (364). The declassed Indian majority, who are "suffering and mute, waiting for the future in a pathetic immobility of patience" and who still "looked all alike" to Emelia Gould, are drawn into the conflict. They have only Pedrito Montero to lead them, an avaricious and comic barbarian, but he fails to discredit their cause and at least speaks to the real nature of their oppression.[75] His Caesarism, with its aim of "imperial rule based upon the direct popular vote," may be ludicrous, but Pedrito is only mimicking the bad faith of his liberal upper-class enemies and is not just indulging in crude demagoguery when he describes the Blancos as "Gothic remnants, sinister mummies, who plotted with foreigners for the surrender of the lands and the slavery of the people" (150). Montero encounters mass support as he advances on the Blanco stronghold of Sulaco; indeed, despite himself, Conrad's image of the "liberation forces" entering the city is tinged with grudging admiration:

> Emaciated greybeards rode by the side of lean, dark youths, marked by all the hardships of campaigning, with strips of raw beef twined round the crowns of their hats, and huge iron spurs fastened to their naked heels. Those that in the passes of the mountain had lost their lances had provided themselves with the goads used by the Campo cattlemen: slender shafts of palm fully ten feet long, with a lot of loose rings jingling under the ironshod point. They were armed with knives and revolvers. A haggard fearlessness characterized the expressions of all these sun-blacked countenances; they glared down haughtily with their scorched eyes at the crowd, or, blinking upwards insolently, pointed out to each other some particular head amongst the women at the windows. (362-63)

By mid-century these "bandits" will be more disciplined and ideologically equipped, their leaders inspired not by third-rate historical romances but the writings of Regis Debray. As it is, they are defeated by the combined forces of Gould, the Blanco aristocrats, and

General Barrios, who prevail only by recruiting their own "lawless" elements, Hernandez and Father Corbellan.[76] Yet while a fragile social order has been restored, we are left with a feeling that the civil war has been just a scrimmage for the cataclysm to come. At last glimpse the San Tome mine, having attracted the foreign capital that ignited the civil war, has become a focus of hatred for the workers, with a "democratic" opposition growing again, this time not in the barracks but in the anarchist meetings and coffee shops of Sulaco, beefed up now by foreign workers, Italian socialists, a burgeoning lumpen proletariat, and four spectacular defections: the Corbellans, the Avellanos, Hernandez, and Nostromo. But the Ribierists too have gained a formidable ally in the inevitable renewal of conflict: the imperial U.S. is the first nation to recognize the republic as the so-called "legitimate" government of Costaguana.[77] Indeed, there is a foreshadowing of the seventeen U.S. military interventions to come in Central and South America, even shades of Saigon, in the sudden appearance of the U.S.S. *Powhattan* in the harbor, of exclusively American bars in Sulaco. Perhaps Dr. Monygham puts it best in his trenchant response to Emilia Gould's weary desire for peace:

> There is no peace and no rest in the development of material interests. They have their laws and their justice. But it is founded on expediency, and is inhuman; it is without rectitude, without the continuity and the force that can be found only in a moral principle. Mrs. Gould, the time approaches when all that the Gould Concession stands for shall weigh as heavily upon the people as the barbarism, cruelty, and misrule of a few years back. (481)

As a political fable of imperialism, *Nostromo* unfolds with a sense of dispassionate justice and concludes on a note of unqualified pessimism, fully justified by the march of events in the Third World in the twentieth century.[78]

What is arresting for our inquiry, however, is the way Conrad deflects any nascent revolutionary impulses via a succession of "secret selves" who all find themselves on the wrong side in the civil war and cling to political formulae he adopted in exile to disavow his origins. Take Charles Gould, a native Costaguanan "haunted by a fixed idea" of the mine for which he will sacrifice his wife, the integrity of government, the lives of the Indians, virtually everything. Is Conrad not alluding to his own situation as a "patriot" who, like Gould, is also an Anglophile whose ideal of "order and stability" is equivalent to selling out his country to foreigners? Take Don Jose Avellanos, whose timid nationalism and effete rectitude provide a rhetorical cover for the financial schemes of Holroyd. Is Conrad not alluding to Tadeusz Bobrowski, and the pathetic irrelevance of his uncle's political mentorship with the image of sheets of "Fifty Years of Misrule" fired as cannon fodder and littering the streets as the Monterist forces enter Sulaco? Take the nostalgic figures of Captain Mitchell and Don Pepe, both epitomes of discipline and fidelity — exactly those maritime virtues that Conrad tried to substitute for his revolutionary legacy. Is Mitchell's wandering recollection of the civil war not egregious for its "official" mis-interpretation of the deeper issues involved, and Don Pepe not just a colorful taskmaster for Gould who wields Conrad's celebrated job sense as an instrument of oppression at the San Tome mine? Take Dr. Monygham, who was tortured under the Bento regime into betraying other resistance fighters and has since turned misanthropic. Is his "outspoken scorn for mankind" not absorbed into the fabric of the narrative itself, thus pointing to "mere recklessness of judgment, the bravado of guilt"? Take Martin Decoud, the ironic intellectual and "adopted child of Western Europe" whose corrosive skepticism toward any ideals leads to his suicide on the Isabels. Does his fate not inform on the urgencies that drove Conrad to attempted suicide in Marseilles and an ironic disengagement from politics thereafter? Or take Nostromo, a "foreign" sailor whose "manly vanity" leads him to acquiesce in the role of flunkey for the Ribierists. Is this not a derisive self-assessment of his creator, who recast himself as a romantic sailor, then a writer of nautical tales at the service of his "foreign" home, imperial England? All these characters deserve what old Giorgio Viola, a "pure" revolutionary consigned by age to the sidelines of the civil war, charges of all those Costaguanans who would fight for the Ribierists: "Blind. Esclavos!" (158)

Conrad's literary credo was "before all to make you see," and what should be apparent by now is the defensive character of his varnished pessimism.[79] "There was something inherent in the necessities of successful action," he writes at the conclusion of *Nostromo*, "which carried with it the moral degradation of the idea" (490). Conrad can sustain this *angst* only by himself promulgating the "fixed idea" of historical fatalism and disguising the motives of his characters (as Decoud sneers about Gould) in "a moral romance derived from the tradition of a pretty fairy tale" (202). There are interludes in the novel that challenge these authorial strategies, but we must search for them beneath the "saving callousness" of the fable and its omnipotent logic of material interests — essentially a denial of human motivation. What rescues *Nostromo* to some degree from its "hollow" reverberations are exactly those deeper psychological undercurrents in characters who threaten to break out of their fixed mold and expand into freedom. This subversion of the fable from within marks the return of latent revolutionary energies that bear upon three characters most closely aligned with the author himself: the obsessional Gould, the virile Nostromo, the neurotic Decoud.

Nostromo has often been called an exhaustive study of self-deception, with Gould as the supreme instance. Yet the fable, which equates motives with ideals, cannot recognize real self-deception which involves a psychological paradox: a person must be lying to himself about his true motives and yet believe the lie. This assumes the existence of an unconscious, into which consciousness banishes one's true motives only to reclaim them in the cloak of "ideals." Is this not operating in Gould's enterprise? "You know he doesn't talk," insinuates the engineer-in-chief. "But we all know his motive, *and he has only one*—the safety of the San Tome mine with the preservation of the Gould Concession in the spirit of his compact with Holroyd" (298). Considering Gould passed his early adulthood in England away from a native land engulfed in revolution, we might expect to fathom his obsession by turning to his family roots. Indeed the parallels with his creator are striking. Not only was Gould's uncle killed in political struggles "out of pure love for rational liberty and from his hatred of oppression" (62), but his father was hounded to his death by corrupt post-Bento regimes that forced him against his will to operate the Concession during which "whole tribes of Indians had perished in the exploitation." Moreover, the impact of his father's death threatened Gould with the same survivor guilt and sense of inner dissolution that menaced Conrad upon the untimely loss of his own parents: "His breathing image was no longer in his power. This consideration, *closely affecting his own identity*, filled his heart with a mournful and angry desire for action . . . action is consolatory. It is the enemy of thought and the friend of flattering illusions" (63). Gould's form of consolatory action is to disobey his father's dying injunction to abandon the San Tome mine in order to usurp his authority. Indeed his need to reclaim the mine as a victory for "order and stability" is inseparable from a need to see his father "be put completely in the wrong," thus affecting in his own self a "vague idea of rehabilitation." Only these unconscious urgencies can explain Gould's obsession, which as Decoud observes, "he holds to . . . as some men hold to the idea of love or revenge"(230). It is no wonder Conrad keeps this self-disclosure well veiled, for Gould's alliance with Holroyd's "purer form of Christianity" travesties his own revolutionary heritage, and transforms his secret self into a "sham" anarchist with "an adventurer's easy morality" who in a pinch is prepared to see his country "go to hell" and dynamite his own folly into oblivion.[80] Upon inspection, Gould is not so much a conservative cut down by "the necessities of successful action," but rather one too driven by filial guilt and resentment toward his departed elders to allow for more than a tangential encounter with political realities.

Initially, Nostromo also is nourished solely by action, fanning a reputation that is unredeemed by any political principle and so subject to exploitation. He is eager to "run at the heels of his English" and do the dirty work of the Blancos by recruiting Sulacan laborers at gunpoint from their "black, lifeless cluster of huts . . . like dog kennels" (91). This Capataz is no "man of the people," but one destined to die destitute and a "traitor," as Signora Teresa never tires of reminding him.[81] Nostromo recognizes this only when he loses his audience during the civil war and, adrift on the lighter with Decoud, finds himself just another fugitive on the Gulfo Placido. This "vast bed of ocean," silent, dark, still, outside history, threatening nonexistence, betokens his creator's own free-floating survivor guilt, and Nostromo's experience on the Gulfo Placido "made everything that had gone before for years appear vain and foolish, like a flattering dream come suddenly to an end" (390). Nostromo now glimpses with partial lucidity that he has been "betrayed" and is burdened with what he lacked earlier: a political awareness. Now he recognizes that "what he had heard Giorgio Viola say once was very true. Kings, ministers, aristocrats, the rich in general, kept the people in poverty and subjection; they kept them as they kept dogs, to fight and hunt for their service" (391). With this perception Nostromo's vanity yields to a grim alienation, based on his nascent sense of class struggle, and he withdraws from his old aristocratic cronies to become an oracle of leaden unhappiness among the anarchists, cursing the mine which "appeared to him hateful and immense, lording it by its vast wealth over the valor, the toil, the fidelity of the poor, over war and peace, over the labors of the town, the sea, and the Campo"(472). At last he is ready to acknowledge his ties to his "father-mentor," recognizing himself as "a republican like old Giorgio, *and a revolutionist at heart* (but in another manner)" (494). This hedge, however, is crucial, for instead of pursuing that lapsed revolutionary mandate, Nostromo is diverted by his selfish scheme to draw off the silver hidden on the Isabels in order to "grow rich slowly," thus in a way "betraying" the people once more by reviving his spiritual kinship with the Blancos.[82] Such a dereliction is also decipherable in his related scheme to abandon the passionately idealistic Linda for the romantically self-indulgent Giselle, and as retribution he is "accidentally" shot and killed by Giorgio Viola.[83] It is as if Conrad were driven with despairing consistency to revive the discredited "superstition" of the silver, and in doing so compromise Nostromo's integrity as an emerging revolutionary in accord with his own personal history.

This vein of distress and subsequent flight into melodrama is especially transparent in the case of Decoud. At the start an exotic dandy of the Parisian boulevards, one who reduces all idealism to the secret urgings of personal advantage, Decoud "was in danger of becoming a sort of non-descript dilettante all his life." Father Corbellan sums him up with terrible curtness: "*You believe neither in stick nor stone* (emphasis mine)" (186). Yet this proves to be something of a pose, for as we soon learn, he "had pushed the habit of universal raillery to a point where it blinded him to the genuine impulses of his own nature" (145). Despite himself, then, Decoud is drawn into the sorrowful destiny of Costaguana. He claims as motive only a desire to win his beloved Antonia, whose political enthusiasm requires a response, but this is no more convincing than most of Conrad's "romantic" stratagems. As the narrator remarks, "He soothed himself by saying he was not a patriot, but a lover" (166). Now Decoud's scorn for his labors as a journalist for the *Porvenir* ("a sort of intellectual death") has as its target not idealism, but the Ribierists, whose political defects he must conceal in his half-hearted denunciations of the Monterists.[84] He knows where the sentiments of the people lie and is swift to fondly mock Avellanos and others when they pontificate otherwise. When subjected to anathemas, Decoud passionately defends himself: "I believe I am a true *hijo del pais*, a true son of the country, whatever Father Corbellan may say. And I'm not so much of an unbeliever as not to have *faith in my own ideas, in my own remedies, in my own desires* (emphasis mine)" (200-01). What his "own ideas" are becomes clear when, with Sulaco under siege, he delivers a stirring proposal for separation to the demoralized Ribierists, who balk initially because this remedy might do justice to both sides. This Decoud insists on action: "There is never any God in a country where men will not help themselves"; indeed he is ready to make the ultimate sacrifice for the achievement of national destiny: "Whoever is allowed to live on in terror, I must die the death" (223).

It is precisely on the brink of self-confrontation that Conrad is impelled to launch Decoud on the lighter with Nostromo, and with no apparent motive unless to escape that sense of immanent death that drove him from his native land. Decoud assures his sister that "I am not running away . . . I am simply going away with that great treasure of silver which must be saved at all costs" (206). Yet this new preoccupation with the silver suggests a subtle lapse of vision. Once alone on the Gulfo Placido, he experiences the world "as still as when you wake up in your bed . . . from a bizarre and agitated dream." What ensues on the Isabels, of course, is Decoud's suicide, where he is "swallowed up in the vast indifference of things." Yet this hardly seems consistent with his steady maturation as a character.[85] During the siege of Sulaco, Decoud displays lucidity, courage, love for another, a sanction for action outside himself—all the ingredients that might give a man a profound grasp on life. But once having "run away," he too, like Nostromo, must bear his creator's own fallen condition. It is revealing that when we rejoin Decoud on the Isabels (after an interruption of some 200 pages), he has oddly regressed to his earlier self, once more called "the spoiled darling of the family," given once more "the affectation of skepticism and irony," viewing again the people of Sulaco as "jibbering and obscene specters." Decoud the revolutionary is gone, to be replaced by a lost soul who is killed by what underlies the persisting misery of this self-avowed autobiographical writer: moral solitude, "the enemy known to but few on this earth, and whom only the simplest of us are fit to withstand" (466).

These analyses of Gould, Nostromo, and Decoud are not meant to detract from the novel, but to expose the undercurrents that define its appeal. Yet few political novels with so much insight provide us with so little hope or incentive for resistant action. The Monterist forces are subjected to demeaning caricature that smacks too much of the *Porvenir*, and when Nostromo and Decoud threaten to "break out" of character as revolutionaries, they are extinguished by melodrama as part of a fictional reenactment of Conrad's own long-nurtured disgrace. But by the end of *Nostromo*, it is revolutionary fervor once again rather than a sense of "fatal necessity" that has taken hold in Costaguana. "And do you know where they [the people] go for the strength, for the necessary force?" Dr. Monygham warns Emilia Gould. "To the secret societies among immigrants and natives" (480).

Conrad himself would turn next to these secret societies, shifting from his "native" seaboard to the sordid London slums. The compassionate irony that encircles *Nostromo* will give way to the scornful caricature of *The Secret Agent*, where a bombing fiasco drives a plot that a reader might cooperate with only at his own peril.

THE SECRET AGENT, CONRAD'S ONLY treatment of revolution arising out of the personal confines of exile, was most likely "crystallized" by the revival of Polish hopes for liberation upon the October Revolution in St. Petersburg, ensuing in the wake of Russia's miraculous defeat by Japan in 1905. "I am greatly moved by the news from Russia," he wrote to Ada Galsworthy. "Certainly a year ago, I never hoped to live to see all that."[86] On one hand, Conrad rallied enthusiastically to these hopes for Poland by writing "Autocracy and War," which not only predicted revolution in Russia, but welcomed it as part of "the real progress of humanitarian ideas."[87] Yet in a sense he also wished he were dead (*"never hoped to live"*), for Conrad was now re-engaging his survivor guilt, now clarified and inflamed by the very events he welcomed. "It was a period," he says in his Author's Note, that "made me feel left behind, aimless amongst mere husks of sensations and lost in a world of other, of inferior values," leading to the "vision of an enormous town . . . a cruel devourer of the world's light . . . with depth enough there for any passion . . . darkness enough to bury five million lives."[88] The pivotal episode in the novel was inspired by Ford Maddox Ford's "few words" recalling an abortive attempt to blow up the Greenwich Observatory in 1894.[89] "I remember . . . remarking on the criminal futility of the whole thing . . . ," Conrad writes, "the half-crazy pose as of a brazen cheat exploiting the poignant miseries and passionate credulities of a mankind so tragically eager for self-destruction" (xxix). While this "remembering" is no more politically defined than the Greenwich fiasco ever was, the central protagonist of *The Secret Agent* will prove a "brazen cheat" doing something of the kind and passing it off as revolution.

But Conrad felt "left behind" in more than a political sense in

1905, for this was the time of Jessie Conrad's second pregnancy. "I could not account to myself," she recalled later, "for the grimly ironic expression I used often to catch on his face, whenever he came to give me a look-in. Could it have reference to the expected baby? No! it was only a reflection of the tone of the book's."[90] That it referred to both is suggested by a bizarre moment during a family vacation to France in 1906 — when Conrad was impulsively moved to throw a package of his new son's clothes from a speeding train, causing Jessie to remark wryly later: "Well, I am sure the man who finds that bundle will be looking for the baby's corpse."[91] This action speaks not only to Conrad's hostility toward the child, but also to the behavior of Mr. Verloc, whose cultivated "father-son" relationship with Stevie unleashes buried passions that result in the latter's grisly death. This is why the political theme in *The Secret Agent* is accompanied, then gradually eclipsed by what the Assistant Commissioner calls a ludicrous "domestic drama," and what Conrad, who alone invented his proletarian heroine and Winnie's suicide, must have viewed as his own inner situation.

Out of this state of utter demoralization — an "air of moral nihilism" which, like Mr. Verloc, is "by no means diabolic" — emerge the authorial strategies of *The Secret Agent*. To enter this realm, Conrad needed psychic distance, namely, both a bewildering self-negating irony that preserves the "impenetrable mystery" and a new, comic, non-solipsistic mode — for as the proverb goes that the narrator suddenly cites midway through the novel: "*truth can be more cruel than caricature* (emphasis mine)" (142). All political ideology, then, is exploded by reducing every personal motive to sloth, vanity, and social self-preservation. Recurring violence is visited upon victims by their own blind stupidity. Misunderstanding and "accident" play such a dominant role in the novel that the issue of personal responsibility is blurred. Evil exists disembodied and projected into the sordid surroundings of London. Such strategies enable Conrad to blot out all moral-political imperatives by divesting his characters of any claim to pity or redemption.[92] Anyone seized by compassion for this "mediocre mankind" must be mad. Anyone who thinks the oppressive social system can be fazed by some quixotic act of indignation must have the naiveté of a child. Indeed it is only Stevie — literally an idiot boy — who shows any such signs of a conscience, and his reward is to be blown to bits amid an overwhelming sense of nausea. On a manifest level, *The Secret Agent* is Conrad's bleakest book, not because moral-political gestures meet with doom, but because the very possibility of their being genuine is denied.

This nihilism, however, is held together only by witty contrivance: in particular by a reductive psychology and reign of chance no less suspect than the band of Soho anarchists in their shady haunts. As Conrad wrote somewhat disingenuously to Graham, "I don't think I've been satirizing the revolutionary world. All these people are not revolutionists — they are mere shams."[93] Karl Yundt, then, is a self-declared terrorist, deformed by gouty swellings, full of impotent fierceness like "the excitement of a senile sensualist," who in fact has never raised a finger against the social edifice.[94] Michaelis is a defunct, "ticket-of-leave" apostle, a hopelessly illogical humanitarian, round "like a distended balloon" who was buried in prison for seven years by a wave of vindictive public opinion and now adopted as the darling of the ruling classes.[95] Comrade Ossipon is a disciple of Lombroso and delegate to the "more or less mysterious" Red Committee, but in fact nothing more than a complacent sensualist living off the dole of desperate women.[96] These anarchists are "shams" because they are afflicted to an exaggerated degree by what Conrad felt to be his own defects as a revolutionary manqué, who, buried in the same "inferior" bourgeoisie values, used scare tactics, resignation, Anglophilia, and a spurious rationality to conceal his real political selfhood. It is their very inertia that forces Mr. Verloc to recruit poor Stevie in order to pull off some real political action. They are ridiculed precisely because they are *not authentic*. In this curious way, what Conrad feared might be "gratuitous outrages" against the revolutionary world threaten to "explode" his *own* defensive realignment with the forces of reaction.

This link exists mainly through Mr. Verloc, who engages the action in a way that parallels Conrad's. He serves the forces of the

Embassy by "betraying the secret and unlawful proceedings of his fellow-men" that would subvert it — whereas his creator serves his own exorbitant need for order by betraying (through caricature) the revolutionary impulses that tyrannized him. Of course Conrad bears the painful burden of self-knowledge, for the teasing ironies that surround the oblivious Mr. Verloc are daggers directed at himself. Thus Mr. Verloc, who "by a mystical accord of temperament and necessity had been a secret agent all his life" (165), is now a dull-minded respectable Anglophile whose only goal in life is to avoid more incarceration and blanket himself in domestic comfort. His meditation on revolutionists blends imperceptibly with Conrad's own "official" views about them:[97]

> The majority of revolutionists are enemies of discipline and fatigue mostly. There are natures, too, to whose sense of justice the price exacted looms up monstrously enormous, odious, oppressive, worrying, humiliating, extortionate, intolerable. Those are the fanatics. The remaining portion of social rebels is accounted for by vanity, the mother of all noble and vile illusions, the companion of poets, reformers, charlatans, prophets, and incendiaries. (48)

This is the vulgar bias of a "protector of society," one who shields "wealth and opulence" from the "demands of unhygienic labor," and if the irony admits of any gradation, this repulsive slug is marked by a greater degree of spiritual sloth than the anarchists: "He was too lazy even for a mere demagogue, for a workman orator, for a leader of labor. He required a more perfect form of ease; or *it might have been that he was a victim of a philosophical unbelief in the effectiveness of every human effort* (emphasis mine)" (12). Conrad is skating on thin ice, for it takes no startling act of recognition to see that this philosophical "unbelief" is the novel's prevailing assumption.[98] Indeed once we consider Mr. Verloc's proper contempt for revolutionaries and "officially" sanctioned betrayal of them, his "inert fanaticism" which insulates him from political reality and allows his appropriation by the forces of counter-revolutionary zeal, his inimical response to sex — all these traits congeal into both a brilliant prefiguration of the Cold War citizen and a scathing self-portrait of the author.[99]

And the plot exacts a full measure of revenge, for it is Mr. Verloc's dogged pursuit of middle-class ease that leads to his demise. That ease is threatened when his employer, the Embassy, pressures him to commit an outrage meant to force the British government to replace tolerance with repressive legislation against refugee radicals. As Vladimir blurts out in exasperation: "This country is absurd with its sentimental regard for individual liberty" (25). In Mr. Verloc's secret interview with this agent of a "European power," Conrad comes perilously close to self-confrontation once again. For beneath the comic disguises and rhetorical exaggerations, which even "dawn" on Mr. Verloc at one point as "an elaborate joke" (30), we can detect Conrad dueling with his Polish origins. After all, the imperative for revolutionary action issues from the Embassy, and it is Mr. Verloc's fear of getting "chucked" by them that motivates him. Under the late Baron Stott-Wartenheim (whose name in German means a stuttering stay-at-home) Mr. Verloc was allowed his indolence, and it is not hard to discern here the paternalistic shade of Tadeusz Bobrowski.[101] "His Excellency had social revolution on the brain. He imagined himself to be a diplomat set apart by special dispensation to watch the end of diplomacy . . . in a horrid, democratic upheaval. His prophetic and doleful dispatches had been for years the joke of Foreign Offices" (24). But the First Secretary, Vladimir, is more suave and menacing, with no doubts about the need for revolutionary action, nor about Mr. Verloc's derelictions on this score. As such, he would appear to be the mocking shade of Apollo Korzeniowski. That Valdimir should be a counter-revolutionary in favor of "universal repressive legislation" is not just part of Conrad's "elaborate joke," but a covert admission of the distortions to which he had subjected his father's ideals. This is embodied in Vladimir's insane proposal to "Go for the First Meridian" — based on his darkly sane grasp of the moral consequences of sheer revolutionary terror: "Madness alone is truly terrifying, inasmuch as you can't placate it either by threats, persuasion, or bribes" (29).[102]

What issues from the Embassy, then, the Greenwich fiasco, is hardly a revolutionary action but rather part of a reactionary plot to assassinate the reputation of its foes. While his creator writhed under these duplicities, Mr. Verloc's "official" obligation to do the dirty work of the totalitarians in no way disturbs his allegiance to English mores. Still, they share the same moral culpability; and it is just before his murder that Mr. Verloc proudly blurts out his accomplishments to his wife: "There isn't a murdering plot for the last eleven years that I haven't had my fingers in at the risk of my life. There's scores of these revolutionists I've sent off with bombs in their blamed pockets to get themselves caught on the frontier" (217). Mr. Verloc's moral sense does not extend beyond the dictates of his career, a grim, quasi-Marxist insight about human nature; yet as part of Conrad's manifest need to shore up his immobilization, it too is "exploded" by Karl Yundt, of all people, who protests it is marked by "the taint of that resigned pessimism which rots the world," leading to the perpetuation of squalid social inequities: "Do you know how I would call the nature of the present economic conditions? I would call it cannibalistic. That's what it is! They are nourishing their greed on the quivering flesh and the warm blood of the people — nothing else" (46). This vision, corroborated by the imaginative weight of *The Secret Agent*, is what Mr. Verloc is shoring up as a "protector of society" — a standard of political conduct more morally bankrupt than any misdeeds of the revolutionaries.

Conrad is less malicious, yet just as deadly, in his treatment of the hospitable edifice of English legality. The great elder statesman, Sir Ethelred, is a living tribute to England's inept insularity, and he sums up his wisdom in comic refrains: "Be lucid, please. No. No details, please" (198). Actually Sir Ethelred's alarm over the threat of revolution invading the West has no basis in fact; and moreover, the British have managed to outflank their "shams" rather well. This is made clear when Conrad, with more insight and self-referential scorn, gives us a glimpse into the "official" mind of Inspector Heat. After all, he too is in the business of "betraying" revolutionists, and Conrad is repeatedly projecting his own sins onto his characters and then mocking them. The first to discover a link between Mr. Verloc and the bombing, Inspector Heat is reluctant to turn over the information, thus exposing the clandestine contact upon which he has built his reputation. (A.J.P. Taylor was not the first man to see that the real motive behind the sophisticated nonsense indulged in by the likes of the C.I.A. is not the protection of society, but simply Jobs for the Boys.) When the Assistant Commissioner extorts the truth from him in intense cross-examination, Inspector Heat feels like a "betrayed tightrope artist" — an accurate metaphor for Conrad's own virtuosity here — for this "servant of the law," in walking a fine line between legality and lawlessness, is only demonstrating what his creator offered to Graham years earlier as his own "conviction": *"L'homme est un animal mechant. Sa mechancete doit etre organisee. La societe est essentiellement criminelle — ou elle n'existerait pas."*[103] Inspector Heat is compared to a native chief in the colonies who was "not precisely a traitor, but still a man of many dangerous reservations in his fidelity, caused by a due regard for his own advantage, comfort, and safety" (108). This might double as Conrad's own view of himself in exile — which he tried to extenuate by universalizing his own perversity (*mechancete*) and then allowing "society" the appropriate sanctions. Beneath his naive duplicity, then, Inspector Heat is acting out a policy without conscience. Indeed his "solution" to the bombing outrage at the Observatory, which is his own misdeed through his illegal link with Mr. Verloc, is to blame the revolutionists. Rankled by the acclaim bestowed upon Michaelis, wary of dealing with a man of conviction like the Professor, alarmed for his own career, Inspector Heat tries to shunt blame for the whole affair onto an innocent humanitarian — an especially "perverse" move since Michaelis has already been unjustly imprisoned once by the English legal system.

All of this imbecility leaves the full range of ideological options in ruin, and it is all generated by the "madness and despair" inside the claustrophobic Verloc household, with its "secret" quotient of anarchism (Stevie), treason and infanticide (Adolph), and avenging retribution (Winnie). The reign of "accident" and misstated relationship conceals what assailed both the Verlocs and Conrad at this time: the unconscious enmity between a father, a mother, and their child. For it is plain that psychologically Stevie is Winnie's child, whom she has shielded since he was small from their cruel father (a man "bad enough for murder"), and that Mr. Verloc, in being responsible for his death, is an appropriate surrogate for Stevie's actual father.[104] It is just Winnie's cultivation of this bond *as reality*, in order to insure Stevie's future, premised on her husband's "supreme wisdom and goodness," that leads Mr. Verloc to reciprocate by recruiting his "boy" to deliver a can of deadly explosives to the Observatory. There is some truth, then, in Mr. Verloc's accusation to his grief-crazed wife after the grisly truth comes out— "Don't you make any mistake about it; if you will have it that I killed the boy, then you've killed him as much as I" (235). This Oedipal fantasy is submerged virtually beyond recognition in *The Secret Agent*, but it does surface in the form of Conrad's misogynous treatment of Winnie which deprives this beleaguered outcast of any sympathy. Winnie breaks her unfathomable reserve on politics only once, and makes an ingenuously revolutionary observation: "Don't you know what the police are for, Stevie? They are there so that them as have nothing shouldn't take anything away from them who have" (158). But what impresses us most is simply the dull tenacity of her loyalties, capable of erupting into resolute violence under the stress of terror. After murdering Mr. Verloc, Winnie's "maternal" compassion for Stevie hardens into a more ludicrous, yet equally fanatical fear of the gallows: "The drop given was fourteen feet." And after her farcical collision with Comrade Ossipon in the maze of London streets, we are likely to share his swelling horror and disgust for this "degenerate" woman. This trace of misogyny also marks Conrad's handling of the other women in *The Secret Agent*, who, seemingly paragons of self-sacrifice, are actually emasculating figures who figuratively "kill" the selfhood of their men, all "lapsed" revolutionaries (Yundt, Michaelis, the Professor), with acts of compassion.

Of course the real issue is male inadequacy. While Mr. Verloc takes his wife for granted, his sex life is a morass of inhibition as he dreads "facing the darkness and reticence that follows the extinguishing of the lamp" (52). These doubts about his manhood stem from his dual roles as an *agent provocateur* and betrayed husband, and hence he will assuage them by killing off Stevie — simultaneously a real "anarchist" and usurping "son." This is hardly a manly solution, however, and in the famous eleventh chapter Conrad ghoulishly dispenses with his alter ego by having Mr. Verloc, "with no other idea than that of being loved for himself" (229), take the lead in provoking his own murder. Now converted by the "unexpected march of events . . . to the doctrine of fatalism" (210), he injects the idea of murder into Winnie's fevered brain by bragging of all the revolutionaries he has led to destruction. He injects the idea of violent revenge upon himself by seeking her sympathy for his plight as a marked man. He tries to detain Winnie by asserting his physical supremacy in a way that only cements her hatred and paranoia: "He advanced, and stretching out his hand, dragged the veil off, unmasking a still unreadable face, against which his nervous exasperation was shattered like a glass bubble flung against a rock" (234). All else failing, Mr. Verloc pulls the fatal trump card of seduction, as he calls to his wife in a tone "intimately known to Mrs. Verloc as the note of wooing" (238). Given the primitive passions at large, this is his most ironic miscalculation to date, and Winnie now makes those passions clear. In an "astonishing" reversal of sexual roles, her face now mystically fused with Stevie's, she reciprocates by planting the bone-handled carving knife in his fat carcass. The style refuses to become alarmed or compassionate at the moment of Mr. Verloc's death, for Conrad feels he deserves none:

> His wife had gone raving mad — murdering mad. They were leisurely enough for the first paralyzing effect of this discovery to pass away before a resolute determination to come out victorious from the ghastly struggle with that armed lunatic . . . But they were not leisurely enough to allow Mr. Verloc the time to move either hand or foot. The knife was already planted in his breast. It met no resistance on its way. Hazard has such accuracies. Into that plunging blow, delivered over the side of the couch, Mrs. Verloc had put all the inheritance of her immemorial and obscure descent, the simple ferocity of the age of caverns, and the unbalanced nervous fury of the age of bar-rooms. Mr. Verloc, the Secret Agent . . . expired without stirring a limb, in the muttered sound of the word "Don't" by way of protest. (239-40)

Hazard has such accuracies indeed.

On a manifest level, then, *The Secret Agent* frees us from politics by grounding its social vision in the invincibility of human error. Yet Conrad can sustain this grimly humorous vision only by resorting to a reductive psychology of "idiotic vanity" that verges on the banal. Ultimately his paralysis of motivation is no more sane than the reactionary plot to demolish "Time" at the Greenwich Observatory.[105] In this sense the corrosive irony negates itself by throwing into doubt the very authorial strategies Conrad uses to assail politics in general. If any political imperative is latent in *The Secret Agent*, then, we must look for it beyond the reach of caricature, in those characters that have in some measure been "liberated" into free will and historical time. A few verge this way, but in allegiance to the simpler ironies of the plot, they prove to be a fanatic, an adventurer, and an idiot.

Virtually all the insights we glean into politics in *The Secret Agent* are anticipated by the Professor, as if he and the narrator were shaking hands behind the scenes. The Soho anarchists he dismisses as "slaves" of the same conventions as the police: "The terrorist and the policeman both come from the same basket. Revolution, legality — counter moves in the same game; forms of idleness at bottom identical" (64). He recognizes that character is fate, that "the way of even the most justifiable revolutions is prepared by personal impulses disguised into creeds" (74). He knows that the Embassy's aim of provoking British repression would only strengthen the revolutionary cause: "Nothing would please me more than to see Inspector Heat and his likes take to shooting us down in broad daylight with the approval of the public. Half our battle would be won then" (67). He cannot accept the bombing of the Observatory as a revolutionary action: "Solidarity with the extremist form of action is one thing, and silly recklessness is another" (70). His desire to "break up the superstition and worship of legality" and be rid of the "old morality" seems a half-conscious intention of his creator. Finally, the Professor's discourse on the weak as the source of evil is all but substantiated by the novel itself: "Do you understand, Ossipon? The source of all evil? They are our sinister masters — the weak, the flabby, the silly, the cowardly, the faint of heart, and the slavish of mind. They have power. They are the multitude. Theirs is the kingdom of earth" (276).

The Professor operates inside the plot, then, as a derisive projection of his creator, one who used scare tactics — "Exterminate, exterminate! That is the only way of progress" — to discredit a political option that his own insights mandate. The disturbing genocidal rage of the Professor brings to mind Kurtz, and each functions simultaneously as caricature and truth. Parentage is normative: the Professor's father, we are told, "a delicate dark enthusiast with a sloping forehead had been an itinerant and roving preacher of some obscure and rigid Christian sect — a man supremely confident in the privileges of his righteousness" (73). Conrad wrote to Graham that his creation was not meant to be "despicable. He is incorruptible at any rate. In making him say: 'Madness and despair, give me that for a lever and I will move the world', I wanted to give him a note of perfect sincerity. At the worst he is a megalomaniac of an extreme type. And every extremist is respectable."[106] Such a clarification vanishes in its own irony. Yet we can recognize this death-cultist as Conrad's own standard *misrepresentation of revolution*, a seedy lunatic ready to take on society with an "intelligent detonator" so that his creator could pretend to a chilly disengagement. As we are told rather disingenuously at one point, the Professor "had genius, but lacked the great social virtue of resignation" (69).

Another reliable truth-teller is the Assistant Commissioner, who, chained to his desk in "a litter of paper," emerges from professional obscurity to take a personal hand in exposing the bombing plot. He is well-equipped for the task because he has a "mistrust of established reputations" and "no saving illusions about himself." As the narrator remarks in rueful reference to Conrad's own vocation as a political writer: "*It is only when our appointed activities seem by a lucky accident to obey the particular earnestness of our temperament can we taste the comfort of a complete self-deception* (emphasis mine)" (103). For this reason the Assistant Commissioner is able to unmask Inspector Heat and, once in possession of his information, offer to

Sir Ethelred an accurate assessment of the bombing as "barefaced audacity amounting to childishness of a peculiar sort . . . not a work of anarchism at all, but something else altogether — some species of authorized scoundrelism" (126-28). Armed now with "a new man's antagonism to old methods," he traces the "gratuitous outrage" back to the despairing side of Conrad's mind: Mr. Verloc. His final recommendation to Sir Ethelred underscores the negative political impact of secret agents, whether their actions are incendiary or literary:

> "What is your general idea, stated shortly? No need to go into details."
> "No, Sir Ethelred. In principle, I should lay it down that the existence of secret agents should not be tolerated, as tending to augment the positive dangers of the evil against which they are used. That the spy will fabricate his information is a mere commonplace. But in the sphere of political and revolutionary action, relying partly on violence, the professional spy has every facility to fabricate the very facts themselves, and will spread the double evil of emulation in one direction, and of panic, hasty legislation, unreflecting hate on the other. However, this is an imperfect world — " (126-27).

But as percipient as the Assistant Commissioner might be, he too is circumscribed by Conrad's own fancied derelictions in exile. His lapse into action is a matter of facile adventurism, escape from the tedium of an "official" political identity that remains intact. He frees Michaelis from any blame in the bombing not to shield the innocent but to preserve his ties with the famous radical's wealthy benefactress. There is no hope for conversion because the "instinct for self-preservation was strong within him." Descending into the "immoral atmosphere" of the London streets, the Assistant Commissioner inherits his creator's tag-in-exile as a "cool reflective Don Quixote," as he seems to "lose some more of his identity" to a pleasant "sense of loneliness and evil freedom" (134-35).[107] Here truth is surely more cruel than caricature, for this escape into nihilism that led Conrad to a lifetime of survivor guilt works with amusing success for the Assistant Commissioner, who is allowed to vanish into the realm of ethical insignificance:

> He felt lighthearted, as though he had been ambushed all alone in a jungle many thousands of miles away from departmental desks and official inkstands. This joyousness and dispersion of thought before a task of some importance seems to prove that this world of ours is not such a very serious affair after all. (137)

Ultimately, the only character in *The Secret Agent* acutely sensitive to injustice and oppression is the idiot boy, Stevie.[108] He alone remotely resembles an authentic revolutionary. Stevie cares nothing about careers: in one job he exploded a cache of fireworks upon hearing of the maltreatment of two office boys, thus causing a general panic and his own dismissal. Stevie cares nothing about "official" power: he is outraged upon hearing of a recruit physically abused by a German officer (Poland's traditional oppressor), causing Winnie to relate: "He was shouting and stamping and sobbing. He can't stand the notion of cruelty. He would have stuck that officer like a pig if he had seen him then" (54-55). But as these episodes make clear, Stevie is "degenerate." His sympathy for people is a "form of fear," thus indiscriminate, morbid, and ultimately dangerous. "In the face of anything which affected directly or indirectly his morbid dread of pain, Stevie ended by turning vicious ... The anguish of immoderate compassion was succeeded by the pain of an innocent but pitiless rage" (154). But who is responsible for this? The impulse behind Stevie's creation is disclosed while he is eavesdropping on the Soho anarchists gathered in Mr. Verloc's porn shop. As Michaelis voices his humanitarian sentiments begotten in the penitentiary, that "colossal mortuary for the socially drowned," Mr. Verloc spies upon the boy:

> Mr. Verloc, getting off the sofa with ponderous reluctance, opened the door leading into the kitchen to get more air, and thus disclosed the innocent Stevie, seated very good and quiet at a deal table, drawing circles, circles, circles; innumerable circles, concentric, eccentric; a coruscating whirl of circles that by their tangled multitude of repeated curves, uniformity of form, and confusion of intersecting lines suggested a rendering of cosmic chaos, the symbolism of a mad art attempting the inconceivable. (41)

These "whirling circles" have many valences. They might symbolize the travesties of revolutionary thought Stevie is overhearing. Or the lunacy he is inheriting by hearing of the world's pain. Yet on a deeper level the "whirling circles" speak to the mental turmoil Conrad inherited from that time long ago when, exiled in the "penitentiary" of Russia, he was educated into a desperately quixotic revolutionary calling by his father. Stevie is the only artist in the novel, and his "symbolism of a mad art attempting the inconceivable" reveals what the composite mosaic of plot has already hinted at: a suicidal defeatism and despair.

This hint of inner madness permeates the London streets. They are a "maze of irrationality," an urban heart of darkness, and Conrad's duplicities can be taken as his own rescue from such a fate. The novel lies in wait to punish all those who pursue an impulse to sink into the "immensity of greasy slime" of the city. Here hope is as unreal as the rusty halos of mist encircling the gaslights. By day "the dust of humanity settles inert and hopeless out of the stream of life," and by night its streets are "a deep trench" where people fumble about abject and lost. The evil that Conrad dare not invest intact in his characters is projected into the landscape of London where it hovers with an elemental permanence. It is the emblem of a mind, Conrad's own, a "secret" psychic basement where impulses of madness and despair lurk like "queer foreign" fish:[109]

> His [the Assistant Commissioner's] descent into the street was like the descent into a slimy aquarium from which the water had run off. A murky, gloomy dampness enveloped him. The walls of the houses were wet, the mud of the roadway glistened with an effect of phosphorescence, and when he emerged into the Strand out of a narrow street by the side of Charing Cross Station the genius of the locality assimilated him. He might have been but one more of the queer foreign fish that can be seen of an evening about there flitting round the dark corners. (134)

The maze of streets are populated with symbols of irremediable misery: the grotesque carriage that takes Winnie's mother to the Charity as a reward for her selflessness ("the Cab of Death"), the old starved horse that draws it ("the stead of apocalyptic misery"), the poor cabman who whips the horse and then drinks up the fare ("This ain't an easy world"). The cabman's pieces of silver "symbolized the insignificant results which reward the ambitious courage and toil of a mankind whose day is short on this earth of evil" (157).

But what is the nature of that evil? Take Winnie's suicide for instance. What is the "impenetrable mystery" that "seems destined to hang for ever" over "this act of madness and despair" (279-80)? Conrad would have us settle for these newspaper clippings and end our investigation on a teasing riddle. I have tried to resist him on this score and trace the "impenetrable mystery" back to an autobiographical writer who always admitted he lurked behind the draperies of his fiction, although "the disclosure is not complete."[110] To accept such a covert invitation to an unmasking is to end up feeling rather like the local constable who shovels up Stevie's remains: "He's all there. Every bit of him. It was a job" (79). Ultimately, this dark comedy is the work of a lacerated conscience. What is even more "alarming," however, is how much of what Conrad meant to be derisive caricature — the curse of government secrecy, the banality of evil, the genocidal impulses bred of social anarchy — has been the cruel truth in our own demoralized era.[111]

In the fading moments of *The Secret Agent*, Conrad gives signals that he would explore his illicit link with revolution once more, and with "a new man's antagonism for old methods" (131). For if his "secret" alignment with Mr. Verloc is a correct surmise, then it speaks of such a degree of mordant self-hate that the urge for uninhibited confession must have been intense. The Assistant Commissioner tells Sir Ethelred that what he came upon in Mr. Verloc was a "psychological state," a broken one, for "most criminals at some time or other feel an irresistible need of confessing — of making a clean breast of it to somebody — to anybody" (198). Likewise, when he is advised by Inspector Heat to "vanish" after his downfall, Mr. Verloc snarls "Where to?" and adds a warning to this bulwark of the English legal system: "No, no, you don't shake me off now. I have been a straight man to those people too long, and now everything must come out" (191). Nothing does come out, however, for only on the lower frequencies does the novel or Mr. Verloc have "enough moral energy to take a resolution of any sort" (201). In the end we must turn to *Under Western Eyes* for a more naked and dignified revelation of Conrad's inner situation. Meanwhile *The Secret Agent* stands as one of the most caustic and bizarre confessions of its kind in modern literature.

UNDER WESTERN EYES IS CONRAD'S only treatment of revolution arising out of the personal confines of his Slavic past. And in shaping the drama of a young Russian's betrayal of a utopian revolutionary, and then his "make-believe" career in the West as a secret agent serving the forces of despotism, Conrad was working at ground zero. "The obligation of absolute fairness," he wrote in his Author's Note, "was imposed on me historically and hereditarily, by the peculiar experience of race and family . . ."[112] This is more than just an allusion to his childhood exile in Russia in the company of his father. At least one more family source for the novel exists — his own cousin, Stanislaw Bobrowski, who was arrested, tried, and sentenced to prison in St. Petersburg in 1892.[113] Tadeusz's letters to his nephew concerning the plight of Stanislaw reveal an unmistakable parallel between him and the "ultra-democratic" Victor Haldin, except that Conrad imposed upon this fictional character *his father's destiny* of being hounded to his death by the czarist authorities. That Razumov is responsible for this death is a stark measure of Conrad's own survivor guilt, and helps us grasp why his struggle with *Under Western Eyes* culminated in a complete mental breakdown, leaving him bedridden and raving at his characters in Polish.[114]

In his Author's Note, Conrad places his official stamp on revolution by seeing it as "senseless desperation provoked by senseless tyranny." But this formulated paradox, that "the ferocity and imbecility of an autocratic rule . . . provokes the no less imbecile and atrocious answer of a purely Utopian revolutionism" (51), leads to a posture of neutrality that ruins Razumov. It invites us to make a travesty of judgment by finding some moral equivalence between the behavior of a Victor Haldin and a mass-executioner like Mr. de P— or a timid czarist functionary like Councilor Mikulin. Conrad would rather have us see both sides stained by "the cynicism of oppression and revolt." This work of self-exculpation is performed from within the novel by his safety-valve, the English professor of languages, who would bias our response with the thesis that "the spirit of Russia is the spirit of cynicism" (105). But one is hard pressed to find this spirit incarnated in the Russians themselves, and it is formulated by a narrator who must also "confess that [he has] no comprehension of the Russian character." The cynical artist, Conrad wrote in 1908, will make a "mere declaration, not of the vanity of things (that would be a too optimistic view), but of the utter futility of existence. Pessimism can go no further. This is the danger of the moralist who has not a faith, however crude, distorted or extravagant, to present to his audience."[115] But faith is exactly what the Russians have in abundance, at least the revolutionaries. Any vein of cynicism is not so much an ineradicable trait of the Russian character as a projection of Conrad's in exile, a way to blindfold his own conscience-stricken "Western" eyes.

The overture of *Under Western Eyes* is taut and trance-like, as if Conrad were imagining what might happen if he had returned as a young man to pre-revolutionary Russia equipped with his vulnerable solitude and skepticism. An illegitimate son and anonymous student at St. Petersburg University, Razumov is "as lonely in the world as a man swimming in the deep sea" (61). Sane and hard-working, he has no more conscious longing in life than an ambition to become "a celebrated old professor." Yet there is a strong trace of defensive caution behind these choices. Eavesdropping on political meetings at the university, he "took the attitude of an inscrutable listener, a listener of the kind that hears you out intelligently and then just changes the subject" (57). Razumov's retreat from the tensions of the times is so calculated that it seems to bespeak a deeper seduction denied out of prudence and dread of dire consequences.

All of this is blown to pieces when Haldin suddenly appears in his lodgings to admit to the assassination attempt and appeal for help. Nor is he too far wrong in assuming that his "brother," by his elusive silence at the university, has marked himself as a secret rebel. Razumov has real cause to resent Haldin's assumption that he has nothing to lose, and so will prove hospitable to a lone terrorist with its enforced complicity; yet his derisive exclamation — "There goes my silver medal!" — is directed as much at that shallow ambition as anything else. Once more an inscrutable listener, Razumov is now instructed by *example* in the moral-political convictions that have already flickered in his conscience and at first he *does* cooperate with Haldin's request to search out Ziemianitch: "Yes, of course, I will go. You must give me precise directions, and for the rest — depend on me" (69). His resolve starts to dissolve into hatred only as he ponders the personal risk, the dismal future he had already imagined in wait for revolutionaries while listening in on Haldin's circle:

> Razumov saw himself shut up in a fortress, worried, badgered, perhaps ill-used. He saw himself deported by an administrative order, his life broken, ruined, and robbed of all hope . . . He saw his youth pass away from him in misery and half-starvation — his strength give way, his mind become an abject thing. He saw himself creeping, broken down and shabby, about the streets — dying unattended in some filthy hole of a room, or on the sordid bed of a Government hospital. (68-69)

Again the shadow of Conrad's own nightmarish exile in Russia with his ailing father is unmistakable. It was to escape the same fate that he quit Poland — like Razumov now, who will turn against Haldin not out of political considerations but out of simple failure of nerve.

Any other reasons we can dismiss, thanks to the precision with which the character of Haldin emerges. The resurrected spirit of Apollo Korzeniowski, he is a messianic populist by conviction, a pre-Marxian nationalist, entirely quixotic in motive, resigned to death, yet naively blind to the danger to others that attends his extreme views. In resorting to terrorism, Haldin has targeted the life of a notorious butcher, Mr. de P—, who served the autocracy by "imprisoning, exiling, or sending to the gallows men and women, young and old, with an equable unwearied industry" (58). As he justifies his action to Razumov that night —

> Yes, Razumov. Yes, brother. Some day you shall help to build. You suppose that I am a terrorist, now — a destructor of what is. But consider that the true destroyers are they who destroy the spirit of progress and truth, not the avengers who merely kill the bodies of the persecutors of human dignity. Men like me are necessary to make room for self-contained, thinking men like you... Look here, brother! Men like me leave no posterity, but their souls are not lost. No man's soul is ever lost. It works for itself — or else where would be the sense of self-sacrifice, or martyrdom, of conviction, of faith — the labors of the soul? What will become of my soul when I die in the way I must die — soon — very soon perhaps? It shall not perish. Don't make a mistake, Razumov. This is not murder — it is war, war. My spirit shall go warring in some Russian body till all falsehood is swept out of the world. The modern civilization is false, but a new revelation shall come out of Russia. (67-69)

Confronted by the might of czarism, already bloated with victims, Haldin's high-minded militancy is an entirely appropriate response, as Conrad himself admitted in "Autocracy and War":

> The revolutions of European States have never been in the nature of absolute protests en masse against the monarchical principle; they were the uprising of the people against the oppressive degeneration of legality. But there never has been any legality in Russia; she is a negation of that as of everything else that has its root in reason or conscience. The ground of every revolution had to be intellectually prepared. A revolution is a short cut in the rational development of national needs in response to the growth of worldwide ideals.[116]

But Haldin discovers that terrorism is a duty hard to swallow ("But God of Justice! This is weary work... ") and the death of innocent people fills him with anguish and grief ("I... I wouldn't hurt a fly!").[117] Hardly the "sanguinary fanatic" that Razumov will describe later, Haldin embodies the real moral-political imperative at the heart of *Under Western Eyes*, and unless we see his action as approaching a kind of pure yet doomed heroism, we will fail to appreciate the political tragedy of this era.

This recognition is not lost on Razumov, whose first response is to help Haldin escape. Setting out on his mission, he feels a horrible sickness, yet urges himself on: "I must be courageous" (73). But upon reaching Ziemianitch's vile den marked by starvation and despair, he catches a glimpse once more of his revolutionary destiny. Haldin's "bright Russian soul" lies drunk in the hay, whereupon his courage collapses, and indulging a "blind rage of self-preservation," Razumov beats the sled-driver senseless. Back on the wintry streets, his overwhelming fear now leads him to the brink of a conversion which alone can rescue him, a belief in Russia's "sacred inertia ... a guarantee of duration, of safety, while the travail of maturing destiny went on — a work not of revolutions with their passionate levity of action and their shifting impulses — but of peace ..." (78) This leads Razumov to the embrace of czarism, a kind of political suicide, a persuasion that it is "better that thousands should suffer than that a people should become a disintegrated mass," that "obscurantism is better than the light of incendiary torches" (79). Walking over Haldin's phantom in the snow, he decides to betray the revolutionary, and instantly his train of rationalizations grows more desperate and defensive: "What is betrayal? All a man can betray is his own conscience ... by what bond of common faith, of common conviction, am I obliged to let that fanatical idiot drag me down with him?"(82)

But Razumov protests too much. Everything that he does from now will be designed, unconsciously, to erode these modes of bad faith; indeed an instant later he is seized by an impulse to rush back to Haldin and pour out "a full confession in passionate words that would stir the whole being of that man to its innermost depths; that would end in embraces and tears; in an incredible fellowship of souls ... " (83). Instead Razumov turns to the palaces of Prince K— and betrays his secret self, and in doing so becomes a tragic instance of what Conrad wrote so movingly about in "Autocracy and War":

> The worse crime against humanity of that system ... is the ruthless destruction of innumerable minds. The greatest horror of the world — madness — walked faithfully in its train. Some of the best

intellects of Russia, after struggling in vain against the spell, ended by throwing themselves at the feet of that hopeless despotism as a giddy man leaps into an abyss.[118]

After the betrayal, then, Razumov is driven by a blend of fear and guilt which leads him to find relief only in alignments that will ensure his own ruin. Earlier his guarded cavils against visionaries before the startled Haldin as he prepares to depart are an unconscious admission of his treachery, imploring his secret self to clear out and escape: "Have I let him slip through my fingers after all?" On the surface his reckless volubility before General T— is a manifestation of shot nerves, but after hearing his own "conversion" embraced with absolute "fidelity" by this goggled thug — "I detest rebels of every kind. I can't help it. It's my nature!" — we can discern a deeper desire to unmask himself. Now he realizes a reason beyond prudence for not including the peasant in his account of the affair: "To mention him at all would mean imprisonment for the 'bright soul,' perhaps cruel floggings, and in the end a journey to Siberia in chains. Razumov, who had beaten Ziemianitch, felt for him now a vague, remorseful tenderness" (90). Once he falls under suspicion, he tries to retreat into his studies, but that same harassment from the czarist police proves his liberalism —

> History not Theory
> Patriotism not Internationalism
> Evolution not Revolution
> Direction not Destruction
> Unity not Disruption

— to be a mere daydream, his notes now "a mere litter of blackened paper." Now he sinks into a "ditch-water stagnation" and contemplates suicide. Reaching back for a "wrathful wisdom," he recovers and returns to the university — only to be idealized and offered courageous aid by one of Haldin's co-conspirators, which leaves "his moral supports falling away one by one." With nowhere else to turn, Razumov suddenly steadies himself for an interview with General T— who "was perfectly capable of shutting him up in the fortress for an indefinite time" (119). Apparently he is ready for uninhibited confession.

But in place of General T— awaits Councilor Mikulin, and in their strained interview Razumov is recruited by sympathy and his own political rationalizations into the czarist secret police. The full details are not revealed until Part IV, but his bad faith is symbolically recorded when Razumov "beheld his own brain suffering on the rack — a long pale figure drawn asunder — whose face he failed to see" (121). This hallucination that merges his brain with the half-disclosed face of Haldin might serve as an image of Conrad's tortured conscience. And like his creator, Razumov's mode of exorcism is a wail of reactionary hysteria: "I hated him! Visionaries work everlasting evil on earth. Their Utopias inspire in the mass of mediocre minds a disgust of reality and contempt for the secular logic of human development" (127). But he has no heart for pursuing this in action, and Part I ends with Mikulin's sinister reply to his wish to "retire" from politics: "Where to?"[118] This question echoes unanswered throughout the novel, for whether the political scene is totalitarian Russia or democratic Europe, *Under Western Eyes* offers no escape from commitment, no sanctuary.[119]

Part II opens in Geneva, with an abrupt shift of perspective that parallels Conrad's own "jump" from a revolutionary graveyard to the perils of exile. And the loss of tension is extreme. Now the issues are deadlocked by talk, stillborn, as the simple "great heart" of Natalia Haldin, who, safely removed from the stage of revolutionary action, is pitted against Conrad's own "cynical" judgment expressed by the English professor of languages. They gently jostle each other, resuming in a mode of over-polite opposition the censored self-debate Conrad rendered with such dramatic daring in Part I. Before Razumov's disruptive reentry into the novel, the Englishman declares what is usually regarded as Conrad's own unequivocal bias on revolution:

> The last thing I want to tell you is this: in a real revolution — not a simple dynastic change or mere reform of institutions — in a real revolution the best characters do not come to the front. A violent

> revolution falls into the hands of narrow-minded fanatics and of tyrannical hypocrites at first. Afterwards comes the turn of all the pretentious intellectual failures of the time. Such are the chiefs and the leaders. You will notice that I have left out the mere rogues. The scrupulous and the just, the noble, humane, and devoted natures; the unselfish and the intelligent may begin a movement — but it passes away from them. They are not the leaders of a revolution. They are its victims: the victims of disgust, of disenchantment — often of remorse. Hopes grotesquely betrayed, ideals caricatured — that is the definition of revolutionary success. (158)

Given the nightmare of Bolshevism to descend upon Russia in the next decade, we might be tempted to credit this passage with a clairvoyant modernity; yet in the world of *Under Western Eyes* it won't do. As George Orwell observed, "All revolutions are failures, but they are not the same failure."[120] By reducing revolution to a determined cycle of failure, the passage frees us from any need to fathom political complexities, and returns us to Conrad's letters to Spiridion Kilszczewski twenty-five years earlier. It would have nothing to say about oppression in czarist Russia, for instance; and the Englishman is struck impotent by Natalia Haldin's valiant reply: "I believe you hate revolution . . . You belong to a people which has made a bargain with fate and wouldn't like to be rude to it . . . I would take liberty from any hand as a hungry man would snatch at a piece of bread" (157-58). By using a platitudinous mouthpiece to gloss over his deeper links with the Russians, Conrad strains to shore up his own "bargain with fate"; however, over and again the Englishman is subjected to one blundering irony after another — cast adrift in a political intrigue that exposes his utter irrelevance.

This process is initiated by Razumov's political "romance" with Natalia, which leaves the Englishman feeling "altogether out of it, on another plane where I could only watch her from afar" (185). He loses his self-righteousness, starts to reflect an uneasy conscience, and acknowledges "it is not for us, the staid lovers calmed by the possession of a conquered liberty, to condemn without appeal the fierceness of thwarted desire" (181). The rudeness Razumov shows him reflects the political vacuity of his lost ambition to be a celebrated professor, and likewise, this prompts in the Englishman a "mistaken" yet prophetic flash of insight: "He puts on the callousness of a stern revolutionist, the insensibility to common emotions of a man devoted to a destructive idea . . . " (200) Now the stage is set for Razumov's verification, and Part II leaves him gazing from a bridge into a reflection of his own mind:

> He hung well over the parapet, as if captivated by the smooth rush of the blue water under the arch. The current there is swift, extremely swift; it makes some people dizzy; I myself can never look at it for any length of time without experiencing a dread of being suddenly snatched away by its destructive force. Some brains cannot resist the suggestion of irresistible power and of headlong motion. It apparently had a charm for Mr. Razumov. (206)

This charm for his own destruction is what we can intuit from Razumov's "headlong" behavior in Part III. Admittedly it is speculation. His alignment with the czarist secret police might reflect a desire to clear himself as a suspect, or a need to confirm his hatred for Haldin by reenacting the crime on his kindred spirits in Geneva. A more inadmissible reason is a need to seek out those with most right to destroy him. In fact, what Razumov calls his "mock-career" becomes necessary only after he has choked an impulse to confess to Mikulin himself: "Go back! What for? Confess! To what? . . . Establish a false complicity and destroy what chance of safety I have won for nothing — what folly!" (284) But this is exactly what he achieves among the Russian émigrés, when he talks with savage curtness to Peter Ivanovitch and Sophia Antonovna. "All sincerity was an imprudence," he warns himself. "*Yet one could not renounce truth altogether* (emphasis mine)." Yet what is the truth? Simply that the suspicion Razumov reads in the émigrés is largely imagined, that his unwise loquacity and suspicious seclusion seem designed to provoke that suspicion, that it is a compulsion he will not recognize and cannot control. "Even as he spoke he reproached himself for his words, for his tone. All day long he had been saying the wrong things. It was folly, worse than folly. It was weakness; it was this disease of perversity overcoming his will" (250). His spiral of duplicities continues right up to when he gains an outward immunity from suspicion with Sophia Antonovna's news of Ziemianitch's suicide by hanging. He scorns her ascription of motive: "Remorse." He welcomes his "perfect safety" with its "freedom from direct lying." Yet it is precisely this piece of good luck that frustrates Razumov's confessional urge, forcing him to take responsibility for his own unmasking. Initially the drunken Ziemianitch served as ironic commentary on Haldin's idealism, but now his "conscientious" suicide in a sense confirms that martyr's estimate of him, which is why Razumov must ascribe it to a brawl over a woman. When this self-deception falls away, he is returned once more to his own revolutionary complicity — "Why the devil did I go to that house? It was an imbecile thing to do" — and instructed by the example of Ziemianitch, he is now ready to call down retribution upon his head.

This is partially disclosed in Part IV of *Under Western Eyes*. For the first time Razumov's official mission is clarified as the narrative flashes back reluctantly — "there is always something ungracious — even disgraceful — in the exhibition of naked truth" — to his recruitment by Councilor Mikulin. It is not hard to discern in this paternalistic figure a final reincarnation of Tadeusz Bobrowski, and like him, Mikulin makes his appeal to moderation instead of dangerous revolutionary alternatives:

> I understand your liberalism. I have an intellect of that kind myself. Reform for me is mainly a question of method. But the principle of revolt is a physical intoxication, a sort of hysteria which must be kept away from the masses. You agree to this without reserve, don't you? . . . We live in difficult times, in times of monstrous chimeras and evil dreams and criminal follies . . . Things are ordered in a wonderful manner . . . You have been already the instrument of Providence. You smile, Kirylo Sidorovitch; you are an *esprit fort*. (Razumov was not conscious of having smiled.) (282-83)

His "unconscious" smile here is Razumov's recognition of the unreality of Mikulin's views, which gloss over what is passive complicity in czarist tyranny.[121] But he yields when later in his room he can mutter to himself: "And, after all, I might have been the chosen

Joseph Conrad

instrument of Providence . . . What if that absurd saying were true in its essence?" (287) Now he is trapped for good in mendacities as the narrative retreats to a safe distance:

> This much said, there is no need to tell anything more of that first interview and of the several others. To the morality of a Western reader an account of these meetings would wear perhaps the sinister character of old legendary tales where the Enemy of Mankind is represented holding subtly mendacious dialogues with some tempted soul. It is not my part to protest. Let me but remark that the Evil One, with his single passion of satanic pride for the only motive, is yet, on a larger, modern view, allowed to be not quite so black as he used to be painted. With what greater latitude, then, should we appraise the exact shade of mere mortal man, with his many passions and his miserable ingenuity in error, always dazzled by the base glitter of mixed motives, everlastingly betrayed by a shortsighted wisdom. (290)

Now the flashback ends and we rejoin Razumov on an island in a Geneva park, now *writing* for the first time to Mikulin, and with a bronze effigy of Rousseau keeping vigil overhead.[122] And isn't this a visual analogue to Conrad's own career as a political writer, exhorted to revolution by his heritage yet isolated in the insipid West, writing novels that seem in harmony with Mikulin's views, yet underneath are confessions of "miserable ingenuity in error," exposing "the base glitter of mixed motives," and with the author himself "everlastingly betrayed by a shortsighted wisdom"? Razumov now, in any case, "could not believe in the reality of his mission," and crushing his notes in his fist, he leaves the park to find Natalia Haldin and unburden himself.

If this surmise is correct, then it helps to unknot the odd puzzle of Razumov's two confessions: the first verbal and offstage to Haldin's mother, the second written to Natalia.[123] Confronting her, he speaks with a turgid incomprehensibility. Only when he touches his own chest does Natalia realize she is looking at the betrayer of her brother, whereupon Razumov retires and returns that night to deliver his diary:

> He, this man who robbed me of my hardworking, purposeful

existence. I, too, had my guiding idea; and remember that, amongst us, it is more difficult to lead a life of toil and self-denial than to go out in the street and kill from conviction . . . I had to confirm myself in my contempt and hate for what I had betrayed . . . Listen — now comes the true confession. The other was nothing. To save me, your trustful eyes had to entice my thought to the very edge of blackest treachery . . . Victor Haldin had stolen the truth of my life from me . . . He talked of you, of your lonely, helpless state, and every word of that friend of yours was egging me on to the unpardonable sin of stealing a soul. Could he have been the devil himself in the shape of an old Englishman? NataliaVictorovna, I was possessed . . . Your light! Your truth! I felt that I must tell you that I had ended by loving you. And to tell you that I must first confess. (331-33)

Razumov is lying here; indeed this is an astonishing piece of authorial censorship that *blots out* the depth of his crime, which is not against just a single man but a whole network of moral-political impulses. Now we are asked to believe Razumov has a clean conscience on that score, that his real mission in Geneva has been to steal Natalia's soul to further his legitimate vengeance, that he was undone by his falling in love with her. But this is sheer melodrama, palpable nonsense belied by both the subtle characterization and sympathetic rendering we have had of Razumov until now. Natalia's adulation of her brother's "comrade" may speak of love, but there has been no convincing trace of reciprocal love on his part. Conrad is resorting to the same sleight of mind Razumov used to escape self-damnation earlier when he strained to interpret Zimianitch's suicide as "a drama of love, not of conscience." Since he does radiate guilt, pretending at the last instant to a scandalous diabolism, thus reviving "the old Father of Lies — our national patron — whom we take with us when we go abroad," is clearly a means whereby Razumov can emerge as a romantic villain rather than a political traitor.[124]

The flaw in characterization is a measure of Conrad's own identification with Razumov. It is darkly relevant that for the first time he is speaking for the young Russian in the first person and that the diary is delivered in Natalia's veil. For as we are warned that night he decided to betray Haldin: "Now and then a fatal conjunction of events may lift the veil for an instant. For an instant only. *No human being could bear a steady view of moral solitude without going mad* (emphasis mine)" (83). This is why the truth must remain veiled, why Razumov, who let his "brother" wander off to certain death and whom he is vainly trying to replace in Geneva, must continue to elevate his moment of weakness into an act of political sanity. This is the "moral discovery" at the heart of *Under Western Eyes*, the truth behind Razumov's final outcry: "It was myself, after all, that I betrayed most basely" (333).

Perhaps this is why his "confession" is no more purgative than it is convincing, and why he can find peace only by delivering himself over to the émigrés assembled at the house of Julius Laspara.[125] They alone can be the suitable agents of Haldin's revenge. Only when his self-accusations have been silenced by his deafening by Nikita, another secret agent, can Razumov regard his mission as over. Sophia Antonovna's tribute to him afterwards accurately traces his moral growth: "But tell me, how many of them would deliver themselves up deliberately to perdition . . . rather than go on living, secretly debased in their own eyes?" (337) There is even a hint of Razumov's "re-conversion" too, especially in his final role as patron saint of the revolutionists. At last glance this tortured soul, who initially "had his being in the *willed*, in the *determined* future — in that future menaced by . . . the lawlessness of revolution," is paid homage in his retreat in southern Russia by revolutionists seeking amends and inspiration: "He is intelligent. He has ideas . . . He talks well, too" (347). Mistaken by them as "one of us" in St. Petersburg and Geneva, Razumov ultimately earns their acceptance upon by his submission to retributive justice.

The work of critical detection also calls into question Conrad's scorn for the Russian émigrés in Geneva. Are they really "apes of a sinister jungle" as he says in his Author's Note?[126] Understanding, even the warmth of admiration filters through willful disgust in his portrait of Sophia Antonovna. Her humane selflessness has been proven by action rather than arrogant ideology; indeed she has "outlived all that nonsense . . . " Nor is Sophia Antonovna quite as wrong-headed as Conrad claims in his Author's Note. She came to Geneva to verify an identity, and she does so in her masterful session with Razumov that ends Part III. There his scorn gradually yields to curiosity, then grudging respect, as the mature Sophia re-educates him into the truth about revolution: "The subservient, submissive life. Life? No! Vegetation on the filthy heap of iniquity which the world is. Life, Razumov, not to be vile must be a revolt — a pitiless protest — all the time" (256). His silence seals this truth, but due to his "unique case," Razumov now drifts into that same region of fatalism that we have seen his creator adopt all his political life to shore up his bargain with fate:

> As if anything could be changed! In this world of men nothing can be changed — neither happiness nor misery. They can only be displaced at the cost of corrupted consciences and broken lives — a futile game for arrogant philosophers and sanguinary triflers. (256)

But to his chagrin, a sanguinary trifler is exactly what Sophia Antonovna is not, and once she announces Ziemianitch's suicide, shrewdly identifying his "devil" as "some police-hound in disguise," Razumov verifies her theory with his confession to her comrades.

The other female revolutionary, Tekla, wins our affection as a simple paragon of suffering and compassion. At the end it is she who calmly accepts the role of nurse and companion to the punished Razumov. In doing so she finds a suitable "double" for her earlier revolutionary lover who informed on his comrades under torture by the czarist police and who was released into Tekla's care to suffer "his remorse stoically" and in isolation. "He ought to have trusted in his political friends when he came out of prison," she tells Razumov earlier. "He had been liked and respected before, and nobody would have dreamed of reproaching him with his indiscretion before the police" (173). Indeed from the start Razumov's declared "hatred" of Haldin has been rooted more in personal shame and loss than political opposition. Gazing on Haldin's mother he asks himself: " ... was it something like enviousness which gripped his heart, as a privilege denied to him alone of all men that had ever passed through this world?" (317) Once he at last secures these lost privileges — both the forgiveness of the revolutionaries and the maternal caresses of Tekla — his reactionary scorn evaporates and he slides into an easeful drift toward death.

But Conrad reserves most of his sympathy for Natalia Haldin, whose valiant "soul" stays faithful to the tragic course of revolution inside Russia:

> That is the true task of real agitators. One has got to give up one's life to it. The degradation of servitude, the absolutist lies must be uprooted and swept out. Reform is impossible. There is nothing to reform. There is no legality, there are no institutions. There are only arbitrary decrees. There is only a handful of cruel — perhaps blind — officials against a nation. (157)

Because the liberal credo he tacks to his wall after the betrayal is a brittle evasion of these realities, Razumov can politically court Natalia but not win her. It is largely because she is banished to the sidelines by her sex that Conrad can pay tribute to her idealism, while seeming to denounce the same in her martyred brother. For the same reason, unfortunately, she remains inert, waxes static against the flow of action. Natalia's hope of reconciliation is moving, yet in the world of *Under Western Eyes* more a naive wish than anything else: "I believe that the future will be merciful to us all. Revolutionist and reactionary, victim and executioner, betrayer and betrayed, they shall all be pitied together when the light breaks on our black sky at last" (327).

Even Peter Ivanovitch, the "peacock" leader of the Russian émigrés, is handled with some equivocation.[127] On the personal side he is ungently mocked: he is patient and flattering before Razumov and Sophia Antonovna, but his feminism is inseparable from domineering vanity before Tekla.[128] Yet allegations of hypocrisy and vanity, as we might recognize from *The Secret Agent*, are for Conrad covertly self-referential; and on political matters Peter Ivanovitch's views have the ring and bite of truth about them: "For us . . . there yawns a chasm between the past and the future. It can never be bridged by foreign liberalism. All attempts at it are either folly or cheating. Bridged it can never be! It has to be filled up." (217) It is revealing that he serves to discredit revolution when prudently self-exiled in Geneva, but proves a far more attractive figure when the narrative returns him to his dramatic past in Russia. The ironic account of his daring trek across Siberia is leavened with a vividness, humor, and sympathy that is unmistakable. And by surviving what Razumov feared most, captivity there, he is able to ward off "an absurd form of morbid pessimism, a form of temporary insanity, originating perhaps in the physical worry and discomfort of the chain" (149). Ultimately, all the potential for moral heroism rests with the revolutionaries. Again when Peter Ivanovitch is projected into the future, our earlier grounds for dismissing him have vanished. By returning to Russia at tremendous risk to live devotedly with a peasant girl, he has in some measure earned the tribute paid to him by Sophia Antonovna: "Peter Ivanovitch is an inspired man."

FOR CONRAD THERE WAS no such touch of grace. He remained marooned in England, recovering slowly from his brush with madness and filled with an abiding fear of its return. Actually he had been living with this fear throughout his most productive decade. "I have long fits of depression that in a lunatic asylum would be called madness," he wrote to Garnett as early as 1896. "I do not know what it is. It springs from nothing. It is ghastly. It lasts an hour or a day and when it departs it leaves a fear."[129] Conrad was challenging that fear in his political works, starting in far-off Costaguana, shifting to the squalid London slums, and then returning to the frozen terror of pre-revolutionary Russia. Each step in this progression was a new surrender of psychic distance, a zeroing in on his survivor guilt — issuing in the horrible nightmare of *Under Western Eyes.*

Most critics agree that Conrad's fiction never recovered, and neither did his politics.[130] His response to World War I was that of a stolid wartime Englishman, filled with bravado and jingoistic pride.[131] Instead of welcoming the outbreak of the Russian Revolution in 1917, as he had the October Revolution in St. Petersburg in 1905, he reacted with a climax of reactionary hysteria, bemoaning the "great cataclysmic forces" on the loose, and actually urging Western intervention by appealing to the moralism of the English tradition.[132] After the war, the most nationalistic proposal he could muster on behalf of his native land was its incorporation as an Anglo-French Protectorate.[133] Even this timid commitment was more verbal than real, for according to Joseph Retinger, when pressed into action in support of Poland, Conrad responded with what now defined his entire way of dealing with the world: "*Il ne faut pas alter contre le courant des choses.*"[134]

During the first decade of the 20th century, Conrad's artistic purpose was exactly the opposite of this, and his decline must be measured against his persisting courage during this period. "Confronted by the ... enigmatic spectacle," he wrote in 1897, "the artist descends within himself, and in that lonely region of stress and strife, if he be deserving and fortunate, he finds the terms of his appeal."[135] Few writers have found this descent more perilous, and yet Conrad managed to rescue from his private hell such superbly curious and insightful works as *Nostromo*, *The Secret Agent*, and *Under Western Eyes*. Whether focused on colonialism, espionage, or totalitarianism, these novels offer a "moral discovery" that subverts traditional political categories. Instead we are engaged as readers in making the discovery for ourselves, often against the undertow of Conrad's willed intentions. We find here a harbinger of our own political world — with its widespread injustice, its totalitarian reach, its secret police, its fear and loneliness, its decadent legalism, its wake of corrupted consciences and broken lives. There is no expiatory truth emerging from these novels, but something less tangible and more profound. For Conrad makes us feel what it is like to be human in a world tyrannized by political imperatives that are either beneath or beyond our capacities, but cannot be escaped. This is the source of his enduring appeal, indeed his warning. Locked in a world where the self is being relentlessly assaulted or seduced by political exigencies, we can learn much by listening to him.

NOTES

1 Quoted by Michael S. Reynolds in *Hemingway's First War* (Princeton: Princeton University Press, 1976), 60.

2 In his essay on Henry James, Conrad compared his labors as a writer to "rescue work carried out in darkness against cross gusts of wind swaying the action of a great multitude," a "snatching of vanishing phrases of turbulence, disguised in fair words, out of a native obscurity into a light where the struggling forms may be seen, seized upon, endowed with the only possible form of permanence in this world of relative values — the permanence of memory." Quoted by Jean-Aubry, G., *Joseph Conrad: Life and Letters, II* (Garden City: Doubleday, 1925), 13.

3 For an elaboration of the thesis that Conrad's political novels are efforts in symbolic disguise to expiate his sense of guilt over deviating from the Polish national cause, see Gustav Morf's underrated *The Polish Shades and Ghosts of Joseph Conrad* (Astra Books: New York, 1976). For corroboration of this thesis, see Bernard Meyer's *Joseph Conrad: A Psychoanalytic Biography* (Princeton: Princeton University Press, 1967), 202-20, 281-7. Further support is provided by a contemporary Polish writer, Czeslaw Milosz, who writes: "As we go more deeply into the biographical materials we come to the conclusion that a carefully hidden complex of treason is discernible in some of Conrad's writings — a feeling he had betrayed the cause so fanatically embraced by his compatriots and above all, by his father." See "Joseph Conrad in Polish Eyes," *Atlantic Monthly*, CC (November 1957), 219.

4 Conrad is most likely alluding to his father when he speaks of his "unconscious response to the still voice of that inexorable past from which his fiction and their personalities are remotely derived." See *A Personal Record* (New York: Harper, 1925), 20.

5 See Zdzislaw Najder's introductory essay in his *Conrad's Polish Background* (London: Oxford University Press, 1964) for an in-depth analysis of the political situation in Poland prior to the Insurrection of 1863.

6 Quoted by Najder, 5.

7 Quoted by Meyer, 24.

8 Quoted by Najder, 9.

9 *A Personal Record*, 36.

10 *Life and Letters, I*, 183.

11 Conrad conspired with his uncle, Tadeusz Bobrowski, to pretend that his wound from the abortive suicide was incurred in a duel over a woman, and wrote *The Arrow of Gold* to present the "romantic" version to his public. This "official" version was accepted without much question by Conrad's biographers, indeed became part of the Conrad legend for sixty years. Then in 1937, a letter came to light written by Bobrowksi on March 24, 1879 to Stefan Buszczynski, an old friend of Conrad's father, which remarks: "Let this detail remain between us, for I have told everyone that he was wounded in a duel." Apparently the young Conrad was involved in smuggling, not for the glorious cause of the Pretender, but for personal gain. And after losing every penny he went on to Monte Carlo, gambled himself further into debt, and returned to Marseilles where he tried to kill himself. Compare with Marlow's feverish misinterpretation of Jim's suicide as a "romantic triumph" in Patusan.

12 Preface to *A Personal Record*, ix.

13 Perhaps this accounts in part for the appalling fatality rate of Conrad's male characters. Meyer notes that in thirty-one stories, Conrad's males survive in only fourteen.

14 J.A. Gee and P.J. Sturm, *Letters of Joseph Conrad to Marguerite Poradowska, 1890-1920* (New Haven: Yale University Press, 1940), 72.

15 Najder observes that "to sympathize with Korzeniowski's desperate determination to subordinate his whole life to a common cause one had to understand his reasons and to share, at least partly, his beliefs. Bobrowski did not share them and hardly ever tried to discover what had led Apollo to his extreme political views. His idea of his brother-in-law as a woolly-headed sentimentalist, who pitied the poor but was not in fact a true democrat or a man who understood politics, is plainly belied by many of Korzeniowski's manuscripts." *Conrad's Polish Background*, 11. For a full exposition of Bobrowski's views, see his letter to Conrad of Nov. 1892 in Najder, 153-54.

16 Thus Bobrowski described Apollo's father Theodore as "nothing but a utopian," deriding him as a man who "considered himself a great politician and a supreme patriot; without listening to common sense he was always ready to saddle a horse and chase the enemy out of the country." Quoted by Jocelyn Baines, *Joseph Conrad, A Critical Biography* (London: Weidenfeld & Nicolson, 1960), 2.

17 Quoted by Najder from Bobrowski's *Memoirs*, 17.

18 Najder, 11.

19 *A Personal Record*, xix.

20 *Life and Letters*, I, 84.

21 *Ibid.*, 321.

22 What Conrad admitted about his gallery of political types seems to apply in equal measure to his more discursive and often "prophetic" pronouncements on contemporary politics — "Writing about them he is only writing about himself." See *A Personal Record*, xv.

23 "Prince Roman," *Tales of Hearsay* (New York, 1925), 48.

24 Gee and Sturm, 64.

25 *Ibid.*, 42.

26 *Life and Letters*, I, 216.

27 *Ibid.*, 222-23.

28 *Ibid.*, 229-30.

29 See Conrad's letter of August 14, 1896, in Edward Garnett's *Letters from Conrad, 1895-1924* (Indianapolis: BobbsMerrill, 1928).

30 *Ibid.*, 155.

31 Marvin Mudrick, ed., *Conrad: A Collection of Critical Essays* (Englewood Cliffs, N.J.: Prentice Hall, 1966), Introduction, 10.

32 Frederick Crews, "Conrad's Uneasiness and Ours," *Out of My System* (New York: Oxford University Press, 1975). My study is deeply indebted to Crews' essay, especially to the terms he coins (self-confrontation vs. self-exculpation) in order to fathom the sense of deadlock in Conrad's works.

33 *The Letters of T.E. Lawrence*, ed. David Garnett (London: Jonathan Cape, 1938), 301-02.

34 See Thomas Moser's *Joseph Conrad: Achievement and Decline* (Cambridge: Harvard University Press, 1957) for an excellent account of Conrad's struggle with the "uncongenial theme" of sexuality in his works.

35 Leo Gurko, *Joseph Conrad: Giant in Exile* (New York: Macmillan, 1979), 1.

36 Avrom Fleishman, *Conrad's Politics* (Baltimore: Johns Hopkins University Press, 1967), 69.

37 Irving Howe, *Politics and the Novel* (Chicago: Ivan R. Dee, 1957), 84.

38 The majority of Conrad's political critics, Leo Gurko. Eloise Hay, Avrom Fleishman, and Albert Guerard to name a few, accept as "sincere" his reactionary "views" embedded in his works. A refreshing exception is Irving Howe's excellent essay on Conrad in his *Politics and the Novel*.

39 See Gustov Morf's *The Polish Heritage of Joseph Conrad* (London: Sampson Low, 1930), 149-66.

40 *A Personal Record*, 12.

41 See Conrad's letter of Nov. 12, 1900 in Garnett's *Letters from Conrad, 1895-1924*.

42 It is astonishing how easily critics too fall into talk of Jim's "cowardice" on the *Patna* — as if it were reasonable to expect Everyman to be an ultimate moral hero, to sacrifice his life for a principle alone. Ultimately this view, which is Jim's, is precisely what is morbid, though admirable, about him.

43 In 1887, while he was serving as first mate on the *Highland Forest*, Conrad was struck on the back by a piece of rigging and immobilized in a Singapore hospital for three months. Conrad's own report on his ailment

in "The Mirror and the Sea" is revealing: "Thereupon followed various and unpleasant consequences of a physical order — 'queer symptoms,' as the captain, who treated them, used to say; inexplicable periods of powerlessness, sudden accesses of mysterious pain; and the patient agreed fully with the regretful mutters of his very attentive captain wishing it had been a straight-forward broken leg." This sounds very much like the post-traumatic neurotic reaction or attack of "Imagination" that Jim suffers after being struck by a falling spar.

44 Joseph Conrad, *Lord Jim* (New York: Alfred A. Knopf, 1935), 65. Page references in the text are to this edition.

45 "Yes!" Conrad wrote to Garnett on Nov. 12, 1900. "You've put your finger on the plague spot. The division of the book into two parts which is the basis of your criticism demonstrates to me once more your amazing insight; and your analysis of the effect of the book puts into words precisely and suggestively the dumb thoughts of every reader — and my own." *Letters from Conrad, 1895-1924.*

46 Thus, upon his arrival by canoe into the depths of Patusan, Jim is armed only with an unloaded revolver, a rather ambiguous precaution, since he has good reason to think that he is entering a hostile environment. Likewise, in order to prove his courage to the Bugis, Jim goes through the daily ritual of taking coffee with the treacherous Rajah, despite the real risk that it might be poisoned. Again, during his conduct of Doramin's martial campaigns, Jim recruits himself for the most dangerous missions, and offers his life as a ransom against their success. In all these instances, he seems to be searching out his own "romantic" self-destruction.

47 *Life and Letters,* I, 270.

48 Jewel's mother was forced to make an unsatisfactory marriage with Cornelius, but before then she was implicated in a "mysterious" way with Stein. "And the woman is dead now," Stein remarks "incomprehensibly" when he first tells Marlow about Patusan. And Marlow goes on: "Of course I don't know that story. I can only guess that once before Patusan had been used as a grave for some sin, transgression, or misfortune. It is impossible to suspect Stein." And yet the fact that Jewel's mother died "weeping" intimates that Stein abandoned her in his pursuit of the "dream," in the same way that Conrad felt that his father was responsible for his mother's death.

49 Conrad returned from the Congo afflicted by the darkest melancholy. He entered a London hospital, and failing to improve there, was advised to undertake a course of hydrotherapy in a sanitarium near Geneva, Switzerland.

50 Joseph Conrad, "Geographers and Some Explorers," *Last Essays* (London: J.M. Dent and Sons, 1955), 18.

51 For a brilliant study of King Leopold's colonization of the Congo, a story of murder and greed cloaked in humanitarian sentiments, see Adam Hochschild's *King Leopold's Ghost* (New York: Mariner Books, 1999), especially pp. 140-49 dealing with Conrad's trip there.

52 *Life and Letters*, I, 268.

53 Joseph Conrad, *Heart of Darkness and Other Tales* (New York: Oxford University Press, 2002), 107. Page references in the text are to this edition.

54 The autobiographical reference among the many characters Marlow meets in his journey to Kurtz is quite astonishing. Thus the air of "intrigue" at the Central Station, vaguely directed at "taking advantage" of Kurtz's rumored illness at the Inner Station, alludes to the political feud in Conrad's political heritage. The "paper-mache Mephistopheles" speaks of Kurtz as a "prodigy" whose belief in "pity, and science, and progress" for the persecuted "natives" should be replaced by a more repressive policy. Described as "young, gentlemanly, a bit reserved, with a forked little beard," this villain is in large measure a derisive self-portrait, recipient of the hatred Conrad must have harbored for his "reactionary" posings.

55 The uncle of the manager would appear to be an allusion to Tadeusz Bobrowski, who will find many reincarnations in Conrad's political novels.

56 Conrad himself admitted in his unguarded moments the role of the "unconscious" in his work. When Garnett suggested alterations to *An Outcast of the Islands*, Conrad replied in 1895: "Nothing can now unmake my mistake. I shall try—but I shall try without faith, because all my work is produced unconsciously (so to speak) and I cannot meddle to any purpose with what is within myself."

57 Jocelyn Baines, despite a perceptive analysis, throws in the towel when it comes to explaining Marlow's "unconscious loyalty" to Kurtz: "His motive for this is obscure to himself... Conrad did not choose to develop Marlow's reasons for this loyalty..." *Joseph Conrad, A Critical Biography*, 222-30. And Douglas Hewitt leaves us with the same teasing riddle: "It is useless to ask what is the quality in Kurtz which is absent in the pilgrims. In one sense he is no more than the logical culmination of the hollowness of them all..." *Conrad: A Reassessment* (Totowa, N.J.: Rowman & Littlefield, 1975), 24.

58 Hochschild writes: "Mr. Kurtz was clearly inspired by several real people, among them Georges Antoine Klein, a French agent for an ivory-gathering firm at Stanley Falls. Klein, mortally ill, died on shipboard, as Kurtz does in the novel, while Conrad was piloting the *Roi des Belges* down the river. Another model closer to Kurtz in character was Major Edmund Barttelot, the man whom Stanley left in charge of the rear column on the Emin Pasha expedition. It was Barttelot... who went mad, began biting, whipping, and killing people, and was finally murdered. Yet another Kurtz prototype was a Belgian, Arthur Hodister, famed for his harem of African women and for gathering huge amounts of ivory. Hodister eventually muscled in too aggressively on the territory of local Afro-Arab warlords and ivory-traders, who captured and beheaded him. However, Conrad's legion of biographers and critics have almost entirely ignored the man who resembles Kurtz most closely of all... the swashbuckling Captain Leon Rom of the Force Publique. It is from Rom that Conrad may have taken the signal feature of his villain: the collection of African heads surrounding Kurtz's house." *King Leopold's Ghost*, 145-46. Hochschild go on to establish the likelihood that Conrad read news-journal accounts of Rom, and furthermore, that the two may have met in the Congo.

59 I am indebted to Frederick Crews for making clear the reference of Kurtz to Apollo Korzeniowski. See *Out of My System*, 59-60, 193-94.

60 "Marlow finds Kurtz attended by a remarkably boyish Russian," writes Crews, "a 'harlequin' with a peeling nose, who sits at Kurtz's feet and tries to think the best of him, as the well-bred, inwardly unforgiving Conrad must have done with his father in Russia. This figure of submission had formerly been rebellious against his father, an arch-priest; he 'had run away from school, had gone to sea in a Russian ship; ran away again; served some time in English ships; was now reconciled with the arch-priest. He made a point of that.' Beyond question this is Conrad's own

story, with the difference that Conrad finds reconciliation less feasible." *Out of My System*, 194.

61 Letter of December, 21, 1903; Zdzislaw Najder, *Joseph Conrad: A Chronicle* (New Brunswick: Rutgers University Press, 1983), 295.

62 *Ibid.*, 296.

63 *Life and Letters*, I, 285.

64 *Ibid.*, 288.

65 Ford Maddox Ford, *Joseph Conrad: A Personal Remembrance* (London: Duckworth, 1924), 70.

66 Morf points out that the 3rd of May, the one date mentioned in *Nostromo* — the holiday of an important battle — is the National Day of Poland. Likewise, as the ship *Patna* echoes its reference, Poland, so Sulaco appears to refer to Cracow, the capital of Poland. Morf shows convincingly that *Nostromo* "is one of the best examples of the compensatory function of artistic creation. All the repressed Polish reminiscences, sentiments, aspirations, and resentments, lying deep under the surface of the artist's conscious mind, had their day of rehabilitation when this book was written." *The Polish Heritage of Joseph Conrad*, 148.

67 Conrad received a copy of his uncle's *Memoirs* immediately after its publication in 1900. In his Author's Note, he remarks that before taking on *Nostromo* he had been afflicted by the sense "that there was nothing more in the world to write about." Perhaps, then, it was his reading of the *Memoirs* that inspired him. In Poland the volume created an uproar, being full of malicious gossip and scornful opinions about most of the people Bobrowski knew. Najder remarks that "the frustration of a clever man, self-confident to the point of conceit, who never achieved anything 'great' and was never sufficiently appreciated by his contemporaries, is clearly seen." *Conrad's Polish Background*, 143.

68 Joseph Conrad, *Nostromo* (New York: Alfred A. Knopf, 1957), 39. Page references in the text are to this edition.

69 *Life and Letters*, II, 84.

70 Albert Guerard, *Conrad the Novelist* (Cambridge: Harvard University

Press, 1958), 176.

71 F.R. Leavis in *The Great Tradition* (London: Chatto and Windus, 1948) accounts for this "hollow" reverberation by citing the novel's lack of "the day-to-day continuities of social living," but I suspect it has more to do with the "vibrant melodrama" he finds so edifying.

72 The disrupted narrative design of *Nostromo* has raised conflicting responses from critics. Guerard remarks that the digressions in fact convey very little information and ask us "to record too many visual impressions." *Conrad the Novelist*, 180. Eloise Hay too complains that the "disorderly presentation of material contributes to the novel's dramatic impenetrability." *The Political Novels of Joseph Conrad* (Chicago: University of Chicago Press, 1963), 176. And Baines argues that the "elimination of progression from one event to another ... has the effect of implying that nothing is ever achieved." *Joseph Conrad, A Critical Biography*, 301. Surely Baines is correct on this point, yet it is time to admit that Conrad's often-praised "aesthetic" techniques are often more muddled than sophisticated, that he was simply not in control much of the time.

73 Conrad wrote to Ernest Bendz in 1923: "Nostromo has never been intended for the hero of the *Tale of the Seaboard*. Silver is the pivot of the moral and material events." *Life and Letters*, II, 296.

74 I am indebted to Irving Howe for his discussion of this aspect of *Nostromo*. For an application of Trotsky's notion of "permanent revolution" to the political situation in Costaguana, see *Politics and the Novel*, 101-03.

75 Howe remarks that "Conrad has struck exactly upon the note of fanatical solemnity which is to vibrate through the bloody comedies of Latin American politics." *Politics and the Novel*, 102.

76 In his loyalty to the masses, his Christian zeal, his severe enthusiasm for justice, his reckless and quixotic activism, and his ultimate alliance with the new revolutionists, Father Corbellan too bears a striking resemblance to Apollo Korzeniowski. It is all the more significant, then, that he should bear the banner of political rectitude at the conclusion of *Nostromo*.

77 Conrad had an irrepressible antipathy for the blatant imperialist policies of the U.S. during this period, especially the thievery of the Roosevelt administration. The Spanish-American War incensed him, and in 1898 he

wrote in *Blackwood's Magazine*: "If one could set the States and Germany by the ears... That would be real fine. I am afraid however that the thieves shall agree in the Philippines. The pity of it!" Quoted by Hay, 167.

78 For a discussion of the parallels between Costaguana and later political developments in Columbia and Panama, see Fleishman, 169-70.

79 See Conrad's Preface to *The Nigger of the Narcissus*.

80 Apparently at one time Conrad was considering a career of business ventures in America. "By Jove!" he wrote to Graham in 1907. "If I had the necessary talent, I would like to go for the true anarchist, which is the millionaire. But it's too big a job." *Life and Letters*, II, 60.

81 Psychologically speaking, Signora Teresa is Nostromo's "mother," and in having him refuse to honor her dying request for a priest, Conrad would seem to be alluding to his own sense of disgrace before the revolutionary voice of his mother and his irrational feeling that he was somehow responsible for her death. See Meyer, 68.

82 By externalizing Nostromo's motives onto the "evil spirit" of the silver, Conrad would seem to be alluding to his career as a smuggler far away from the arena of revolution during his Marseilles period.

83 We are told Giorgio Viola had "lost" a son for whom clearly Nostromo becomes a psychological substitute. It is appropriate, then, that Viola should "execute" him when he betrays his revolutionary consciousness.

84 Compare with Conrad's own reactionary journalism whose secret scorn is for the causes he seems to espouse.

85 Guerard remarks with unfocused suspicion: "There is, generally, a marked discrepancy between what Decoud does and says and is, and what the narrator or omniscient author says about him." *Conrad the Novelist*, 199.

86 *Life and Letters*, II, 40.

87 *Ibid.*, 84.

88 Joseph Conrad, *The Secret Agent* (New York: Alfred A. Knopf, 1961), xxviii. Page references in the text are to this edition.

89 Ford claimed that the famous Russian double agent, Evno Azef, rather than the French anarchist Bourdin's exploit in Greenwich Park, was the original of Conrad's Adolf Verloc. For a discussion of these "documentary sources" behind the novel, see Ian Watt's "The Political and Social Background of *The Secret Agent*" in his *Essays on Conrad* (Cambridge: Cambridge University Press, 2000), 112-26.

90 Jessie Conrad, *Joseph Conrad As I Knew Him* (Garden City, N.J.: Doubleday, 1926), 53.

91 *Ibid.*, 122.

92 For a further discussion of Conrad's tactics of "dehumanization" in *The Secret Agent*, see Jeffrey Herman's *Joseph Conrad: Writing as Rescue* (New York: Astra Books, 1977), 110-28. Berman, however, does not see the complex web of political duplicity out of which these tactics were generated in Conrad's case.

93 *Life and Letters*, I, 60.

94 Yundt is perhaps the most scathing of the self-portraits of the gout-ridden Conrad. He is called a "senile sensualist," and while it may shock some Conradians, Meyer lays bare the sexual aberrations of Conrad and gives some evidence that his *Arrow of Gold* and love scenes in some of his other novels were "inspired" by a reading of *Venus in Furs*, Sacher-Masoch's pornographic classic of this period. See *Joseph Conrad: A Psychoanalytic Biography*, 291-316.

95 Michaelis's humanitarianism bears a faint if wacky resemblance to Korzeniowski's idealism, and while this "apostle" has succumbed to "resignation," he offers a perfect rejoinder to Conrad's "scare tactics" against revolution in *The Secret Agent*: "No one can tell what form the social organization may take in the future. Then why indulge in prophetic fantasies. At best they can only interpret the mind of the prophet, and can have no objective value. *Leave that pastime to the moralists, my boy* (emphasis mine)" (46).

96 Ossipon's confidence in hygienic science as a mode of perception is challenged by virtually every underlying truth in the tale.

97 This is usually taken by critics as the voice of Conrad, but it is followed

immediately by "Lost for a whole minute in the abyss of meditation, Mr. Verloc did not reach the depth of these abstract considerations. Perhaps he was not able" (55).

98 The "cynical" artist, Conrad wrote in 1908, will make a "mere declaration, not of the vanity of things (that would be a too optimistic view), but of the utter futility of existence. Pessimism can go no further." *Life and Letters, II*, 77-78.

99 It is no accident that Mr. Verloc's shop on Brett Street, supposedly an "anarchist" stronghold, is actually in the business of selling pornography. Such was the scorn Conrad held for his own political duplicities. Mr. Verloc's name, in French, suggests a syphilitic.

100 This would seem to be the Russian Embassy, Poland's oppressor, and the strategy of *The Secret Agent*, as well as its imagery, was anticipated by Conrad a full decade earlier defining the effect of Garnett's words of criticism for *The Rescue*: "They exploded like stored powder barrels — while another man's words would have fizzled out in speaking and left darkness unrelieved by a forgotten spurt of futile sparks. An explosion is the most lasting thing in the universe. It leaves disorder, remembrance, room to move, a clear space. Ask your Nihilist friends. But I am afraid you haven't blown me to pieces. I am afraid I am like the Russian governmental system. It will take a good many bursting charges to make me change my ways." *Letters from Conrad*, 79.

101 Hay suggests that Conrad is caricaturing himself in the German Ambassador Stott-Wartenheim. Actually, as his name suggests (a stuttering stay-at-home), Stott-Wartenheim is an allusion to Tadeusz Bobrowski, the anti-revolutionary "boss-man" of the duplicitous Conrad-Verloc.

102 Vladimir's vision of irrationalism used to wield control over a demoralized public mass has found its disciples in brands of both revolutionary violence and Fascist oppression in our own era.

103 *Life and Letters, I*, 269.

104 For a full discussion of the "family romance" configuration in *The Secret Agent*, see Meyer, 185-96.

105 In *Lord Jim* (Brierly) and *Nostromo* (Captain Mitchell) timepieces

"stop" at moments of moral failure, an attempt to stave off the return of these repressed memories. The reactionary plot to attack "Time" at the Greenwich Observatory can be viewed as Conrad's wry symbolic admission that he was trying to "freeze" history and "paralyze" action in severing himself from his guilt-edged revolutionary loyalties.

106 *Life and Letters*, II, 60.

107 "I have been charged," Conrad wrote, "with the want of patriotism, the want of sense, and the want of heart too . . . and have been called an 'incorrigible Don Quixote', in allusion to the book-born madness of the knight." *A Personal Record*, 44.

108 Stevie's name can be traced back to Conrad's own cousin, the "ultra-democratic" Stanislaw Bobrowski, who was arrested, tried, and sentenced to prison in St. Petersburg in 1892. On the other hand, Stevie is also, by way of Mr. Verloc, Conrad's fictional "son," and a clue to the origin of his stutter is contained in a letter to Galsworthy in which Conrad wrote: "Poor B. (Borys) stutters painfully on some days and on others not at all. Something will have to be done with his nose and throat." Quoted by Meyer, 194.

109 The epithet "queer foreign fish" is Conrad's wry allusion to himself as an exile in England. As he wrote in his Author's Note: "For the surroundings (for the tale) hints were not lacking. I had to fight hard to keep at arm's length the memories of my solitary and nocturnal walks all over London in my early days, lest they should rush in and overwhelm each page of the story as they emerged one after another from a mood as serious in feeling and thought as any in which I ever wrote a line." Thus the Assistant Commissioner tells Toodles he is using Mr. Verloc as bait to catch a "whale," but clarifies this by admitting his own target is a "witty fish." This would seem a derisive call for the self-revelation of the author.

110 "A novelist lives in his work . . ." Conrad wrote "the only reality in an invented world . . . Writing about them he is only writing about himself. But the disclosure is not complete . . . " *A Personal Record*, xv.

111 Perhaps the most ghastly example of this is the Nazi ascendancy to power in Depression Germany and the ensuing policy of extermination of European Jewry.

112 Joseph Conrad, *Under Western Eyes* (Penguin Classics, 1985), 49-50. Page references in the text are to this edition.

113 I am indebted to Avrom Fleishman for bringing attention to the relevance of Stanislaw Bobrowski's plight as a possible source for Conrad's use in *Under Western Eyes* (although Fleishman sees him as a partial model for Razumov (?), not Victor Haldin). See *Conrad's Politics*, 220-21. No doubt Conrad relied on other documentary sources for the building of his plot. Razumov was partially modeled after the famous Russian double agent, Azef, who was apparently involved in the assassination of the infamous Russian Interior Minister, De Plehve, in 1904. For a discussion of this possible link, see Morton Zabel's "Introduction" in the Doubleday Anchor edition of *Under Western Eyes*.

114 "Months of nervous strain have ended in a complete nervous breakdown," Jesse Conrad wrote in her memoir. "Poor Conrad is very ill...There is the M.S. complete but uncorrected and his fierce refusal to let even I touch it. It lays on a table at the foot of the bed and he lives mixed up in the scenes and holds converse with the characters." Quoted by Meyer, 206.

115 *Life and Letters*, II, 77-78.

116 *Ibid.*, 101-02.

117 It is significant, perhaps, that it was not Haldin but his revolutionary comrade who threw the errant bomb that killed innocent bystanders. Still he takes remorseful responsibility for the accident.

118 Compare with Mr. Verloc's response to Inspector Heat in *The Secret Agent* when the policeman advises the secret agent to "vanish" after the Observatory bombing: "Where to?"

119 For an excellent account of this aspect of *Under Western Eyes*, to which I am indebted, see Howe, 86-92.

120 Quoted by Howe, 90.

121 Of course, while Mikulin is actively in the service of czarism, Bobrowski was not, even if his conservatism cooperated with the status quo. Perhaps this is why Conrad grants his fictional surrogate of him in

Under Western Eyes the compassion and affection he deserves.

122 The effigy of Rousseau is a suitable overarching "conscience" for Razumov, both as the author of the *Confessions* and a political writer whose revolutionary zeal is shared in some degree by the Russian émigrés in Geneva.

123 As Meyer reveals, Conrad held the irrational belief that he was somehow responsible for his mother's death — which perhaps is why Razumov's confession of guilt to Haldin's mother is done off-stage. Perhaps this also informs Haldin's mother's odd suspicion that her son did not try to escape, and instead surrendered (like Razumov) to the czarist authorities.

124 We have seen this ruse of reinterpreting a political betrayal as mere romantic intrigue before. In *Nostromo*, Decoud masks his political engagement in the civil war as merely 'love' for Antonia Avellanos, only to kill himself when marooned on the Isabels. Nostromo forsakes his political awareness in pursuit of the "romantic" Giselle, only to be shot by Georgio Viola, a pure revolutionary. Melodrama in Conrad is a retreat from complexity and escape from self-confrontation.

125 Laspara is a firebrand journalist, perhaps another vindictive reference to Apollo Korzeniowski.

126 Among the émigrés, only Madame de S— and Nikita are fair game, sickly caricatures straight out of *The Secret Agent*, and they are denigrated precisely because they are counterfeit revolutionaries. Madame de S— is a pampered aristocrat forced into exile by rumored allegations of complicity in an assassination plot that was imputed to revolutionaries, but in fact the work of a palace intrigue upon which she has sworn revenge. And Nikita is actually a notorious *agent provocateur* (significantly, he, and not one of the real revolutionaries, is the one who deafens Razumov) in the hire of the Russian autocracy.

127 "Peacock leader" is precisely the term Bobrowski applied in ridicule to Polish nationalists in a letter of October 28, 1891 to his seafaring nephew: "Our nation, unfortunately, as Slowacki so truly remarked — is a 'peacock among nations,' which in simple prose means that we are a collection of proclaimed and generally unrecognized celebrities — whom no one knows, no one acknowledges, and no one ever will!" Quoted by Najder, 153.

128 Apparently Conrad used the character of Peter Ivanovitch as a vehicle for pouring ridicule on Leo Tolstoy, whose literary works are parodied in the titles of the works credited to Ivanovitch. Probably he was also patterned after Michael Bakunin, populist, nihilist, and elitist who idealized womankind and himself had escaped imprisonment in Siberia to become an émigré in Switzerland. It is significant, however, that Peter Ivanovitch is exposed as a hypocrite only with regard to his feminism and not his revolutionary idealism.

129 *Letters from Conrad*, 56.

130 See Meyer, 221-23.

131 See "The Dover Patrol," *Last Essays*, 58-65 and "Well Done," *Life and Letters, II*, 179-93.

132 See Conrad's letter of Nov. 11, 1919 to Hugh Walpole in *Life and Letters, II*, 211.

133 See Ludwik Krzyzanowski, "A Note on the Polish Problem," *Joseph Conrad: Centennial Essays* (New York: Polish Institute of Arts and Sciences in America, 1920), 123-33.

134 Joseph Retinger, *Conrad and His Contemporaries* (London, 1941), 65. Another of Conrad's Polish critics, Joseph Ujejski, remarks wistfully with regard to Conrad's position on Poland that "a revelation of a decisive nature, either from within or without, never illuminated his spiritual horizon." Quoted by Hay, 331.

135 See Conrad's preface to *The Nigger of the Narcissus*.

Index

Acmeism, 47, 58
agent provocateur, 3, 40, 207
animal stories, Franz Kafka, 126-27, 129-33, 142-45, 153-57
anti-Semitism, 3, 5, 73, 105, 116-17, 129, 141, 146

Babel, Isaac, ix-x, 1-58
   1920 Diary, 25, 28, 30, 33-35, 54-55
   "Awakening," 4, 9-10
   Benya Krik, 37-38
   "Dante Street," 43-44
   "Di Grasso," 47-48, 58
   "First Love," 6-7
   "Gapa Guzhva," 38
   "Guy de Maupassant," 15-16, 41-42
   "In the Basement," 4, 8-9
   Mariya, 45
   "Old Marescot's Family," 11
   "On the Field of Honor," 11
   Red Cavalry, 4, 7, 11-12, 16, 22, 23-36, 56
   Tales of Odessa, 4, 9, 16-23, 35, 39, 53
   "The End of the Old Folks' Home," 39
   "The Quaker," 11-12, 14
   "The Road," 40-41
   "The Sin of Jesus," 12-14
   "The S.S. *Cow-Wheat*," 38-39
   "The Story of My Dovecot," 4-6
   "Through the Fanlight," 12, 14
   "With Old Man Makhno," 37
Babel, Nathalie, 4, 36, 45, 56
Baines, Jocelyn, 188, 240
Baker, Carlos, 62, 97

Bauer, Felice, 126, 132, 136, 141-42, 145-46, 153
Benjamin, Walter, 118, 126, 158
Beria, Laventrii, 46-47
Berryman, John, 18
Black Hundreds, 16, 19, 52
Bobrowski, Stanislaw, 215, 244-45
Bobrowski, Tadeusz, 171-72, 188, 194, 204, 224, 233-34, 237, 239, 243, 246
Brod, Max, 120, 124-25, 127, 129, 134, 142, 146, 153-56, 164
Budyonny, Semyon, 14, 23, 29, 35
Bullfighting, 74-75, 81-84, 93

Calasso, Robert, 139, 150
Camus, Albert, 85
Casement, Robert, 186
Charyn, Jerome, 19, 37-38, 41, 51, 58
Civil War, American, 73, 109
Civil War, Russian, 10, 14, 23, 39-40
Civil War, Spanish, 51, 93-96
Congo, 182-88, 237-38
Conrad, Jesse, 200-01
Conrad, Joseph, ix-x, 167-247
   A Personal Record, 172, 179, 234, 244
   An Outcast of the Islands, 237
   "Heart of Darkness," 182-88
   Lord Jim, 179-82
   Nostromo, 178, 188-200, 231
   The Arrow of Gold, 233, 242
   "The Mirror and the Sea," 236
   The Rescue, 243
   The Secret Agent, 178, 200-15, 229, 231

Under Western Eyes, 178-79, 215-31, 245-46
Cossacks, 6-7, 21-35, 37, 52-56
Cowley, Malcolm, 65
Crews, Frederick, 177, 235, 238-39
Czar Nicholas II, 6, 40

Diamant, Dora, 117, 132
Dorman-Smith, Eric, 66
Dos Passos, John, 88, 93, 110
Dreyfus Affair, 134, 141, 163
Drinnon, Richard, 106

Eichmann, Adolf, 135
Eisenstein, Sergi, 46

Fitzgerald, F. Scott, 72, 80, 91, 101-02, 107
Fitzgerald, Zelda, 81
Fleishman, Avrom, 178, 245
Ford, Ford Maddox, 101, 187, 200
Fossalta, 64, 67-69, 73, 76, 82-83, 86, 98, 105-07
Freud, Sigmund, 61, 65, 130-31, 189
Fussell, Paul, ix, 69, 78, 103-04, 107-08, 111

Galsworthy, Ada, 200
Garden, Patricia, 24
Garnett, Edward, 177, 179, 230, 237
Garth, John, 97
Gellhorn, Martha, 81
genocide, 8, 33-34, 115, 124, 158
Gorky, Maxim, 10, 35, 43-44
Graham, Cunningham, 174-76, 182-83, 187, 202, 206, 210, 241
Graves, Robert, 67, 69

Great Depression, 91-92
Guerard, Albert, 188-89, 240-41
Gurko, Leo, 178

Hallett, Richard, 28
Hapsburg Empire, ix, 115-16, 153
Hardt, Ludwig, 142
Hay, Eloise, 240-41, 247
Hemingway, Ed, 62, 80, 109
Hemingway, Ernest, ix-x, 51, 59-111, 169
 "A Clean, Well-Lighted Place," 85
 A Farewell to Arms, 64, 76-80, 94, 98, 169
 A Moveable Feast, 62, 101-02
 "A Way You'll Never Be," 86
 Across the River and into the Trees, 98-100
 "Big Two-Hearted River," 69
 Death in the Afternoon, 63, 81-85
 For Whom the Bell Tolls, 94-96, 98
 Green Hills of Africa, 86-88
 "In Another Country," 65-66
 In Our Time, 70-71
 Islands in the Stream, 102-03
 "Now I Lay Me," 68
 "On the Quai at Smyrna," 70
 "The Battler," 70-71
 The Old Man and the Sea, 100-01
 "The Short Happy Life of Francis Macomber," 89-91
 "The Snows of Kilimanjaro," 88-89
 The Sun Also Rises, 72-75
 To Have and Have Not, 91-93
Hemingway, Grace, 62, 68-69, 108-09

Hemingway, Gregory, 101
Hemingway, Hadley, 102
Hilsner, Leopold, 116, 141
Hitler, Adolf, 115
Hochschild, Adam, 237-38
Holocaust, 124, 127-28, 135, 147, 183
Hovey, Richard, 105
Howe, Irving, 178, 191, 240

imperialism, 183, 186-87, 190-91, 193, 238, 240-41

Janouch, Gustav, 155-56, 158
Jesenska, Milena, 126, 129, 146-47, 153, 158
Jewish Defense Corps, 7, 49
Jews, assimilation in Europe, 16, 116-18, 123-24, 126, 139-41, 143-45, 147-48, 150, 153, 157
Jones, David, 99

Kafka, Elli, 117, 158
Kafka, Franz, ix-x, 113-165
   "A Hunger Artist," 127
   "A Report to an Academy," 144-45
   Amerika, 120-124, 138
   Diaries 1910-1923, 115, 123-25, 132
   "In the Penal Colony," 127, 134-36
   "Investigations of a Dog," 154-55
   "Jackals and Arabs," 142-44
   "Josephine the Singer, or the Mouse Folk," 155-57
   Letter to His Father, 118, 128, 160, 162
   The Castle, 148-53
   "The Judgment," 118-20, 124, 129, 131
   "The Metamorphosis," 129-31
   The Trial, 124, 136-41, 148
   "The Village Schoolmaster (The Giant Mole)," 132-33
Kafka, Hermann, 117-18, 124, 128, 160, 162
Kafka, Ottla, 146, 158
Kalmykov, Betal, 38
Kierkegaard, Soren, 117, 142
Kilszczewski, Spiridion, 172-73, 222
King Leopold II, 182-83, 186
Korzeniowski, Apollo, 169-71, 174, 185, 188, 204, 217, 233, 238, 240, 242, 246
Kurowsky, Agnes von, 66, 68

Lawrence, T.E., 177
Lenin, Vladimir, 10, 14, 17, 23, 27, 32, 34-35
Lewis, Cecil, 61
Lewis, Wyndham, 71, 101
Lowy, Yetzhak, 141, 158`
Lynn, Kenneth, 62, 64, 68-69, 78, 80, 108-09
Lyttelton, Oliver, 111

Macdonald, Dwight, 61
Mandelstam, Nadezhda, 15, 36, 41, 46, 48-50, 55-58
Mandelstam, Osip, 47-48, 51, 58
McKey, Edward, 76, 107
metamorphosis, 3, 121, 125, 128-31, 133, 136-38, 140, 142, 147-48, 153, 156, 158
Meyer, Bernard, 232, 241, 243, 246
Meyers, Jeffery, 67
Mickiewicz, Adam, 169

Mikhoels, Solomon, 46
Milosz, Czeslaw, 232
Montefiore, Simon, 17
Morf, Gustov, 178, 188, 239
Mudrick, Marvin, 177

Najder, Zdzislaw, 169, 172-73, 233, 239
Nazism, 115, 135, 153
nihilism, 127, 174, 180, 201-02

O'Connor, Frank, 28
Olesha, Yuri, 46
Orwell, George, 222
Owen, Wilfred, 103

pacifism, 3, 8, 27, 76
Packer, George, 93-94
Pasley, Malcolm, 124
Passchendaele, 63, 99, 100, 110
Paustovsky, Konstantin, 3, 5, 15
Pawel, Ernst, 115-17, 159
Pilnyak, Boris, 46
Pilsudski, Josef, 23
Pirozhkova, Antonina, 4, 38, 44-45, 47
Poggioli, Renato, 53
pogroms, 4-6, 18-19, 25, 27, 33-34, 49, 52-54, 116
Polish Insurrection of 1863, ix, 169
Poradowska, Marguerite, 171, 174
Pound, Ezra, 70, 78, 82, 107-08

Red Army, 23-35, 39, 53, 56
Red Cavalryman, 27, 29, 53-54, 56
Retinger, Joseph, 231
Rosenthal, Raymond, 20-21

Russian Revolution, ix, 3, 8, 10, 17, 22-23, 26, 34-38, 41, 45-46, 230-31

Sassoon Siegfried, 65, 67
Sinyavsky, Andrei, 4-5, 23, 50
socialist realism, 35, 43, 55, 58
Somme, 63, 77, 103
Sorley, Charles, 91
Spanish influenza, 146
Spanish-American War, 241
Stalin, Josef, 3-4, 8, 17, 23, 34-36, 38, 41, 43-46, 50-51, 55, 58, 82, 93
Stein, Gertrude, 70, 101
survival guilt, ix, 66, 79, 99, 128, 169, 171-72, 179, 181, 196-97, 200, 211, 215, 230, 232

Thompson, John, 69
Trilling, Lionel, 12, 54
Trotsky, Leon, 34-35, 47, 55, 240
tuberculosis, 145-46, 153, 170
Tucholsky, Kurt, 135-36

Wells, H.G., 173
Weltsch, Felix, 128, 133
Wilson, Edmund, 81
World War I (The Great War), ix-x, 61-71, 78-79, 81-83, 87, 92, 95, 97-100, 103-05, 107-08, 110, 169
World War II, 50, 96-100

Yagoda, Genrikh, 45-46
Yeats, William Butler, 15, 61
Yezhov, Nikolai, 3, 46-47
Young, Philip, 104-05

Zagorska, Aniela, 187
Zionism, 129, 143, 153

ABOUT THE AUTHOR

PETER STINE has taught at South Carolina State University, Wayne State University, University of Michigan, and Oakland Community College. He founded the literary journal *Witness* in 1987 and was editor-in-chief through 2007. *Witness* was awarded eight grants from the National Endowment for the Arts, and four volumes were reissued as books by university presses. His fiction, poetry, literary essays and journalism have appeared in many publications, including *The Iowa Review*, *Boulevard*, *The Threepenny Review*, *Contemporary Literature*, *The Cambridge Quarterly*, *The New York Times*, *Sport Literate*, and Harold Bloom's *Modern Critical Views*.

Basic Idea:

Happy, Event, experience direct who you are:
  Can't explain — Focuses — to infinite, couples
    ∴ Conclude live in the moment, doesn't matter what
      personal history is — just accept happenstance,
        uncertainty & give in to it & think about why.
          Become indifferent and don't judge — be free